Withdrawn

UP, UP, & AWAY

Also by Jonah Keri

*The Extra 2%: How Wall Street Strategies Took a
Major League Baseball Team From Worst to First*

UP, UP, & AWAY

The Kid, The Hawk, Rock, Vladi,
Pedro, Le Grand Orange, Youppi!,
The Crazy Business of Baseball,
& the Ill-fated but Unforgettable
Montreal Expos

JONAH KERI

Random House Canada

PUBLISHED BY RANDOM HOUSE CANADA

Copyright © 2014 Jonah Keri

www.randomhouse.ca

Random House Canada and colophon are registered trademarks.

Library and Archives Canada Cataloguing in Publication

Keri, Jonah, author
Up, up, and away : the Kid, the Hawk, Rock, Vladi, Pedro, le Grand Orange, Youppi!, the crazy business of baseball, and the ill-fated but unforgettable Montreal Expos / Jonah Keri.

Issued in print and electronic formats.

ISBN 978-0-307-36135-6

1. Montreal Expos (Baseball team)—History.
2. Baseball—Québec (Province)—Montréal—History. I. Title.

GV875.M6K47 2014   796.357'640971428   C2013-905452-9

Cover and text design by Five Seventeen

Cover images: (Andre Dawson) © Rich Pilling / Getty Images;
(baseball) © Arkela / Shutterstock.com
Interior images courtesy of Russ Hansen
Interior cartoons courtesy of Terry Mosher ("Aislin") and the *Montreal Gazette*

Printed and bound in the United States of America

2 4 6 8 9 7 5 3

*To Papa Alec, who took me to the Big O
to see Tim Raines hit for the cycle,
and Papa Max, who had the best nickname
for Rodney Scott ("The Woodchopper")*

Contents

Prologue

Before the Montreal Expos actually lived, they almost died.

Blame it on big dreams. In the 1960s, few cities anywhere dreamed bigger than Montreal. During his second stint as mayor, Jean Drapeau and his executive committee spearheaded a staggering number of wildly ambitious projects. Place des Arts opened in 1963, giving Montreal a sprawling performing arts centre that expanded and shifted the city's downtown core eastward—a big deal given that anglophone power and wealth had been consolidated in the city's west end. The Montreal Metro made its maiden voyage in 1966, more than half a century after the idea for a subway was first proposed, and grew to become the most widely used rapid transit system in Canada.

But by far the biggest and ballsiest venture was Expo 67. Montreal had previously bid to host the World's Fair in 1960, only to lose out to Moscow. Two years later, after Moscow dropped out, Drapeau pushed for another bid. On November 13, 1962, he got his wish: Montreal would host the six-month exhibition from April to October 1967 to celebrate Canada's centennial and Montreal's reach-for-the-sky mentality.

Problem was, Drapeau often acted first and asked questions later. The mayor eschewed existing locations within the city as sites for the exposition. Instead, he proposed a gigantic public works project: Montreal would build a large, man-made island from scratch in the middle of the St. Lawrence River (Île Notre-Dame), greatly expand an existing one (Île Sainte-Hélène), and host Expo there. Despite its audacity, the guts of the plan were a stroke of genius, with the city moving the mountains of rock and rubble dug up during concurrent construction of the Metro, along with silt and gravel dredged from the river, to build out the islands.

But the plan's actual execution was fraught with seemingly overwhelming problems. Several top organizing officials resigned after a computer program predicted that all the necessary ground-work—building the islands, completing the Metro, erecting a bridge, then setting up the enormous exhibition itself—couldn't possibly be completed in less than four and a half years for the opening ceremony in April 1967. There were also environmental objections, complaints from other Canadian cities over funding huge and potentially wasteful projects in Montreal, and major financial concerns as a preliminary budget of $167 million in 1963 swelled to $439 million four years later.

The city got it done anyway. The mass resignations opened the door for a committed new group. A diplomat named Pierre Dupuy assumed the role of commissioner general, and the man overseeing day-to-day construction, Robert Fletcher Shaw, was a hard-nosed engineer. The management group led by Dupuy and Shaw came to be known as *Les Durs:* the tough guys. Under their stewardship, Expo 67 became the largest world exposition ever held in North America, drawing more than 50 million visitors, with a record 569,500 in one day. When asked early in the process what he hoped to accomplish by bringing Expo to Montreal, Drapeau said he wanted the city to host "one of the finest exhibitions of its kind that the world has ever seen."

What the world got was both a six-month party and a paean to progress. There were grand performances of all stripes, including jazz, opera, and ballet. The Grateful Dead performed, as did Jefferson Airplane. The *Ed Sullivan Show* broadcast live for two weeks from on site, headlined by acts like The Supremes. For many visitors, however, it was Expo's educational components that resonated the loudest. Sprawling exhibits playing on the fair's "Man and his World" theme dominated the grounds. As *The Canadian Press* described it at the time: "All over the mid-river 1,000-acre site strange shapes and unfamiliar sounds heralded the breaking of new ground in the fields of design, architecture, transport, construction, cinema and communication of ideas." Expo 67 was fun. But it also conveyed an image of being *important*.

It was with that same ambitious spirit that the city of Montreal, Mayor Drapeau, and the head of the city's executive committee, Gerry Snyder, fervently pursued a Major League Baseball expansion team. Bid now, work out the details later.

This latest big dream had its roots in another baseball team that had come and gone: the Montreal Royals. The first iteration of the franchise played in Montreal from 1897 to 1917, with affiliations in the Eastern and International leagues and a list of managers that included future Hall of Famer Ed Barrow. But it was the second version of the Royals that ultimately gained acclaim in the baseball world, and, for a time, a rabid following in *la belle province*. The Royals of 1928 to 1960 retained affiliation with a single circuit, the International League, but didn't truly flourish until well into this second stint, after the major league's Brooklyn Dodgers bought the Royals in 1939. The Royals won the league title soon after, in 1941. A year later, legendary baseball executive Branch Rickey jumped from the St. Louis Cardinals to the Dodgers, after becoming the first operator to build an elaborate and highly successful farm system of minor league teams. When he took over the general manager's role with the Dodgers after the 1942 season, Rickey immediately set to work building a similar killer farm system for his new organization—with the Royals as its crown jewel. The Royals went on to win six more league titles, led by a cavalcade of future National League stars. Don Drysdale, Roy Campanella, and Duke Snider all matriculated for the Dodgers' Triple-A club in Montreal while future World Series–winning operator Buzzie Bavasi ran the club, and future Hall of Fame manager Walter Alston skippered it for four seasons. Though he'd eventually forge his Hall of Fame career in Pittsburgh, with the Pirates, Roberto Clemente also came through Montreal.

But the main attraction—the man who won the hearts and minds of Montrealers—was Jackie Robinson. It's entirely possible that Robinson could've achieved instant stardom in the big leagues even without a year honing his craft in Triple-A. But Rickey rightly saw Robinson's eventual transition to the majors as a mental and emotional challenge as well as (or more than) a physical one. Rickey deemed Montreal an inviting and progressive enough place to welcome the man destined to become the first African-American player of his era to break Major League Baseball's long-standing colour barrier. Fans flocked to Delorimier Downs to see the phenom in action, and he didn't disappoint. In his one year in Montreal, Robinson batted .349 with a .468 on-base percentage (OBP), stealing 40 bases and showing an amazing eye at the plate: 92 walks versus just 27 strikeouts in 124 games.

The Royals went on to win the Little World Series that year, beating the American Association champion Louisville Colonels four games to two. The clinching game came on October 4, 1946, before a record home crowd of 19,171. Sam Maltin, a writer and friend of Robinson's, detailed in the *Pittsburgh Courier* what happened after the Royals won the deciding game 2–0.

> Ushers and police couldn't keep the crowd from the field. They refused to move and sang *Il a gagné ses Epaulettes* ("He won his bars") and "We want Robinson." It was a mob ready to riot . . . Jackie came out and the crowd surged on him. Men and women of all ages threw their arms around him, kissed him, pulled and tore at his clothes, and then carried him around the infield on their shoulders, shouting themselves hoarse. Jackie, tears streaming down his face, tried to beg off further honors. They carried him back to the clubhouse. There, he had a tough time packing his gear as people came trooping in to wish him luck. They all said they wanted him back.

When Robinson finally left the ballpark, those delirious fans chased him all the way to his train. Describing the scene, Maltin continued: "It was probably the only day in history that a black man ran from a white mob with love instead of lynching on its mind."

Robinson's stint in Montreal and the locals' hospitality produced a halo effect for the city, one that lasted for decades. But as Robinson and later Dodger greats graduated to the big club, the Royals' talent base started to slip, and with it the team's attendance. By 1960, the Dodgers decided they could make do with two Triple-A teams instead of three. On September 7 of that year, the Royals played their final game, and that was that for high-level professional baseball in Montreal.

This didn't sit well with Drapeau, or with Snyder. Not long after the last pair of spikes was lugged out of Delorimier Downs, the two men set to work trying to bring baseball back to the city. It was a venture that would span nearly the entire decade.

Snyder's first major step was a meeting with MLB Commissioner Ford Frick. He and the city were too late to vie for an expansion team in 1962, when the New York Mets and Houston Colt .45s (later renamed the Astros) entered the league. But Snyder wanted to take the league's temperature anyway, to see if another round of expansion might be coming and if Montreal could be a viable candidate. Frick told Snyder that if Montreal wanted a future expansion franchise, it would need a suitable stadium in which to host that team, something the city most certainly did not then have.

Still, what Snyder never heard in that meeting was "no." For a city that would pull off several huge-scale projects in the '60s—often with little more than political will and a few powerful allies at the start—"not no" meant "yes." That optimism would soon grow, after Frick's successor, William Eckert, said in 1966 that baseball *would* consider expansion at some point in the next few years. The league's owners were happy to collect expansion fees from new franchises, but baseball also sought to grow its regional presence, especially with the NFL rapidly gaining in popularity. Expansion was going to happen, and Montreal was going to make its play.

When Major League Baseball's owners convened in Mexico City in December 1967, Montreal made its official pitch for a team. Snyder touted Montreal as a cosmopolitan city and a growing economic power, with the population base and fan fervour to help a major league ball club flourish. Drapeau followed with his own spiel. One of the league representatives listening to the city's pitch was John McHale, MLB's deputy commissioner and someone who would later play an instrumental role in Montreal baseball history.

"I went to the first meeting when [Drapeau] addressed the chief executive and the owners of the NL clubs," McHale recounted in Alain Usereau's book, *The Expos in Their Prime: The Short-Lived*

Glory of Montreal's Team, 1977–1984. "He was a very good sales-man, he painted a beautiful picture of Montreal. Walter O'Malley had had teams there for Brooklyn and was impressed by the size of the city and they just came off Expo 67. . . . It all sounded very good. He also had said there were owners that would put up $10 million to buy the expansion franchise from the league and every-body left the meeting quite happy."

The history and success of the Royals was a strong point in Montreal's favour, giving the city a puncher's chance against the National League's other expansion candidates—Buffalo, Dallas-Fort Worth, Denver, Milwaukee, San Diego, and Toronto. O'Malley, the owner of the Dodgers and the man who'd presided over many of those Royals teams, hadn't forgotten. In one of those happy and profitable coincidences that blessed Montreal for much of the '60s, it was O'Malley who chaired the National League's expansion committee, O'Malley whose voice would speak loudest while the league deliberated on which two teams would join for the 1969 season.

Still, a major league team in Canada—*French* Canada—was something else altogether, at least in the eyes of some observers at the time. When O'Malley stepped to the podium to announce the two newest members of the National League on May 27, 1968, San Diego was considered a lock, with Milwaukee, Dallas, and Buffalo the best bets for number two. San Diego did indeed get its franchise, and would sail from there to Opening Day 1969 more or less without a hitch. But the second choice was a surprise: Montreal. And things would not sail nearly as smoothly. If Expo 67 took hundreds of millions in cost overruns, obliterating the core group of people expected to be in charge, overcoming multiple protests, and building two islands from the muck to get done, getting a Major League Baseball team ready to play actual games in less than a year would take a damn miracle.

Montreal's first gigantic problem was lining up an ownership group to finance and run the team. One of the most promising candidates was Charles Bronfman, who had gotten his first call from Snyder just a few weeks before the announcement in late May. Bronfman was heir to the Seagram's distilling fortune, a 36-year-old executive with the money to make a big investment—and, as it would later turn out, the will to go out on his own and make a name for himself in something other than the liquor business. Though the timing was both sudden and late, Snyder's initial request wasn't beyond Bronfman's means. Snyder wanted to build a team of 10 owners, each one kicking in $1 million. Would Bronfman be interested?

"I said, if there's a covered stadium, I'm in," Bronfman said in a 2011 interview at his New York office. "So my wife said to me, 'What was that again?' I said, 'Well, Gerry Snyder wants a million-dollar commitment.' She said, 'A million dollars and you just say yes?' I said, 'Well, it's never going to happen anyway.' And then, I heard really nothing else until one night, my wife and I are in bed, and on CJAD I hear the announcers say, 'And now we hear the news about baseball in Montreal.' I looked at her and said, 'Oh shit, now we're in the glue.'"

A week after the announcement, Snyder finally convened an owners meeting. Instead of 10 partners showing up, however, there were only six. Of the six, Bronfman figured only two had what he called "leadership ability": himself and entrepreneur Jean-Louis Lévesque. Bronfman spoke first. "I said [to Lévesque], 'Congratulations, you're the chairman.' And he said, 'Whoa, what do you mean I'm the chairman?' And I said, 'You're the chairman. We need a francophone to be the chairman, you're the chairman.'"

A self-made man, Lévesque had forged his way up through the banking industry, eventually forming the company that would become Lévesque, Beaubien Inc., the largest French

Canadian–owned securities firm in the country. He sat on numerous prestigious boards, had the respect of the Montreal, Quebec, and Canadian business communities, was hailed for his philanthropy, and even made Canada's Sports Hall of Fame years later for his accomplishments as a thoroughbred owner and breeder. "He was very well known, a very wealthy Montrealer," said Bronfman. "He was quite a guy, and he was the right choice." And yes, in a city that then (as now) was both bilingual but nonetheless French-speaking by a large majority, it didn't hurt to have a surname like Lévesque at the top of the masthead.

But even with Bronfman and Lévesque seemingly on board, things were far from stable. In focusing again on big picture first and key details later, Snyder had thrust the future of baseball of Montreal into peril—with MLB at least partly to blame for not doing more due diligence and failing to realize the shaky nature of the city's candidacy. The first communication between prospective owners not happening until after the bid had been approved, only six showing up instead of 10, repeatedly missing key organizational deadlines as the summer days ticked by . . . all of this would be enough to spook even a true believer. Industrialist Robert Irsay, initially expected to buy into the team's ownership group, backed out, not to be heard from again in professional sports until he bought the Los Angeles Rams in 1972 (then swapping franchises to land the Baltimore Colts, whom he would move to Indianapolis in the middle of the night 12 years later). The bigger blow, however, came from Lévesque. The would-be face of Montreal's new baseball franchise pulled out of the partnership on July 31, 1968, thanks somewhat to a conflict with local politician Lucien Saulnier (who was heavily involved with the baseball project) but more broadly because of the group's collective inability to get anything done quickly.

The timing of Lévesque's departure couldn't have been worse. The group now had just 15 days to hand over $1,120,000 to the

National League as a deposit, or else a different city would get a big-league franchise for the following spring. Fortunately, even without Lévesque the group had more than enough funds to pay that first installment. The bigger problem, the one that no one could seem to solve, was the same concern Bronfman voiced to Snyder the first time the two men spoke about baseball in Montreal, and the same one Ford Frick had told Snyder to address six years earlier: Where the hell was the team going to play?

The idea of a domed stadium that would protect fans and players from Montreal's harsh early-spring and early-fall weather was one that had floated through the minds of Snyder and Drapeau for years. As the city progressed in its bid for a team, that thought had intensified; when Montreal gained approval for a team, it blossomed. Drapeau was so confident that the city could pull it off, he wrote a letter to the National League promising that the future Montreal baseball franchise would open the 1971 season in a shiny new covered ballpark—no doubt about it. That letter, along with the tiny window the league now had to get San Diego's expansion partner (*any* partner) on the field in eight months' time, were the main reasons the NL stuck with Montreal, while reassuring anyone who asked that all would be well soon.

All was not well. Bronfman and his remaining partners weren't going to fork over the hold money needed to keep the team alive, much less hire a team president or really do much of anything, until they could get a handle on the stadium situation.

"So I'm going back and forth between Drapeau and Saulnier," said Bronfman. "Drapeau, who at one point tells me I'm his best friend in the world—which was sort of strange to me: I had never been to his house, he had never been to my house—and Saulnier, whose two favourite words were 'definitely not.' So one day, I said to Saulnier, 'What about the covered stadium?' He said, 'What covered stadium?' I said, 'Well, the mayor wrote a letter to the National League, saying that we would have a covered stadium in two years.' He said, 'Well, that's nice. Show me where he's authorized to write that letter by the city council or the executive committee.'

"I said, 'What? He would write a letter without any authorization?' He said, 'Look. You can write a letter; I can write a letter; the guy who cleans the floor can write a letter. He wrote the letter. He was not authorized.' I thought, 'Oh my god.'"

With the August 15 deadline looming, the league breathing down Montreal's neck, and Drapeau's grand ballpark plan amounting to an apparently empty promise typed into a memo, Bronfman set to work writing a note of his own: his resignation from the partnership. He visited the mayor in person to deliver the news. Instead, he got a lecture himself.

"I was taught by my father never to make a rash decision," Drapeau told Bronfman, attempting to guilt him into staying.

Bronfman's decision was hardly rash, however. The mayor and his minions had offered nothing but words for months, and Bronfman saw no way to salvage the entire operation in a matter of days. But Drapeau asked for a little leeway. Give me 24 hours, he pleaded, and maybe something will happen. What the hell, figured Bronfman, *why not*? The next morning, Bronfman and his about-to-be-ex-partners met at his office to say their goodbyes. The phone rang. It was Drapeau. "I would like you to please come down to City Hall," the mayor said. "Only you. Nobody else."

Had Drapeau's Hail Mary been answered? Or would this be just another smokescreen in a summer full of them? Bronfman headed over, if only as a courtesy. What he saw floored him. It was a spectacular colour drawing of a new stadium. Drapeau had called a group of city engineers and architects to his office right after the previous day's meeting with Bronfman, and told them to work around the clock until they had something they could present with pride. Still, a drawing alone—no matter how pretty—wasn't going to solve everything. Drapeau doubled down, agreeing to team up with Bronfman to negotiate with Saulnier, the key city official who stood between the team and a stadium deal.

With Lévesque out of the picture, Bronfman partnered with prominent local businessmen Lorne Webster, Hugh Hallward, Paul and Charlemagne Beaudry, and Sydney Maislin to form the board of investors, with Bronfman serving as chairman and majority owner. With the city's support, the partners were now reinvigorated and determined to bring baseball back to Montreal. As for Bronfman, this was his chance to do something for, as he said, his "city and province and country." Getting the stadium assurance clinched his decision. (Bronfman would later learn that Drapeau had ulterior motives, that building a stadium was largely about winning the Olympics, maybe even wooing an NFL team to Montreal. But none of that mattered at that moment.)

"My mother had wanted me to do stuff for the symphony orchestra," he said, "but I didn't like symphony orchestras too well at that time. Or with the museums, but I didn't like museums. All of a sudden, here was an opportunity to do what I'd always wanted to, in an area that I loved."

Unfortunately, this wasn't enough to assuage the National League's fears. While Bronfman and city leaders hashed everything out behind the scenes, rumours began swirling that the league would strip Montreal of its franchise, and send it instead to Buffalo. The reason was simple: Buffalo had a stadium that was ready to go in War Memorial Stadium, and Montreal did not. Even with a long-term stadium plan in place and a league-granted extension 'til 1972 to open it, Montreal still needed a temporary home for the team's first three years (much longer, in fact, as it would turn out, though no one knew that at the time).

Delorimier Downs, the old home of the Royals, was briefly considered. But the 20,000-seat park lacked the capacity and the modern amenities needed to host major league games. It was located right in the middle of a densely populated residential area, parking was scarce, and a major renovation would be impossible. Also, by then the city had bought the property, with plans to convert the building into a school.

For a while, the Autostade seemed the most likely candidate. Built by five car companies in preparation for Expo 67, the Autostade was an odd duck of a building, oval-shaped, with 19 distinct concrete grandstands spread around the field that could be taken apart and rebuilt to accommodate different events. But even with its flexibility and versatility, it was nearly impossible to imagine it being recast as a fully functional baseball stadium. City planners tried to make it work nonetheless. In phase one, they'd knock out seats in two sections to allow space for foul lines. They would then drastically expand the seating capacity, from about 25,000 after that initial reduction in seats to 37,000 upon completion. The planners believed the renovation could be done in a few months, in time for Opening Day 1969. And they believed it could be done affordably.

But the price grew in a hurry when talk turned to adding a roof in addition to the 12,000-seat expansion—a move some advocates felt was essential given that the Autostade was nearly brand new, and would be needed to host other sports and events after the Expos left. Worse, the Canadian Football League's Montreal Alouettes held the stadium's lease and demanded steep payment for the three years that the baseball team intended to stay. Not surprisingly, the city rejected the proposal.

Now scrambling to find *any* kind of half-decent plan, Drapeau ultimately turned his attention to Jarry Park. Located about three miles northeast of the downtown core, the large municipal park sat in the middle of the Villeray neighbourhood, surrounded by duplexes and triplexes. If the Autostade offered a good-sized facility that was simply ill-suited for baseball in its present state, Jarry Park delivered even less: though the larger park did contain a true baseball diamond, that field wasn't even big enough or in any way suitable for high-level minor league play, let alone the big leagues. With Montreal's bid down to its last licks, Drapeau and company would need to convince Major League Baseball that a 3,000-seat amateur ballfield could be converted into a big league–quality stadium—with 10 times the capacity, better lighting, workable clubhouses, concessions, scoreboard, and everything else—in just eight months.

Drapeau was on the case, and the mayor invited National League president Warren Giles for a visit. He talked up the stadium's location: less than a mile from the Metropolitan Expressway, walking distance from a commuter rail station. Giles appreciated all those features, but really, the league was *looking* for a reason to grant its approval. That late in the process, stripping the franchise from Montreal and shipping it somewhere else—even to a city with a usable stadium—would have been problematic for many reasons. In fact, the league's supposed make-or-break deadline had largely been intended to turn up the heat on Montreal. Finally, it was Drapeau the charmer who sealed the deal, convincing Giles to accept Jarry Park, and the city, once and for all.

"Drapeau's late grand slam saves ball club," read Ted Blackman's August 9, 1968 column in the *Montreal Gazette*. Bronfman's reaction was equally to the point: "We're going to play ball. Yes, we did it."

One major step remained before the team could take the field, however: it needed a name. "Royals" emerged as an early favourite and a worthy nod to the city's baseball history, but coincidentally, Kansas City's expansion team had already adopted the name for the following season. Other proposed names included suggestions in both English and French. "Voyageurs" had a certain ring to it. One of the leading English-language candidates would presage a pivotal event in franchise history decades later: "Nationals."

In the end, however, the afterglow of the World's Fair would become the inspiration for the decision, offering a team name that worked in both English and French. It was a nod to that era, to taking wildly ambitious ideas that lacked details or serious planning—potentially disastrous boondoggles—and turning them into huge wins. The club created from that ambition would see plenty of its own triumphs in the years that followed, and plenty of heartbreak too. But first, it was time to celebrate. The city of big dreams had done it again, and Montreal had a team to call its own.

CHAPTER ONE

Opening Day (1969)

Charles Bronfman and the Expos' board of directors hired their first employee on August 14, 1968, naming John McHale as the team's president and CEO. This came just a few days after Jean Drapeau convinced Warren Giles and the National League to take a leap of faith on Montreal, and on Jarry Park. It also gave the newborn organization exactly eight months to get ready to play. They'd have six months to hire an office staff, hire a manager and coaches, build a scouting department, and get everything set for spring training. Oh, and they'd need actual players to fill an actual roster.

This was an ambitious timeline. No, wait. Not ambitious. Completely insane.

McHale was the man charged with overseeing this seemingly impossible set of tasks. Born and raised in Detroit, McHale signed with the Tigers as a first baseman in 1941. He made his big-league debut two years later, at age 21, but didn't last long in the majors, appearing in only 64 games thinly spread over five seasons. His playing days over, he stayed in baseball, eventually seizing the role of Detroit's director of minor league operations. At 35, he was running the Tigers as general manager. In 1959, he took the same job with the Milwaukee Braves, where he presided over a roster that included Hank Aaron and Eddie Mathews just entering their primes, and Warren Spahn still going strong at age 38. With the Braves coming off two straight trips to the World Series, and three of the game's top players riding high, McHale had landed the second-most attractive job for a baseball operator at the time, trailing only the Yankees.

However, despite winning 83 games or more for eight straight years, the Braves would finish no better than second in that stretch, and wouldn't see the post-season again for more than a decade. In those days there were no Wild Cards, and no divisions, either: only the two league champions made the playoffs, advancing straight to the World Series. Meanwhile, the Braves developed few impact players to complement Aaron, Matthews, and Spahn, save for up-and-coming catcher Joe Torre. But by the time Torre emerged as a top player, the Braves' core had aged and the team was going nowhere. Nowhere, that is, except Atlanta, as apathy in Milwaukee drove the club to move after the 1965 season. The Braves had led the National League in attendance in each of their first six seasons in Milwaukee, while also winning two NL pennants and a World Series. To see the team skip town a few years later was a shock, and a big black mark against McHale's tenure as GM. By 1966, McHale was gone, ousted from the Braves GM job and headed to the MLB offices to serve as an aide to Commissioner William Eckert.

McHale's baseball legacy had once seemed destined to be written by those three future Hall of Famers in Milwaukee. Instead, he would make his biggest mark as the man presiding over the first major league team outside the United States. He was also someone who learned from his mistakes. Though McHale would remain heavily involved in final decisions throughout his tenure with the Expos, he'd trust many of the day-to-day decisions on player acquisitions and roster building to someone else—his Chicago-born, Iowa-raised assistant from those Braves days, the man who would become the first general manager in Expos history.

When Jim Fanning grabbed the reins in Montreal, he had less than two months to prepare for one of the most important moments of the team's first decade: the expansion draft. Each of the existing major league teams could protect 15 players, while the four expansion teams—the Kansas City Royals and Seattle Pilots in the American League, the San Diego Padres and the Expos in the National League—would then be free to draft those players left unprotected. There are two schools of thought when planning an expansion draft: The first theory holds that fans want to immediately see a competitive and recognizable team, which makes drafting unprotected veterans the way to go, even when they're a few years past their prime. The problem there is that while your team might be recognizable, there's no guarantee that it will be competitive (see the pre-1969 Mets). The second school of thought posits that young talent is the way to go, that a few lean years can be worth it if you can poach a bunch of 22-year-olds and hope one or two of them become hidden gems.

The Expos' strategy was . . . to show up, for starters. All the scrambling with stadium logistics and the early turmoil within the ownership group had set the franchise back several months, and the Expos were way behind their expansion cousins in every facet of the game. Fortunately, Fanning had served as the Braves' de facto scouting director and farm director under McHale, helping him hone his eye for talent. McHale himself, despite some of his ill-advised decisions running the Braves, could still offer some useful feedback leading up to the expansion draft. But that was it.

As draft day approached, the Expos still employed a grand total of zero scouts.

"We just had to hire as many scouts as we could," recalled Fanning in a 2011 phone interview. "That late in the season, it wasn't easy to find really good scouts who were also available. You end up hiring guys who are about to retire, or maybe they already have. But we got lucky. We got Johnny Moore, a great scout from the Braves. We got Bobby Bragan, who'd managed with the Braves and other places, and had a good eye. Larry Doby, Eddie Lopat, this was a good group. This was the busiest time John and I ever had—we did well to find all of these guys."

Once they'd hurriedly assembled a staff, McHale, Fanning, and company hashed out how the Expos would approach their first round of player acquisitions. They finally decided to take as many brand-name veterans as possible—but for craftier reasons than you'd think. McHale and Fanning figured people would flock to Jarry Park at first regardless of the names pencilled into the lineup. What the Expos really wanted was to land players with market value. Draft a bunch of players maybe a bit past their prime, shine 'em up, then trade 'em for players who might actually contribute to winning seasons down the road.

The McHale-Fanning strategy of drafting known commodities and flipping them for something better would pay off in a big way a few months later. Before that could happen, though, the Expos would have to handle basic necessities—like getting Jarry Park renovated in time for the team's first home game.

Montreal is one of the coldest major cities in the Western Hemisphere. On top of that, the winter of 1968–69 was one of the coldest, snowiest, and longest that locals had seen in years. Turning a 3,000-seat amateur park with a couple of grandstands into a fully-equipped, 28,546-seat major league ballpark in eight months would be tough enough under ideal conditions. Ferocious

☞ 1968 ☜
NATIONAL LEAGUE EXPANSION
DRAFT RESULTS

	Player	Position	Former Team	Drafting Team
2	Manny Mota	OF	Pirates	Expos
4	Mack Jones	OF	Reds	Expos
6	John Bateman	C	Astros	Expos
8	Gary Sutherland	2B	Phillies	Expos
10	Jack Billingham	P	Dodgers	Expos
11	Donn Clendenon	OF	Pirates	Expos
13	Jesus Alou	OF	Giants	Expos
15	Mike Wegener	P	Phillies	Expos
17	Skip Guinn	P	Braves	Expos
19	Bill Stoneman	P	Cubs	Expos
21	Maury Wills	SS	Pirates	Expos
23*	Larry Jackson	P	Phillies	Expos
25	Bob Reynolds	P	Giants	Expos
27	Dan McGinn	P	Reds	Expos
29	Jose Herrera	OF	Astros	Expos
32	Jimy Williams	SS	Reds	Expos
34	Remy Hermoso	2B	Braves	Expos
36	Mudcat Grant	P	Dodgers	Expos
38	Jerry Robertson	P	Cardinals	Expos
40	Don Shaw	P	Mets	Expos
41	Ty Cline	OF	Giants	Expos
43	Garry Jestadt	3B	Cubs	Expos
45	Carl Morton	P	Braves	Expos
47	Larry Jaster	P	Cardinals	Expos
49	Ernie McAnally	P	Mets	Expos
52	Jim Fairey	OF	Dodgers	Expos
54	Coco Laboy	3B	Cardinals	Expos
56	John Boccabella	C	Cubs	Expos
58	Ron Brand	C	Astros	Expos
60	John Glass	P	Mets	Expos
April 7, 1969				
23*	Bobby Wine	SS	Phillies	Expos

(Bobby Wine was offered to the Expos as compensation after Larry Jackson decided to retire rather than report to Montreal) blizzards and -20 degrees Celsius (-4°F) temperatures made the job damn near impossible. *The Associated Press* sent a reporter to assess the situation in mid-February 1969, two months before the first regular-season game was slated for Montreal. The reporter saw construction crews splitting the work between two shifts and toiling from 5 a.m. to 10 p.m. daily, yet they still had a long way to go. Work hadn't yet started on the locker rooms, nor were there tunnels leading to the dugouts. There were non-weather-related setbacks, too, including a bizarre incident in which steel that was supposed to be used to build the stands got sent to the wrong place. That set everything back another three weeks. As *AP* described it: "'We'll be ready,' insisted Lou Martin, Expos director of operations, as he looked Thursday over the snow-covered expanse that resembles a disaster area more than a future diamond."

Reporting on March 29, 1969—just 16 days before the scheduled home opener—*AP* bagged another quote from Martin, this one less optimistic. "We must have eight to 10 days of good, warm weather in the next two weeks to allow our new field to dry out. It is extremely hard and could become unplayable if the frost doesn't get out of it in a hurry."

Just four days later, Martin offered an even gloomier outlook. "Frustrating, frustrating, frustrating. We had the field in excellent shape and the 10 tons of straw I had on the infield all winter left everything fine." Fine, that is, until another snowstorm blasted the city. Martin's crew had just finished clearing all the snow from the newly erected bleachers when another six inches floated down on April 2. Less than two weeks before the Expos' grand coronation, no one knew if the team would play on a well-manicured field . . . or a vast, Arctic wasteland.

All of that would be left to Martin, and the crew of four hundred workers he assembled for that final, 12-day mad dash to the finish line. Meanwhile, McHale, Fanning, and the roster they'd assembled flew to New York for Opening Day, ready to take on the Mets. The man picked to lead the Expos onto the field for the first time was one who could run a tight ship, an old-school manager dismissed by the Phillies a year earlier: Gene Mauch.

On temperament alone, you could call Mauch the National League's version of Hall of Fame Orioles manager Earl Weaver. Generously listed at five foot seven, Weaver would often argue calls with umpires, firing spittle and vitriol and kicking dirt on any who dared oppose him. He'd cast scorn on umps, players, and even himself when things didn't go right. That was Mauch, too. A five-foot-ten bundle of nerves, he too argued calls with vigour and anger. But Mauch's critics claimed he was wound so tight that he'd sometimes psyche out his own team. Many of those criticisms seemed justified when Mauch presided over one of the worst collapses in baseball history.

In his book *October 1964*, David Halberstam described the wild pennant race that took shape in the National League that year. The Phillies racked up a 90–60 record heading into the home stretch, leading the league by 6½ games with 12 to play and a seven-game homestand coming up. Fans of baseball history know what happened next.

In the first game of that homestand, the Phillies faced the Reds. Tied 0–0 in the sixth inning, Reds third baseman Chico Ruiz made it to third base with two outs. Right-hander Art Mahaffey was pitching for the Phils. Stealing home under any circumstances takes uncommon anticipation, and guts. In a big spot, Ruiz read the play perfectly, dashed for home, and scored, giving the Reds a 1–0 lead that would hold up for the rest of the game, slicing Philly's league lead to 5½. "The play broke our humps," Phillies slugger Dick Allen said years later.

It's never easy to pinpoint exactly what causes a losing streak, let alone one of the biggest collapses in baseball history. But as the losses piled up following that first hump-breaker game, Mauch grew increasingly shell-shocked, lashing out at anyone he could in an attempt to bail his team out. Whether Mauch's agitated demeanour was a cause or merely a symptom, the Phillies ended up losing the pennant by a single game to St. Louis.

When Mauch took the Expos job five years later, little had changed.

"I broke in with the Cubbies under Leo Durocher," recalled Bill Stoneman, the little righty who became a member of the Expos' inaugural starting rotation (and almost immediately crafted one of the team's most memorable moments—more on that later). "Durocher was a tough, tough guy, and Gene Mauch was a tough guy, but I never had a problem with Gene. I understood his thinking, especially after playing a couple years for Durocher. He was a pretty demanding guy, so you learned a lot playing for him. There weren't any punches pulled when something didn't quite go the way that it should have, especially with mental errors. Physical errors are physical errors, but if you made a mental error, Gene got on you real quick."

Mauch was also considered a shrewd strategist. At a time when pitching ruled the game and bunting, stealing, and scratching out single runs was a universal approach, Mauch was the small-ball master. During the eight seasons in which he managed either all or most of the year in Philadelphia, Mauch's teams finished first in the National League in sacrifice bunts three times, second once, and never lower than fourth. You could argue that treating outs as precious rather than willingly giving them up is always sound strategy—even during the low-scoring '60s. But ask those who played for Mauch and they'll praise their skipper's extreme attention to detail.

"At Jarry Park you'd come into the clubhouse and have to walk right by his office," said Dan McGinn, a lefty swingman and original

Expo who played for three years under Mauch in Montreal. "There was this big board up there, and I mean it had everything. If it's the sixth inning and Pitcher X is pitching, pinch-hit with this guy. All the smallest details, he had it figured it out to a tee. Way ahead of the game."

Just learning to crawl in those first few years, those early, talent-starved Expos teams would push Mauch to the limits of his sanity. But the team wasn't all bad. McHale and Fanning were on to something when they roughly translated the prevailing theory of the expansion draft to "one man's trash is another man's treasure." Cobble together enough attractive, unprotected players from various teams and maybe you could somehow turn them into something better. It would require perfect circumstances, where a team possessing that kind of front-line player either didn't appreciate that player's talent, or was so spectacularly stupid that it would let ill-founded biases get in the way of sound player evaluation. The Houston Astros, it turned out, were happy to oblige. In a tremendous coup, the Expos would leverage three of its newly acquired rejects into its first star, one of the best and most popular players the franchise would ever know: the man who'd become known as Le Grand Orange.

The entire Astros brain trust disliked Rusty Staub, mostly for ridiculous reasons. It started when they gave him $90,000 as an 18-year-old bonus baby, stamping him as the boy destined to become the man who would lead Houston's expansion franchise to glory. Staub got the usual jealous glares and condescending jabs from teammates for being that young and that wealthy (at least for the time). But big bonuses also make managers and general managers expect big things out of players, even when they might be several years shy of their prime. Thrust into the everyday lineup at 19 for the 1963 season, Staub hit just .224 with minimal power. Reduced to part-time work the next year he was even worse, hitting .216 while also struggling defensively as the Astros shuttled him between first base and the outfield.

He took a big step forward in his third season, batting .256 with 14 home runs. And the next year, he set new career bests in multiple categories, making his first All-Star team, settling in as an everyday right fielder, and finishing fifth in the league with a .333 batting average.

During Staub's '67 campaign, *Sports Illustrated* ran a feature story in August on the big redhead; at the time, he was hitting in the .350s and in hot pursuit of the batting crown. The article contained the usual superlatives: Former Reds manager Fred Hutchinson claimed to have pegged Staub years earlier as a future star. Ted Williams called Staub one of the best hitters he'd ever seen. But one quote now pops off the page: "I see the Astros hired Harry Walker as a batting coach," said Mauch, then managing the Phillies. "Well, I'll tell you this: the best batting coach Houston ever had is Rusty Staub. That boy made himself into a hitter, and he did one hell of a job."

Staub could be stubborn, though. He was a tinkerer, and went from an upright stance—in which he held the bat high above his head and near the knob, swinging from his heels—to a crouch, in which he choked up and tried to spray the ball to all fields. Harry Walker was even more stubborn, objecting to Staub's self-diagnosis, even as the hits kept coming for the pupil he hadn't really helped. Staub didn't get along with manager Grady Hatton either. But beyond a mere clash of personalities, Hatton and Astros GM Spec Richardson simply didn't appreciate Staub's skills. Though he didn't hit for a high average until 1967, Staub always owned a good batting eye and a high-contact approach; he walked 52 times against 57 strikeouts in '65, drew 58 bases on balls against 61 whiffs in '66, and walked 60 times versus just 47 punchouts in '67 (albeit with 21 of those walks being intentional).

Houston management hoped for more power from their bonus baby as well, but didn't get it: though Staub posted a .398 on-base percentage (fourth-best in the league) and slugged .473 in 1967, he managed just 10 home runs. This too was a miscalculation, in which management knew the Astrodome was a tough place in which to hit home runs, but didn't realize how much power Staub could produce playing half his home games somewhere else—not to mention what might happen once he'd gained more experience.

The Astros fired Hatton as manager in the middle of 1968, replacing him with Walker. Meanwhile, Staub was in the midst of a disappointing downturn. Some of his lesser numbers were due to luck catching up with him—he'd been fortunate on balls in play in '67—and some were due to the Year of the Pitcher, when things were so tough on the hitters that the mound was lowered for the '69 season. But the bottom line is that Staub was still just 24, and already had four good seasons to his credit. Astros management saw something else, though.

Nuance was not Harry "The Hat" Walker's forte. Seizing on an opportunity to bail on a player he didn't like, Walker huddled with Richardson on trade possibilities that could whisk Staub out of town, preferably in exchange for proven veteran talent. The Expos, by their own design, would prove to be the perfect fit. McHale and Fanning were both big Staub fans, and they'd collected multiple flippable veterans to dangle in trade for just such an opportunity. Staub, of course, had one other admirer who helped seal the deal: the same man who'd praised the ginger-domed outfielder's skill while taking a subtle jab at Walker's instructional abilities in *SI*. Now skippering the Expos and drooling to get Staub, Gene Mauch went to meet with the Astros, leveraging contacts he had within the organization.

The Astros liked Jesus Alou, the 13th overall pick in the expansion draft. This was peculiar, given Alou made Staub's supposedly disappointing stats look stellar, coming off a .263/.278/.317 (average, on-base percentage, slugging) fiasco in '68. But Alou still had youth and potential on his side as well, just two years older than Staub at 26. The Expos were willing to add another expansion draft pickup, 33-year-old former Pirate Donn Clendenon, to seal the deal.

The two teams made the trade official on January 22. Clendenon flew to Houston to tour the facilities and meet the Astros' brass. A few days later, he announced that he would . . . retire. Clendenon claimed he could make as much money working for the Scripto pen company as he could playing for the Astros, and he backed up his words by going to Atlanta to do just that. But the skinny around baseball was that from his visit alone, Clendenon had already come to loathe the Astros brain trust almost as much as Staub did.

Whatever the reason, the Expos were now in trouble, because the Astros wanted Clendenon and wouldn't take anyone else. The trade looked stillborn, leaving the Expos without their potential franchise player.

Time for shenanigans.

"So John McHale had worked with Bowie Kuhn [who had replaced Eckert] in the commissioner's office, he was his number-two guy," said Bronfman. "I'd invited Bowie to spring training. Now Bowie, it was his first year as commissioner. He was the new kid on the block. So I remember, we were in a meeting for some time, we were told Kuhn was about to arrive. McHale said to me, 'Go put your uniform on.' 'You're kidding.' 'Do what I asked you. Go put your uniform on.' Staub had arrived, and McHale said the same thing to him. 'Rusty, go put a uniform on and go throw a ball. Play catch or something.'"

Even though the trade was unofficial, Staub already had an Expos uniform. And then . . .

"We see Kuhn arriving. So we go out to the field to greet

Kuhn, and there's McHale, Fanny, me. And I'm standing with Kuhn, and all of a sudden someone pulls me by the back of the scruff of the neck. It was [Expos travelling secretary] Gene Kirby. All of a sudden, I'm not next to Kuhn anymore, and a guy with an Expos uniform with flaming red hair is standing next to Kuhn, and the rest of us are standing next to them, wearing Expos uniforms too."

"I always had a contact with an *AP* photographer," recalled Fanning. "It dated back to my days with the Braves, who also trained in West Palm Beach. So whenever we needed a picture on the wire, I always called the guy to do it—we staged these things for him. So this time he comes out and takes this picture of Bowie, John, Charles, Rusty, and me. The photographer sent that all over the world. And John had a huge grin on his face, 'Well, that's that,' John always said. We publicized this picture, and it was tantamount to Rusty being a Montreal Expo."

The scheme drove the Astros—especially their outspoken owner "Judge" Roy Hofheinz—mad. With one publicity stunt, the Expos cemented the deal as far as Kuhn, and the rest of baseball, were concerned; the commissioner wanted the trade done, for fear of greater backlash if Houston backed out. The Expos and Astros would eventually make a revised deal official, just before Opening Day. McHale went to Atlanta and convinced Clendenon to unretire and play for the Expos. Montreal traded him later in the year to the eventual World Series champion Mets. The Expos then flipped Jack Billingham, Skip Guinn, and $100,000 to Houston to complete the Staub trade. It was a colossal relief for the deal's centrepiece.

"I knew nothing about Montreal," said Staub. "What got me was how much respect I had for Mauch, and how much he wanted me on his ball club. I knew I had to get out of Houston because of how they were operating—they brought my family into it, it was sick. While everybody was deciding my fate in terms of Clendenon playing or not, I told the commissioner I would not go back to Houston, I would not play for them."

Le Grand Orange would become a local hero on a team that struggled mightily for the first several years of its existence. But for Montrealers, the thrill of seeing baseball *chez nous* trumped any fleeting disappointment over any one loss, or even one hundred losses. One of the first, and greatest, thrills happened on April 8, 1969—the first time the Expos ever took the field for a regular-season game.

On a sunny day at Shea Stadium, the Expos sent 33-year-old veteran cast-off Mudcat Grant to the mound to face Tom Seaver. No big deal—all Seaver had done in his first two big-league seasons was win 32 games, post a 2.47 ERA, win National League Rookie of the Year, and make the All-Star team twice. He would remain a beast in '69, going 25–7 and winning his first Cy Young Award while leading the Mets to one of the most dramatic and surprising World Series titles in baseball history. This, then, was what you might call a colossal mismatch.

The team's architects hardly cared. This was going to be a momentous day, even if the Expos lost 20–0.

"It's still one of my biggest thrills in baseball," recalled Fanning. "Opening Day at Shea Stadium, brand-new unis no one had ever seen, these crisp uniforms on a beautiful day in New York City. Mayor Drapeau throwing out the first pitch next to Charles and McHale. The Canadian flag. The Canadian national anthem being sung. Those were thrills that brought tears to my eyes."

☞ OPENING DAY 1969 STARTING LINEUP ☜

The nine men who started for the Expos in the first regular-season game in franchise history formed a ragtag group of cast-offs. Some of them never amounted to much, while a few others offered colourful backstories but few major contributions to their new team's cause. Here are the Opening Day Nine:

Maury Wills, SS: The 21st pick in the NL expansion draft, Wills was 36 years old when the Expos picked him, six years removed from winning an ill-begotten MVP award, and past his physical prime. He could still play, though, having swiped 52 bases the year before, still playing respectable defence and legging out his share of hits.

But he sure as hell didn't want to play in Montreal. Wills jaked plays blatantly, making half-hearted efforts on defence, failing to run out groundballs, and drawing boos from the usually fawning first-year crowd. Jacques Doucet, who started his career covering the Expos as a beat writer for *La Presse* before going on to call games as the team's primary French-language play-by-play man for 33 seasons, counts Wills as one of the few players with whom he didn't get along in all his years covering the team and announcing its games. Everything came to a head when Wills slugged beat writer Ted Blackman on the team bus a few weeks into the season.

Was Wills frustrated that his best days were behind him? Not according to Bronfman.

"Bullshit," said the owner. "Hell no. To him, he had gone from the Los Angeles Dodgers, where he was famous, to goddamn Pittsburgh, and now he's going to this honky-tonk joint in Montreal where they goddamn spoke French, and the infield

31

is terrible, and you're playing in a bandbox, it was a Triple-A stadium. Who needs that? So he played like he didn't give a damn, and he didn't."

Wills played 47 games for the Expos, posted the worst numbers of his career, then got traded back to the Dodgers (along with Manny Mota, for Ron Fairly and Paul Popovich). Like magic, Wills' performance shot back up immediately.

"I said to John McHale after, 'John, this teaches us a lesson: never trade for anybody unless that guy feels it's a promotion,'" recalled Bronfman, who'd tossed a subtle compliment Staub's way. "'Wills obviously felt like it was a demotion. They've got to feel like it's a promotion to come to Montreal.'"

Gary Sutherland, 2B: At 24, Sutherland was one of the youngest players left unprotected by any NL team. The Phillies saw him as a light-hitting second baseman who might be able to hit for a decent average thanks to a high-contact approach, but with little to no power and below-average defence—and thus limited upside. The Expos ended up getting all of that, except without the decent batting average. Lacking both speed and pop, Sutherland was an easily-defensed player who'd go on to post low batting averages (.239, .206, .257) and poor on-base percentages (.289, .271, .302) in his three years in Montreal.

Sutherland was a popular teammate, though, and is still highly regarded by ex-mates to this day. You could live with him as your 25th man. But as the Expos' everyday man at the deuce in '69, he was overexposed: the kind of player an expansion team was bound to carry as a placeholder until someone better came along.

Rusty Staub, RF: Having long ago abandoned his given name of Daniel Joseph, Rusty earned a nickname on top of a nickname when Blackman playfully dubbed him Le Grand Orange. (The proper article in front of "orange" would normally be the feminine "la," but as Blackman said, "If you think I was going to put a feminine article on his name, you're crazy.") Staub was one of the best players in the league during the Expos' inaugural season, batting .302/.426/.526: monstrous numbers at a time when pitchers still ruled the game. He became the Expos' first superstar, nearly as much for what he did off the field as what he did on it. (Much more on Staub later.)

Mack Jones, LF: It might seem odd to think of an Atlanta-born, African-American man as a doppelgänger for a ginger-pated, pale-skinned New Orleans native, but Jones and Staub formed perfect bookends for those early Expos teams. Reduced to part-time duty with the Reds in 1968, Jones was left unprotected in the expansion draft and became the Expos' second pick after Manny Mota. Still just 30 when he took the field at Shea Stadium to start the '69 season, Jones showed he had plenty left in the tank. He hit .270/.379/.488 that year, mirroring Staub's profile as a high on-base, good-power guy in putting up the best numbers of his career. Slowed by injuries, however, he'd be out of baseball just two years later.

Bob Bailey, 1B: If it seems like John McHale and Jim Fanning had a little Billy Beane in them . . . well, it's mostly a coincidence. If walks and on-base percentage were underappreciated during the *Moneyball* A's era, they were flat-out ignored 45 years ago by nearly everyone except Earl Weaver. But the Expos' front office didn't search under rocks for OBP sources the way Beane and his Oakland predecessor Sandy Alderson did. They simply looked for underrated players. Just as Staub and Jones provided value that wasn't obviously reflected in their batting averages (especially their early-career batting averages), Bailey too was a low-to-moderate batting-average guy who had a strong batting eye. Mostly, though, he was just a guy no one wanted.

The Pirates signed Bailey in 1961 out of Woodrow Wilson High School in Long Beach, California for $135,000, the richest signing bonus ever given to a player to that point. In his first full season in 1963, he hit .228/.303/.328, a crushing disappointment that, as with Staub's early-career scuffles, ignored the reality that most players aren't anywhere close to finished products in their early 20s. Bailey had weaknesses certainly, playing poor defence at third base and averaging a merely decent 12 homers a year in his first four full major league seasons, not remotely enough to live up to this early hype.

What he could do, though, was walk. In his third full season with the Pirates at age 22, Bailey drew 70 bases on balls. He struggled with injuries the following year but actually boosted his walk rate, drawing a free pass in about 11 percent of his times at bat and posting an impressive .279/.360/.447 line (24 percent better than league-average results based on advanced, park-adjusted stats). That still wasn't enough for the Buccos, who traded him to the Dodgers for . . . future Expos teammate Maury Wills. Nagging injuries ate into Bailey's playing time and hurt his performance over the next two years, certainly. But the Dodgers, like the Pirates, were fed up with a player widely believed to be a bust. Even with blank rosters coming into the expansion draft, neither the Padres nor their expansion cousins in Montreal bothered to use one of the top 60 picks on Bailey. Instead, the Dodgers more or less gave him away.

Surprisingly, Bailey quickly became one of the most potent hitters on his new team. Though sidetracked again by injuries, he still hit .265/.337/.419 over 111 games in 1969; the Expos recognized he could do less harm defensively at first base than at third, so that helped too. The next season, all that bonus-baby potential finally rampaged through the rest of the league. In 1970, Bailey flashed a .407 on-base percentage (sixth-best in the NL for players with 400 or more plate appearances), while finishing second in slugging average (.597), and tied for 14th in home runs (28, the same total as the 39-year-old Willie Mays). Though that season proved to be the best of Bailey's career, he became a reliable right-handed power hitter who also ranked among the top 10 in walks three times.

Bob Bailey might've been a flawed player—if you're grading on a steep curve, perhaps he really was a bit of a disappointment—but the man could do some things well. And when you're a brand-new franchise trying to build something from nothing, that's saying a lot.

John Bateman, C: A bruiser listed at six foot three, 220 pounds—at a time when that was actually huge and not just the dimensions of CC Sabathia's left leg—Bateman smacked 17 homers in 1966 with the Astros. Unfortunately, he had few other obvious skills. Bateman couldn't stay healthy either, playing in just 74 games during the Expos' debut season and angering Mauch for ballooning well past his reputed playing weight. A plodder even by catcher standards, Bateman managed to lead the league by hitting into 27 double plays in 1971. Like most of his team-mates, Bateman soaked up playing time and fit in well on a close-knit group, lived in Montreal year-round, grew to love the city, and became a central part of the community. But he too was a standby, dutifully squatting through April shiverfests at Jarry and August scorchers in St. Louis while the Expos built a farm system that would produce more talented replacements. Few would work out better than Bateman's eventual successor.

Jose "Coco" Laboy, 3B: Laboy had never played a major league game when the Expos grabbed him with the 54th pick of the expansion draft at 28, long past the age at which most prospects make the Show. With Bailey moving to first base and no better options, the Expos rolled out the Puerto Rico–born Laboy on Opening Day at third base . . . and got more than they expected. Appearing in 157 games, Laboy cracked 18 homers and drove in 83 runs. In a weak first-year class, Laboy finished second in Rookie of the Year voting, losing out to the Dodgers' Ted Sizemore.

Then it all fell apart. Laboy hit just .199 the next year, lost his everyday job, and played his last major league game in 1973. Despite the speed with which he came and went, Laboy left an impression on old-time Expos fans and ex-teammates that has yet to fade. "He played his heart out," gushed McGinn.

Don Hahn, CF: Another player who made his big-league debut in the Expos' first game, Hahn started all three games of that first series against the Mets . . . and no more that whole season, the great majority of which he spent in the minors. In a reversal of the bonus-baby phenomenon, Hahn was just 20 when he broke in, but also a modestly-paid rookie who'd been a 17th-round draft choice by the Giants three years earlier. The Expos needed a body to man centre field on Opening Day, settled briefly on Hahn, then spent most of the next decade scrambling to find someone who'd stick.

Jim "Mudcat" Grant, SP: One of the first successful African-American starting pitchers in the majors, Grant broke in with the Indians in 1958. He earned his nickname after roommate Larry Doby declared him "ugly as a Mississippi mudcat." Grant made the All-Star team in 1963 and 1965 as a starter, but by the end of the 1968 season he had become almost exclusively a relief pitcher. Still, he'd put up strong numbers in '68, posting a 2.08 ERA and allowing just one home run in 95 innings for the Dodgers. They left him unprotected in the expansion draft anyway, and the Expos took a flyer, eventually deciding on Grant as the man who'd throw the franchise's first-ever official pitch.

It didn't take long to realize this was a mistake. Grant got blasted for 33 runs and 64 hits in his first 51 innings. On June 3, the Expos swapped Grant to St. Louis for fellow pitcher Gary Waslewski. A year after getting that Opening Day start, Grant split the 1970 season between Oakland and Pittsburgh, working exclusively as a reliever—where he belonged at that point in his career. He had a huge year, tossing a staggering 135 innings with a 1.86 ERA. This was a classic case of talent scarcity forcing Montreal into putting a player in the wrong spot. It would take several more years for the Expos to develop enough quality talent to curb those kinds of mistakes.

The first regular-season game the Expos ever played started auspiciously for the underdogs. After Maury Wills led off and struck out looking, Gary Sutherland reached on an error. With two outs, Mack Jones walked. Bob Bailey followed with the franchise's first-ever RBI, lacing a double to drive home Sutherland, with an error by Mets second baseman Ken Boswell cashing a second run. (That would be the first of three errors committed by Boswell that day, still an Opening Day record.)

The game turned into a slugfest, with Grant foreshadowing the rapid demise of his Expos career by getting knocked out after 1⅓ innings pitched. Despite the pitching troubles, the Expos benefitted from a most unlikely hitting highlight. Tied 3–3 heading to the fourth, Mauch left McGinn in to bat against Seaver—a relief pitcher, facing one of the greatest arms of all time. Seaver left a pitch up, and the lefty-swinging McGinn hammered it. The ball carried and carried, all the way to the wall in right-centre. It hit the top of the wall . . . and popped right over for a home run.

McGinn was a first-round pick by the Reds in the 1966 secondary draft (MLB used to hold two amateur drafts, in June and then another, lesser draft in January), a great athlete who lettered as a punter at Notre Dame and also excelled at baseball. He wound up lasting five seasons in the majors, with a lofty 5.11 ERA. Still, he'll always have his big moment.

The Expos kept pouring it on, getting two doubles from Jones and homers from Laboy and Staub, with Le Grand Orange reaching base five times. They led 11–6 heading to the bottom of the ninth, their first-ever win seemingly in the bag—until it wasn't. This was years before every team had a designated closer, and a brand-new team like the Expos wasn't going to have a Mariano Rivera trotting into games anyway. Instead, they tried to ride Don Shaw, who'd been left unprotected by the Mets in the expansion draft. Shaw had pitched three scoreless innings to that point, and Mauch had nothing resembling a true fireman behind him, so what the hell, see if he can get three more outs. The Mets jumped all over Shaw in the ninth, stringing together two singles, a walk, and a homer on their way to a four-run rally.

Now leading by just one run, Mauch called on Carroll Sembera, a rail-thin Texan who hadn't pitched a single major league game the year before and was so lightly regarded that he went unclaimed in the expansion draft and was instead taken in December's Rule 5 draft—an annual clearinghouse for organizational rejects, or at least players who don't fit. Sembera quickly poured gas on the fire, walking Amos Otis and giving up a single to Tommie Agee, putting the potential tying and winning runs on base.

That brought rookie right fielder Rod Gaspar to the plate. Looking back decades later, it seems crazy that the Mets won the 1969 World Series. Gaspar was one of several Opening Day starters who had little business starting for a championship team; he would hit just .228 with one home run that year. In the battle of resistible force versus moveable object, Sembera prevailed, striking out Gaspar to end the game. The Expos were undefeated.

For baseball-loving Montrealers, this was a big deal.

"I was in elementary school in Chambly, I'm 12 years old," said Expos superfan Katie Hynes, cradling a pint while recounting one of her favourite baseball memories. "My principal—and every time I see him . . . he came to my dad's funeral, and we still talk about this every time we see each other—he let us listen to the game on the school intercom!

"In those days, we wore funky hats, it was the '60s. I remember, he made us stand up at our lockers. We were lining up at our lockers and he said, 'Ladies and gentlemen, the Expos have just won their first game.' And reflex action—every kid picked up their hat and threw it in the air. And it wasn't rehearsed. It was a natural reaction. We were hugging each other. I could cry, you know?"

After that first road trip, the team flew to Montreal for another major event: the first home game for the team, the city, and the country.

Still, there was a problem. Teams of workers had toiled around the clock to clear away the early-spring snow while others laboured to coax the grass and dirt into playable shape. But Martin and his crew had run out of time to bolt thousands of permanent seats into place. So the night before the big game, everyone dropped what they were doing and rushed to set up folding chairs—six thousand of them, all told. Sensing the urgency of the deadline, even Fanning joined the effort. Let's see Connie Mack do that.

The birth of the Expos in '69 and that long-awaited home opener delivered a jolt of electricity to the city's baseball-hungry fans. It also gave many people—the players, McHale, Fanning, Mauch—a golden opportunity to prove themselves, or in some cases re-prove themselves. Beyond the men swinging bats, throwing balls, and making decisions, it was a heady time for others too. Few more so than Dave Van Horne.

Born and raised in Easton, Pennsylvania, Van Horne established himself at an early age as a broadcaster, calling baseball, basketball, and football games right out of college in Virginia. When the Richmond Braves Triple-A franchise debuted in 1966, Van Horne was the one calling the games, a job he would hold for three years. At the end of the '68 season, with the Braves done for the year and the four new MLB expansion clubs announced, Van Horne sent out two applications, one to Kansas City and one to Montreal. He had a slight connection with McHale, who'd been ousted as Atlanta's GM midway through the 1966 season, shortly after Van Horne started doing games for Richmond. Still, as the calendar ticked over to 1969, Van Horne hadn't heard anything, nor did the Expos have any idea who'd be broadcasting their games. With three hundred applications sitting in a drawer and only a few days to go until the start of spring training, McHale still hadn't hired an English-language broadcast team.

Still, it wouldn't be the 1969 Expos without a story of slapdash operations and last-minute stress. It was Lou Martin who would again step up to fix a potentially dicey situation. The man in charge of whipping Jarry Park into shape had McHale's ear on other matters too. Martin had served as the Richmond Braves' GM while McHale ran the big club. Hire the Van Horne kid, Martin advised. That was that. At 27 years old, Van Horne landed a gig calling baseball games for a brand-new team, in a city he'd never seen.

Van Horne would have just five days to develop a rapport with broadcast partner Russ Taylor before heading to New York for Opening Day. The broadcast went relatively smoothly anyway. Problem was, in the rush to simply produce a professional broadcast, no one had stopped to reflect on its historical nature . . . so no one bothered to tape the broadcast back home at the radio station.

When Taylor and Van Horne flew up to Montreal, they were better prepared. They were also blown away by the spectacle that unfolded.

"They had an Opening Day parade," Van Horne recounted over coffee in Miami in January 2012. "You had a couple hundred thousand people out to see a team they've never seen and see players they've never heard of except for one or two guys. The park was jam-packed—well, 'jam-packed' meaning they got 28,000-plus people for the opener, as full as it could get. Lou always had the knack of bumping that up to 30,000 or 31,000, which may have counted the people standing on the snow bank beyond the right-field fence to watch the games.

"What I remember is based mostly on what Russ told me. Because I saw limos pulling up and people getting out dressed to the nines. I said, 'Russ, this is like an event that's caught on here. All the high rollers seem to be coming out.' And he said, it's all of Charles' friends. The community would not dare turn its back on this enterprise that Charles is involved in, and he said he is greatly involved in the community here in Montreal. He never said the Jewish community. Everything that Charles was involved in in Montreal, from corporations to hospitals to museums, they all came out because it was Charles. Not that there weren't some baseball fans amongst them. There were, of course. But most of them came because this was Charles' baby."

☞ THE LOGO ☜

MD/TM

Ever looked at an Expos cap? Like, *really* looked at one? What do you see?

For the first 19 years of my life, I saw the letters "elb", and nothing else. Others have put forth various alternate interpretations. Some have claimed the logo is simply "eb." A few pointed to "mb." Still others squinted and somehow saw "cb."

Each of those interpretations has required theories as to what the initials might mean. The "eb" combination was easy to decipher—that had to be "Expos Baseball." The "mb" camp had it as "Montreal Baseball." Little Jonah and teenage Jonah figured "elb" must mean "Expos Limited Baseball." Conspiracy theorists had their own ideas. Those who saw "cb" figured this was some self-serving callback for owner Charles Bronfman. And if you were way out there, you had "eb" pegged for Ellen Bronfman, the name of Charles' daughter.

It took my college girlfriend—not much of a baseball fan when we met and barely aware of the Expos' existence, much less their logo—to finally set me straight. "Don't you see," she said. The lower-case letters were "eb," for "Expos Baseball." Take a step back and eyeball the larger pattern, and you can see that it's a giant "M." For "Montreal."

Turned out she was right—as both Charles Bronfman and his son, Stephen, confirmed.

The pomp and circumstance at the parade mesmerized the players too.

"You thought you were at an inauguration," McGinn told me in 2013. "There was confetti coming down, the parade went through the heart of downtown. We were all dressed in uniform. The whole thing felt like we'd just won the World Series. Most of the guys still talk about it."

The first game at Jarry Park was an even bigger party.

"Drapeau was on a roll," said legendary quipster Tim Burke, sitting on a bar patio on Bishop Street in downtown Montreal, recalling his years covering the Expos for the *Montreal Star* (and later the *Montreal Gazette*). "The day before was a blizzard. He must have waved a wand or something, it was such a glorious day. Everything kept building up after that first game in New York. They won, and you couldn't believe how it all happened, McGinn hitting that famous home run, and then just hanging on for dear life. It was the most exciting thing you could imagine. Then they come home for that first game. It was such a scene, it felt like everybody all across North America was watching."

The players themselves came together from all across North America. Simply being in Montreal was a new experience for everyone on the roster—at least until the team acquired its first Quebec-born player four months later.

"We had no idea about Montreal," said Stoneman. "So somebody said, 'Well, use the subway. You can get around real easy.' I remember going out to the park with some of the other guys. We were all in what was then the Windsor Hotel down on Peel between Dorchester and Sainte-Catherine. It was a nice old hotel and you could get on the subway not far from there and we kind of figured out how to get out near the stadium. We made a mistake on our first trip out, got off at the wrong station. But it was a heck of a nice day, so we had a nice walk.

"The one thing I remember about the park was there was still a snow bank behind the right-field wall. Right between the pool and the outside fence was a big pile of snow. It was April, so the ground was thawing out. So, the field was really soft. I mean really soft. It was a bit rough. It was the first major league game played on that field and it was rougher than other major league parks. The ground was so soft that behind home plate, the catcher was John Bateman—I forget who the umpire was that day—but both of them ended up standing about two or three inches lower at the end of the game than they were at the start of the game, just sinking into the ground as the game went on."

Quicksand field aside, the home opener was another wild game. In the bottom of the first, the Expos put two men on for Jones. Cardinals right-hander Nelson Briles delivered, and Jones launched a three-run homer. Funny thing about first impressions: Montreal's fans were ready to embrace the home nine just for showing up to play—but when your first at-bat in front of the hometown faithful results in a three-run bomb? Well, that's how legends are born. Fans would christen the left-field stands as "Jonesville," and for the two-plus seasons that he remained an Expo, Mack Jones was simply the Mayor of Jonesville.

Montreal piled up three more runs, taking a 6–0 lead into the fourth. As they would do all year long, the Expos again reminded everyone how tough it is to collect enough top-quality starting pitching. The club's rotation would finish with the highest ERA (4.34) and highest walk rate in the National League, and in the home opener foisted lefty Larry Jaster upon the unsuspecting crowd. It wasn't pretty. After holding St. Louis scoreless for three innings, Jaster got creamed for seven runs in the fourth, the big blows coming on a Joe Torre home run and a grand slam by banjo-hitting Dal Maxvill, one of just six homers he'd hit in his 14-year career. Save some blame for the Expos' defence, though: in one of the worst defensive displays in major league history, Montreal committed *five* errors in that disastrous fourth inning.

The Expos tied the score in the bottom of the fourth, scoring a single run on a wild pitch but failing to tack on more, despite loading the bases with nobody out. Meanwhile, the Cardinals suddenly couldn't buy a run. Taking over in the fourth, McGinn went on to allow just three hits and one walk over 5⅓ innings, without giving up a single score.

Montreal still needed a hitting hero, though. With two outs and Laboy on second in the bottom of the seventh, the pitcher's spot was due up. McGinn had already thrown 3⅓ innings and done more than anyone could've reasonably hoped. Mauch the constant string-puller could now pinch-hit, then set up his bullpen to get the matchups he wanted. That is, if he had some actual viable options. Mauch's bullpen consisted of the leftovers of leftovers, the pitchers not good enough to make a leaky rotation. There were no ace pinch-hitters waiting eagerly on the bench. Meanwhile, his southpaw reliever was mowing down every Cardinal in sight. The last time the Expos' skipper faced a similar decision, he left McGinn in and got rewarded with the team's first home run. What the hell, might as well roll the dice again.

Waslewski—the St. Louis pitcher who would get traded for Mudcat Grant a few weeks later—tried to sneak a fastball by his mound counterpart. Instead, McGinn slapped a single to left, scoring Laboy and providing what would turn out to be the winning run in an 8–7 victory. In a season in which they would win just 52 times, the Expos still managed to win the two most important contests of the year: their first game, and their first home game.

"You just couldn't believe it—they won the friggin' game," said Burke. "The happening was so total that when we were driving home, out of the clear blue sky, we see all these kids with gloves on. Driving from Jean-Talon all the way out to N.D.G., every kid was out playing baseball, throwing the ball around. It seemed like every single kid had an Expos hat on."

Just eight games later, Expos fans would celebrate again, this time for the first real baseball milestone in the team's existence.

The ball club flew to Philadelphia to get a first look at the Phillies. Starting for Montreal in the series opener was Stoneman, a 31st-round pick in 1966 who had been a long shot just to make it to the Show. He was tiny for a pitcher of his era (or most other eras) at just five-foot-ten, 170 pounds. But his assortment of breaking pitches served him well in pro ball. He cracked the big leagues just a year after being drafted, debuting in July of '67. Stoneman became a key reliever with a Cubs team that held a share of first place into late July. Things didn't go nearly as well in '68. He posted a 5.52 ERA, pitching himself out of favour in Chicago, and especially with legendary manager Leo Durocher. Stoneman had an excellent reason for his struggles, even if the Cubs didn't care one way or another.

"I didn't go to spring training because of my military obligations," Stoneman said. "So I started the season late, and just could never get it going. There wasn't really any reason for it, no injuries, or anything like that. When I showed up they stuck me straight into the major leagues—I didn't even go to the minor leagues straight out of basic training. That didn't work too well."

Whether or not Stoneman's National Guard stint contributed to his lousy 1968 season, the Cubs left him unprotected for the expansion draft, which is how the Expos landed him. But despite his modest pedigree, Stoneman had talent: he'd shown he could hack it in the majors in his rookie season, and he was just 24 years old when the Expos scooped him up. Here was an opportunity for McHale and Fanning to make good on one of those hidden gems they hoped to find.

Stoneman and McGinn, roommates for three years with the Expos, also served in the same Army National Guard unit in Winooski, Vermont—a two-hour drive from Montreal. The commitment at that time required six months of training to start, then five-and-a-half years of 39 round-trips a year. With that many drives to Vermont required, Stoneman and McGinn were bound to miss the odd game.

"The majority of the hard stuff was during the two weeks in the off-season we had to do," said McGinn. "Drills, marches. Activities camouflaging people out in the woods where you'd have to find them. Marching. Building small buildings. A lot of manual stuff. I remember we had guard duty one night. We had to get it done to defer from being drafted [into service for the Vietnam War]. Most clubs put enough money in you, they obviously didn't want you to end up in the draft."

Things really got crazy when Stoneman and McGinn—as well as teammates Mike Wegener and Terry Humphrey—had to drive across the border to fulfill their military commitment, then hustle back up to Montreal to play the same night. Players would wake at 3:30 or four in the morning, get in the car, and make it to formation 6:30 a.m., ready to start their duty day. They'd clock out at 4:30 p.m., then drive back to Montreal.

"One time I did all that, and I had to pitch that night," Stoneman said. "I got up early in the morning, drove to Vermont and drove back, same as usual. It went great. I don't know to this day how. We were facing the Pirates at Jarry Park. I'm driving back and I mean really fighting traffic. Everybody's pulling into the parking lot, fans, everybody. I'm trying to get past those people so I can get in, pull one uniform off and put the other uniform on. I remember facing Bob Veale of the Pirates. And it just went great. I threw a shutout. That was probably my proudest moment, but I was totally exhausted. So what happened the next day? I had to get up at 3:30 the next morning to make it down to Vermont for more duty."

Military obligations aside, his first season with the Expos didn't start well for Stoney. In his first start, the Mets crushed him for four runs right out of the gate, and Mauch pulled his right-hander after just a third of an inning. Stoneman pitched better in his second start against his old club in Chicago, going 8⅔ innings and striking out nine. But he still gave up seven runs in a 7–6 Expos loss.

His third start wasn't supposed to happen. There'd been a rainout the day before in Philly, the elements so harsh that the Expos didn't even bother leaving their hotel. The next day, April 17, Grant was supposed to start against the Phillies. Instead, Mauch made a change.

"When I got to the ballpark, the ball was in my shoe," Stoneman recalled. "Everybody's shoes were sitting in front of the locker in every clubhouse and the starting pitcher always had a ball in his shoe. That's not how you found out, but that was just kind of a traditional thing, the ball would be in your shoe. But I knew before going to the ballpark because I got a call that morning from the pitching coach. I told Mud. He wasn't too pleased."

The day didn't start auspiciously, as leadoff man Tony Taylor drew a walk. But Stoneman quickly began carving through the Phillies' lineup. He struck out Philly's 3 and 4 hitters, John Briggs and Deron Johnson, to end the first. He induced several ground-outs and lazy flyouts (nine groundball outs and nine flyball outs in total). Stoneman did walk five, but there were only two close calls, both early in the game. In the second, Phillies shortstop Don Money hit a flyball off the end of his bat to centre. Expos centre fielder Don Bosch misplayed it, thinking it was hit harder than it was. Bosch broke back, then came racing in for a shoestring catch. The other scare came in the third, as Stoneman left a ball up to Taylor, who stung a line drive to right . . . but right at Staub.

As the innings wore on and Stoneman piled up routine outs, a buzz started rippling through the Expos dugout.

"We knew what was going on," said Staub. "I had three doubles and a home run in that game, so I was really focused. It was one of the great nights of my career. Really it was one of *the* great evenings, especially for a new franchise."

The Expos built a 7–0 lead, leaving Stoneman to focus on the task at hand. In the ninth inning, he had to get through the meat of the order: number-two hitter Ron Stone, followed by Briggs and Johnson. In the end, it was shockingly routine. Stoneman struck out the first two batters, then got Johnson to roll over on a gimme groundout to short.

The totals for the game: seven runs on 13 hits for the Expos, zero runs and zero hits for the Phillies. In a two-hour, 24-minute game played in front of just 6,496 people at old Connie Mack Stadium—just the ninth regular-season game in Expos history—Stoneman twirled a no-hitter.

"The greatest thing I remember," recalled his roommate McGinn, "is we were staying at the Chase Park Plaza hotel in St. Louis a few days later, and they sent him an eight-inch cheesecake. They were famous for it. That's what I remember, this big huge cake from the hotel, congratulating him. That's how we celebrated."

No other expansion team has ever come close to bagging a no-hitter so soon into their team's history. The Mets waited 50 years before Johan Santana finally pulled it off in Queens. This, then, was a big moment for the Expos, an on-field breakthrough to go with the team's other, more incidental firsts that year. Montreal fans were over the moon that baseball had returned. With a thin roster that would lose a lot of games and take years to build up, those fans would take any real baseball they could get.

CHAPTER TWO

Swimming in Their Own Pool (1970–1973)

O ver time, the Expos would become known locally as *Nos Amours*—the ones we love. As with almost any expansion team, though, the losses piled up in the beginning, and star power was scarce. Baseball-hungry fans streamed into Jarry Park in the early years for another reason: to see visiting stars do their thing.

Those who packed old Delorimier Downs to see the Montreal Royals had never stopped pining for baseball. They parked themselves in front of their TVs every Saturday to watch the MLB Game of the Week. They flipped through the newspapers—English and French alike—to scan the box scores, and they devoured the game stories to follow their favourite players and teams.

Jacques Doucet recalled starting at *La Presse* in 1962, the youngest person on the sports desk by several years. His boss insisted he stay 'til the wee hours every night during baseball season, writing up not only the score but a detailed recap of every game, including those played on the West Coast. When the Expos finally arrived in '69, Doucet became the team's beat writer for *La*

Presse, while also serving as official scorer at Jarry Park and occasionally filling in for Jean-Pierre Roy doing colour commentary for the French-language radio station CKLM 1570. The baseball diehards who would read his accounts—plus those in the *Montreal Gazette*, *Montreal Star*, and *le Journal de Montréal*—could now do something they couldn't before.

"They had the opportunity to see, to almost touch the top players of the National League," said Doucet, sitting in his living room in Montreal's South Shore. "It was a novelty, that you could see Willie Mays, or a Steve Carlton, or a Tom Seaver, or a Willie Stargell, the big names that you had read about, watched on TV. Now you could see them in the flesh. You could get an autograph or take a picture with them too, because way back then, when the players were not making millions and millions of dollars, they were more accessible than they are today."

It didn't matter how close you were to the Expos at first. You, or somebody close to you, had already built allegiances to other teams and players, forged over years of watching baseball without a hometown team.

"This was a few years in, and I remember my own son Stephen, he was eight," said Bronfman. "He obviously was a big baseball fan by then, so I said to him, 'Do you want a [jersey with a] number?' He said number eight. I said, 'Steve, [light-hitting Expos outfielder] Boots Day is a nice little player, but he's not a great player. Why don't you choose some other number on our team? He said, 'Dad, this is not our team.' I said, 'Then who's number eight for?' He said, 'Willie Stargell.' Even my own son wanted some other team's All-Star's number."

It wasn't hard to figure out why Stargell was popular in Montreal (or why he was notorious, depending on your point of view). Aside from being one of the league's most powerful hitters on one of the best teams, Stargell hit 17 home runs at Jarry Park, more homers than any other visiting player. The elements heavily impacted results on the field in Montreal, and right-handed hitters frequently complained about the stiff wind that would knock down flyballs headed to left field. Lefty swingers like Stargell, on the other hand, often benefitted from the wind, which carried many seemingly routine flyballs over the wall.

"You would do your best," said Steve Rogers, a right-handed starter who called Jarry Park home for the first four years of his career and would become one of the best pitchers in Expos history. "The flags would be whipping to right field, but you at least had left field and centre field to pitch to. If the wind was calm, it was just a bandbox. With a little fence too, so you'd get these balls that would be doubles most other places, they'd fly out for home runs there."

Stargell rarely hit cheapies, though. On July 16, 1969, he launched a shot over the right-field wall that travelled an estimated 495 feet. The ball flew so far that it soared out of the entire stadium, landing in a municipal swimming pool outside the ballpark. That blast marked the first time anyone had hit a ball into the pool, and quickly cemented Stargell's reputation as the beast of Jarry Park. The chlorinated resting place for his home runs would come to be known as *la piscine de Willie*—Willie's pool. When Stargell and the Pirates visited Montreal in 1982, his final season, the city of Montreal presented him with a life preserver, honouring the baseball he sent to a watery grave.

The Expos did have one bona fide star of their own, however. He would become one of the deadliest hitters in the league, and a hero to the entire province. Rusty Staub, Le Grand Orange himself, was the one player the Expos could put up against just about anybody.

Staub had to endure big changes upon arriving in Montreal. The day he flew in to meet his new bosses, it was 78 degrees

Fahrenheit in Houston . . . and below the freezing mark in *la belle province*. And on a team that hadn't yet played a major league game, he'd have to take on new responsibilities: star player, and beacon to the entire community. Staub was up to the task.

"He had so much charisma," said Bronfman. "He liked the fans, and he learned a few words of French to help. He had been sort of a semi-star in Houston; now he wanted to be a big star. He found the place where he could be that big star."

Free of the poisonous relationship he'd endured with Astros management, Staub thrived. In '69, he cranked 29 homers and drew 110 walks against just 61 strikeouts. Going by OPS+ (an advanced metric that accounts for a player's on-base and slugging ability, and also adjusts for park effects), Staub tied for the fourth-best hitting performance in the National League that year, trailing only future Hall of Famers Willie McCovey, Hank Aaron, and Roberto Clemente. He posted impressive numbers the next two years too, hitting .274/.394/.497 (with 30 home runs) in 1970, and .311/.392/.482 in 1971, making the All-Star team in each of his first three years in Montreal.

"He was our only All-Star," said McGinn, Staub's teammate in Montreal from 1969 through 1971. "They had to pick a guy from every team, of course. But he was by far the best we had—very deserving. He was a great hitter, had a strong arm. And as Gene Mauch put it, he led the league in fantastic catches of routine flyballs. Always sliding and diving. Gene would say to him, 'Why don't you take a couple steps up and catch the ball!'—instead of running and sliding. That's how it always was with Rusty, though. In '68 I faced him when I was with the Reds and he was with the Astros. He could really hit. But he had so many people wanting him to do other things, tearing him one way and another."

In Houston, his hitting coach and manager tried to screw with his swing almost every day, but in Montreal, the expectations were different. The Expos trusted Staub to hit as he saw fit. They embraced his eccentricities, such as Staub bringing a full set of cooking implements on every road trip (a few years later, he would become a restaurateur). But they did place a different kind of demand on him, sometimes tacitly, sometimes more overtly. They urged Staub to become the face of the team, and an ambassador to the community. This was a challenge he happily embraced.

Staub's first step was to learn to speak French—some French anyway, somewhere between knowing what his own nickname meant and true fluency. He'd go out to lunch with francophone friends and insist that they speak French the whole meal. "Comment dit-on"—"How do you say"—became his go-to phrase. Staub sought practical knowledge in particular. He wanted to get around town, order in restaurants, tell cabbies where to go. What he wanted most of all was to learn baseball terms in French, to be able to converse with French-speaking media and fans.

So he started taking French lessons: 25 half-hour sessions. Learning was slow and painful at first. Beat writers for French-language newspapers made things easier, asking questions in English, then writing their stories in French. Out on the street, it wasn't so simple.

"I felt like a buffoon," he said. "Eight-year-old kids would talk to me [in French], and I couldn't answer."

It got better as the weeks ticked by. Staub began to feel like he could converse in the city's predominant language. He was the star attraction for the team's winter caravan, making stops in Trois-Rivières, Chicoutimi, Rimouski, Val d'Or—all overwhelmingly French-speaking towns with far fewer bilingual residents than Montreal. Jean-Pierre Roy, the Montreal-born TV commentator for French-language Expos broadcasts, travelled with Staub and was expected to do the talking. But Staub found that he could understand what both Roy and the fans were saying. Better still, thanks to his hard work, Staub was able to prepare two-minute speeches in French, then deliver those speeches to audiences.

As Staub's confidence in *la langue locale* grew, so too did the number of opportunities to practise. He appeared on the *Pierre Lalonde Show* and answered questions in both French and English from the popular bilingual TV host. He guested on the iconic *Hockey Night in Canada,* answering questions during the first intermission in French, then the second intermission in English. People noticed.

"It was great; I got letters from all over the country," he said. More than just the recognition, Staub was thrilled with the bonds he established with the city, and the province. "It was one of the best decisions of my entire life. It meant so much to me, to build that rapport between myself and the people of Montreal and Quebec. To this day, it still means a lot to me."

☞ BASEBALL EN FRANÇAIS ☜

Jacques Doucet and Claude Raymond took over as the French-language broadcast team for Expos games in 1972. In the days and weeks leading up to their first time on air, Carling O'Keefe—the title sponsor for the Telemedia network's broadcasts—tried something different. The beer brewer organized a summit consisting of writers and broadcasters from all across Quebec. The goal? To establish a vocabulary of baseball terms *en français.*

"When the old Montreal Royals were on radio and TV, they had pretty good broadcasters in French," said Doucet. "But a lot of terms were used in English. When I took over the job, I was really keen on using French as much as possible."

After collecting ideas from that meeting, O'Keefe published a little manual of baseball terms in French. Doucet and Raymond ran with it from there. They'd discuss ideas for new terms in cabs, on plane rides, sometimes on the air. For awhile, they struggled to describe the act of a pitcher (or catcher) picking a runner off base. So in the middle of a game, they asked their listeners for ideas. A professor from l'Université de Montréal suggested *"prendre quelqu'un à contre-pied"*—catching someone on the wrong foot.

"Jacques and me would say to ourselves, 'Why say this, when we could say this?'" recalled Raymond. "We didn't make it too complicated. When I was raised it was 'ball,' 'strike,' 'home run,' so we just put out words to say it in French. Sometimes we'd say it in English too, to make people understand that 'home run' was *'coup de circuit.'* It was easy."

Though the goal was to find the right French phrase for everything, that wasn't always possible—or at least not always practical. Doucet and Raymond racked their brains to find the right way to describe a squeeze play. Finally, they realized that the squeeze is such a lightning-quick play, there isn't time for some multi-word description. "Squeeze," they decided, worked just as well in both languages.

It can be tough for broadcasters to properly gauge the impact they've had on their viewers and listeners, explained Doucet. You might get complimented at a restaurant here and there, but you're not listening to yourself on your porch every night, not absorbing the impact of your own words. Really, you don't have much time to consume any kind of baseball other than the games you're covering, because you're on the air from late February through the end of September (or later, in a playoff season) every year. But during the strike year in 1981, Doucet found himself with a hole in his schedule, right in the middle of the summer. So he went to see his nephew play.

"I sat in the stands, and I was so pleasantly surprised to hear fans use all those expressions, all that baseball lingo in French," he beamed. "French to me is a beautiful language. If I'm doing something in French, I want to do it correctly."

A lexicon of French baseball terms could fill an entire book. So here's an abridged version, featuring some of the basics, plus some of the more delightful ones to roll off your tongue.

Arrêt-court: shortstop

Balle: ball

Balle cassante: breaking ball

Balle courbe: curveball

Balle glissante: slider

Balle papillon: knuckleball ("papillon" in French means butterfly—"butterfly ball" has my vote for coolest French baseball term)

Balle rapide: fastball

But volé: stolen base

Cercle d'attente: on-deck circle

Champ centre: centre field

Champ droite: right field

Champ gauche: left field

Changement de vitesse: changeup

Coup à l'entre-champ: Texas Leaguer (a bloop hit between the infield and outfield)

Coup de circuit: home run

Coup sûr: hit

Deuxième but: second base

Double: double

Double jeu: double play

Fausse balle: foul ball

Flèche: line drive

Frappeur désigné: designated hitter

Gant: glove

Gérant: manager

Manche: inning

Marbre: mound

Mauvais lancer: wild pitch

Piste d'avertissement: warning track

Premier but: first base

Prise: strike

Releveur: reliever

Receveur: catcher

Retrait: out

Retrait sur trois prises: strikeout

Sauf: safe

Sauvetage: save

Série mondiale: World Series	**Troisième but:** third base
Simple: single	**Victoire:** win
Stade: stadium	**Vol au sol:** shoestring catch
Triple: triple	**Voltigeur:** outfielder

For newly minted Expos fans, watching Staub and friends play every night was a drug. Jarry Park was the delivery system.

La piscine de Willie was just a small part of the ballpark's charm. With old-fashioned wooden ballparks phased out of the game, Jarry was smaller than every other big-league stadium. It wasn't just that it seated fewer than 30,000 fans. Its footprint was tiny. There was no upper deck. There was nothing but a low-slung fence circling the exterior of the park from the right-field foul pole all the way to dead centre. On a summer weekend you could watch Rusty Staub and Bob Bailey, then look across the way and see families everywhere, picnics, kids playing soccer—everything you'd expect from a July Sunday afternoon in Montreal.

The park's cozy confines made for fine acoustics, which came in handy with Claude Mouton on the mic. The team's first public-address announcer, Mouton showed uncommon flair, delighting fans by introducing players with wildly unorthodox pronunciations. In French, a word starting in *H* usually leaves the *H* silent; so when some native French speakers pronounce names in English, they might occasionally compensate by adding an *H* sound to the beginning of words with no *H* in them. As Ted Blackman explained in a column for the *Montreal Gazette*, Mouton would introduce Pirates outfielder/first baseman Al Oliver as "Hal Holiver." In another *H*-related hiccup, the man occupying the left-most infield spot would be recognized as the "tird baseman."

But Mouton saved his very best intro for one of the original Expos, John Boccabella. Marshalling a level of enthusiasm you might use on a future Hall of Famer, Mouton's greeting for the light-hitting, part-time catcher remains one of the most indelible memories for any old-time Expos fan. *"Le receveur*, the catcher, *numero neuf*, number nine . . . JOHHHNNNN BOCK-[extremely long pause]-a-BELLLLLL-a!!!"

Mouton needed the right musical accompaniment to amplify his enthusiastic cadence. One day during the 1968 Christmas holidays, future Expos director of operations Marc Cloutier strolled through Alexis Nihon Plaza. A slight, redheaded man had set up in the middle of the mall, entertaining passing shoppers on his Hammond organ. He made an impression: when the Expos' initial choice to play at games failed to impress after the first month of the season, Cloutier called the mall organist and asked if he'd be interested in a new gig at Jarry Park. To that point, he'd played mostly private parties and weddings . . . and never seen a baseball game. But the job sounded fun, and it was steady work, so the organist accepted the offer. Just like that, the legend of Fern Lapierre was born.

Unaccustomed at first to the usual rituals of a stadium organist, Lapierre learned quickly. He played the old standards, leading cries of "Charge!" when the Expos mounted a rally. But there was more. With just a few bars, he would gently mock visiting managers when they strolled to the mound. He persuaded fans to pop out of their seats and dance in the aisles. A hospital cook named Claude Desjardins was so inspired by Lapierre's notes that he became a legend himself, earning the nickname "The Dancer." The Expos began marketing Lapierre as part of the attraction, urging fans to show up for games an hour early to hear him play. Other teams took notice, even in the American League. When A's owner Charlie Finley heard the organist play, he proclaimed Lapierre the most valuable member of the Expos.

Fans got fired up to meet the players too, as the ballpark offered a level of intimacy that larger and more functional stadiums of that era couldn't. Originally, the clubhouse sat behind the stands, and it was tiny—so small that for the first few home games of 1969, players could touch the lockers on both sides of the room with outstretched arms. When the Expos moved the clubhouse farther down the line, players had to come out and walk past the fans. The walk took awhile, as players stopped to sign autographs. Whether you believe the Expos happened to find 25 nice guys to populate each of those early teams, or that they simply fielded a roster full of players just happy to be in the big leagues (probably a little of both), this was something you saw far less often at other parks.

For many, those quirky Jarry features—the PA man who revelled in rolling his *l*'s and *r*'s, the skilled organist, The Dancer, the intimate setting in which fans were practically on top of the action and conversed often with players—all added up to a great night out.

"Everybody was dancing, everybody was having fun," said Raymond. "French people who didn't speak English sat next to English people who didn't speak French, and everybody had fun. It was like a party. You'd go to Jarry Park on a Friday, catch a doubleheader, listen to Fern Lapierre on the organ, and you were going to have a good time."

In their first three years of existence, the Expos finished seventh, sixth, and eighth in National League attendance out of 12 teams, respectable results given that they played in the smallest ballpark in the league. As the honeymoon period wore off, though, attendance started to slip, dropping by 9 percent in 1972, seeing a brief uptick in '73 as the team played better, followed by sharp drops over the next three seasons. Jarry Park may have had its charms, but it was a minor league facility, in good ways and bad.

The elements posed the biggest problem, and for more than just the pitchers. With the coldest climate of any major league city, games in April, parts of May, and September were bound to be cold no matter what. But where future parks would be built with much higher exterior facades and various studies on wind patterns to guide construction, Jarry Park was tiny and poorly planned in that regard. No one addressed the gap between the left-field bleachers and the seats running down the third-base line. Cold winds whipped through that opening, and the two players who got the worst of it were often the second baseman and the shortstop.

"I remember clearly, seeing Bobby Wine and Gary Sutherland putting cotton in their right ears," recalled Dave Van Horne. "The wind was so strong and so wicked and so cold and damp that they had cotton in there, because they were coming out of games with earaches, headaches, and colds. There was a lot to battle there."

When it wasn't cold, it was often blindingly sunny. For a few weeks every season, games would start right as the sun zapped the first baseman's face with the brightness of a supernova. At first, the Expos tried to play through it. Then, you'd see Coco Laboy try to throw to first on one hop, since there was no way in hell Bailey would be able to see a ball coming at him on the fly. Not that bouncing did much good either: no stadium's infield and outfield grass were kept in worse shape than Jarry Park's. Eventually, everyone decided the best course of action was to delay games until the sun had set low enough to avoid burning the players' retinas.

For all the problems Jarry Park gave players, it could be rough on fans too. If you sat right behind home plate, you had a terrific view; down the baselines, you had to contort yourself into a pretzel to follow the action. On those frigid days in April and September, the players could at least move around to keep warm; fans could only bundle up and hope for the best. The stadium also sounded like an aluminum factory, as the walkways clanged with every step. The aluminum seats were far worse. On hot days, they were instruments of torture, soaking up the sun and broiling those parked on them.

"When they stopped the game because of the sun, that would embarrass me," said Katie Hynes. "There are some people who praise Jarry Park. They'll say, 'Oohh, my god, the intimacy, blah blah blah.' I am one of the few people who don't romanticize about it. Mack Jones: that's what I take away from Jarry Park. That's it."

Really, Jarry Park was both worthy and unworthy of nostalgia. It was a charming place to watch a game. It was, as famed sports-writer and author Roger Angell described it upon his first visit, "a handsome little field that much resembles a country fairground." It was also poorly built, a slapdash stadium that was uncomfortable for fans and at times nearly untenable for players—meant to be a stopgap solution that would end up being needed for much longer, thanks to botched efforts by the city.

"There's a French expression, 'belle/laide,'" said Rory Costello, a baseball historian who's written several Expos-related profiles for SABR's Baseball BioProject. "It means *beautiful/ugly*. It wasn't right, it wasn't perfect, it was kind of funny looking, but it had a lot of charm, and in its own way, it was attractive."

Playing with a patchwork roster in their first few years, the Expos held modest goals. In their second season, the objective was 70 in '70, something they achieved with a 73-win season—21 more wins than the year before.

The team's offence led the way, with Staub affirming his status as the Expos' one true star, and veterans Bob Bailey, Ron Fairly, and Mack Jones adding ample punch. The pitching rotation, in theory, offered more potential for improvement, given that the top four starters were all 26 or younger. Carl Morton, a 26-year-old right-hander acquired in the bottom half of the expansion draft who'd tossed just a handful of innings the year before, had a breakthrough season in 1970. A converted outfielder, Morton went 18-11 with a 3.60 ERA in the Expos' second season, tossing 284⅔ innings: the 10th-highest total in the majors. For his efforts, Morton aced Cincinnati outfielder Bernie Carbo for National League Rookie of the Year honours. That year, unfortunately, would prove to be Morton's best in Montreal. After disappointing '71 and '72 campaigns, the Expos dealt him to the Braves for a little right-hander named Pat Jarvis.

Following the trade, Jarvis lasted just 39⅓ more innings in the big leagues himself. Meanwhile, Morton revitalized his career in Atlanta, posting a better-than-average 3.35 ERA from 1973 through 1975 and throwing more innings than future Hall of Famers Tom Seaver, Jim Palmer, or Don Sutton during that span. The Expos showed more patience with Morton's rotation mate Steve Renko, reaping solid seasons from him in '73 and '74, followed by a lousy showing in '75. The Expos then made another trade, flipping Renko (and Larry Biittner) to Cleveland for first baseman Andre Thornton. Thornton played just 69 games in Montreal, hit .191, got dealt at season's end, then went on to post big power numbers with the Indians, making two All-Star teams.

Despite flashes of competence from a few players, the Expos wouldn't be able to aim higher until they started producing top-flight players through their farm system. While they waited for a more permanent home to replace Jarry Park, the club also needed to find and develop talent that could have more enduring value.

To execute that strategy, the Expos needed only to emulate the man who helped mould Montreal's previous professional baseball team into a powerhouse: Branch Rickey. Starting in 1921, Rickey's St. Louis Cardinals began buying up minor league teams with two goals in mind: reduce the cost of acquiring players, and implement system-wide standards and practices for coaching and instruction, so that the best young players could get the right training before making it to the majors. Using that combination of quantity (more prospects and minor league teams and instructors to help those prospects develop than anyone else) and quality (innovative approaches to instruction that helped young players hone their skills), Rickey oversaw the development of hordes of Hall of Famers. Stan Musial, Johnny Mize, and Enos Slaughter led the pack of future Hall of Famers who came up through the Cardinals system, before Jackie Robinson and all those other Dodger greats hopped from Montreal to Brooklyn to Cooperstown.

Unfortunately, the Expos didn't have a deep stable of farm teams and top prospects when they took the field for the first time in 1969. In fact, they didn't even have their own Triple-A team. During the Expos' first season, they actually shared their Triple-A club (the Vancouver Mounties) with their American League expansion counterparts, the Seattle Pilots. Meanwhile, they had no Double-A club at all. The Expos simply didn't have enough players to fill a traditional farm system. Before they could start thinking about developing future stars, they needed to acquire the right infrastructure: the ballparks, the coaches, and the bodies on the field.

To protect the interests of the existing 20 teams, Major League Baseball ruled that the expansion Expos, Padres, Royals, and Pilots would be barred from picking in the first three rounds of the 1968 amateur draft. The original Montreal Screwjob thus saw the Expos—with a skeleton crew of a scouting staff that early into the team's existence—forced to wait until the 81st overall selection to make their first-ever draft pick. Though late-round choices do sometimes work out, none did this time. Of the 15 players chosen by Montreal in the '68 draft, not a single one ever played a game in the Show.

It was only with their first pick in the 1969 draft that the Expos landed a player who would actually play in the major leagues. With the 22nd overall selection, Montreal nabbed a six-foot-two left-hander from Texas's Deer Park High School, Balor Moore. On the surface, you could find some similarities between Moore and the prototypical Texas high-school phenom, Nolan Ryan: The two played high-school ball just 25 miles away from each other. They served in the Army Reserve together in the early '70s, and would later play together with the Angels. Like Ryan, Moore cracked the big leagues at age 19, and like Ryan, Moore was a hard thrower with command problems early in his professional career. Legendary scout Red Murff must have liked that type—he signed both pitchers.

Moore's pro debut was strong. In 21 starts spread across three levels of A-ball, he struck out 140 batters and walked just 52 over 146 innings, posting a sparkling 1.17 ERA. The next season, Moore struggled with his control. In 21 more starts, most of them in Triple-A, he walked a staggering 108 batters in 144 innings. Pitch-count tracking was notoriously unreliable back then, but anecdotal evidence—plus some back-of-the-napkin math—tell us that averaging seven innings a start while walking that many batters is bound to thrust a pitcher into a lot more stressful situations than is good for any 19-year-old.

A few pitchers can and do withstand heavy workloads and go on to long, healthy careers. Nolan Ryan fired 658⅔ innings over the 1973 and 1974 seasons, striking out an unreal 750 batters and walking 364. Yet Ryan still went on to toss nearly four thousand more innings in his career, breezing into the Hall of Fame. But here's the thing about pitchers' ability to carry gigantic workloads: We remember freaks of nature like Ryan. We forget the thousands and thousands of arms shredded by overuse.

Moore actually fared well in the major leagues at first. In his first full season, in 1972, he flashed a slightly-better-than-average 3.47 ERA and struck out 161 batters in 147⅔ innings. Only one other pitcher in all of baseball wielded a better strikeout rate that year among pitchers with that many innings—Nolan Ryan. But Moore would be done in by a combination of things.

First, teams at the time believed pitchers could never get enough work in.

"It wasn't uncommon for a starting pitcher to throw 30 innings in spring training," Moore recalled. "Then you've got your workload for the regular season. Then it's off to winter ball in Puerto Rico for a 60-game schedule, where you'll start another 12 to 15 games. Then back to spring training to start all over again. If you were lucky, you'd get three weeks of rest all year."

Teams also didn't appreciate pitchers bringing up pain. This was the rub-some-dirt-on-it era, where managers and pitching coaches didn't exercise enough caution when injuries occurred, and pitchers responded by trying to gut their way through everything. In 1973, Moore suffered an early-season ankle injury. Given insufficient time to heal, Moore's ailing ankle messed up the timing and mechanics of his delivery, led to poor results, and put undue stress on his arm, leading to chronic pain. Today, Moore would've been diagnosed, treated, and sent for Tommy John surgery within a matter of weeks. Unfortunately, the procedure wasn't invented until 1974.

Moore did eventually get the surgery. Next came a long and painful rehab. For a long time he couldn't even crack 80 on the radar gun. A two-pitch pitcher with a blazing fastball when healthy, he eventually started throwing more off-speed stuff, hoping to reinvent himself. But Moore pitched poorly for the rest of his career before calling it quits in 1980, his enticing potential wasted.

The man charged with finding better, longer-lasting prospects when the Expos launched was Mel Didier. John McHale had given Didier his first scouting job with the Tigers in 1954. When the time came for the Expos to pick their first scouting director, McHale showed the same loyalty he had with Fanning and many other former colleagues, tapping Didier for the job. In the years that followed, Didier would become known as one of the most resourceful men in baseball—and one of the most well-travelled. As this book went to press, Didier was 86 years old, still working in the Blue Jays system. "I don't know of anyone who has been in more baseball parks throughout the world," former Dodgers general manager Fred Claire told the New Orleans *Times-Picayune*.

Of course, lots of scouts travel. What truly set Didier apart was his desire to take chances, hatching schemes no other teams could've imagined. His shrewdest plan sought to exploit the United States' embargo against Cuba. Canada had no such restrictions, so Didier flew to Havana, via Mexico. There, he gave a talk to a big group of baseball coaches about the Expos' hopes to build a working agreement with Cuba that would allow the team to develop young Cuban prospects. He travelled around the main island, giving clinics to teenage players. He met with Fidel Castro, who seemed receptive to Didier's ideas and was even smitten by the red-white-and-blue Expos cap he was presented. As Didier readied to travel back to Canada, he ran into a problem. Though he made his home in Montreal by this point, he was still a U.S. citizen, and thus faced up to 10 years in prison plus a major fine for his visit. Government officials told Didier he wouldn't be allowed to go back through Mexico or anywhere else for six months. The only way out was a flight to Moscow that stopped in Madrid (where he would disembark)—and the only way to get on that plane was for Castro himself to grant approval. He got his approval, landed in Spain, then flew back to Montreal.

Despite that close call, Didier still had high hopes for an arrangement with Cuba. What if, he asked Castro, the Expos could sign the three best players from the Cuban national team? As Didier recounted in his book, *Podnuh Let Me Tell You a Story*,

Castro liked certain elements of Didier's plan but couldn't sign off, since El Presidente had spent so much time and effort preaching against the evils of capitalism. The plan would've likely failed anyway, considering the reprimand Commissioner Bowie Kuhn levelled at Didier when he learned of the idea. Still, that was Didier's modus operandi: whatever might make his teams better, he was going to try it.

Didier's sense of adventure notwithstanding, the Expos still had to find better players somewhere. Unfortunately, the follow-up to the Balor Moore draft was only marginally better. With the third overall pick in 1970, the Expos selected Barry Foote, a high-school catcher from North Carolina. The team's starting catcher at that point was still John Bateman, another Texan scouted and signed by Red Murff a long eight years earlier. By the summer of 1970, Bateman had turned 30, entering the decline phase of an already unspectacular career. Given his pedigree and what would soon become a screaming need behind the plate, the Expos were going to do everything humanly possible to make Foote into their franchise backstop.

Those efforts failed miserably. After a solid debut season in which he hit .262 with 11 homers and 23 doubles in 125 games, Foote's power evaporated and his flirtations with the Mendoza Line began. Yet the Expos' stake in Foote's future prompted them to cling to their investment. Though they would eventually trade Foote to the Phillies in 1977, it wasn't before shoving another catcher to the outfield, nearly derailing a Hall of Fame career before it ever got going.

The rest of that 1970 draft didn't produce any front-line talent either, with the Expos landing a few bit players but nothing approaching a building block for the future. The two best players drafted by the Expos that year—Phil Garner and Roy Smalley—never even signed with the team, going back to school instead before enjoying impressive careers with other clubs. The 1971 draft was even worse, with only four players ever making it to the Show, and only two of those ever playing for the Expos. It wasn't a total loss, though. With the fourth overall pick in 1971, Montreal landed a four-time All-Star, two-time champion, and Hall of Famer. His name was Condredge Holloway, and he accomplished all of that in the Canadian Football League.

You could forgive the Expos for losing 289 games over their first three seasons, given how little talent they began with; hell, Seattle/Milwaukee lost 287 games in their first three years, while San Diego dropped 309. And of course Montreal wouldn't fully realize the extent of its early draft failures until later. Still, getting nothing out of their first four drafts except a short-lived starting catcher, a few bench jockeys, and a Toronto Argonaut? These were the types of colossal mistakes that could get an entire front office fired.

Instead, patience prevailed. Teams came up empty (or nearly empty) in drafts all the time back then, and still do now, even with far more sophisticated scouting tools at teams' disposal. The one strategy the Expos did implement in those years was a willingness to spend money to produce great players.

"Obviously Charles had the wherewithal to support this," said Van Horne. "More importantly, he had the intelligence—and it's probably one of the reasons he was so successful in the family business—that he knew to surround himself with good people, to trust them, and to give them leeway and encourage them to make decisions. He was very hands-on, but he was hands-on sitting behind John and Jim and Danny Menendez and Mel Didier and all those baseball people, learning.

"He was always there and always had the final word when it came to the purse strings. But he yielded to the baseball people. Charles wanted to give them the finances necessary to build one of the outstanding farm systems and organizations in all of base-ball. He let his fellow partners know that this was the McHale show, so the partners knew where they stood as far as baseball was concerned. Not to say they didn't have input, but Jim and John made all of the baseball decisions. Charles gave them that liberty to do that."

The Expos did offer competitive signing bonuses to their draft picks, which never hurts a team's chances to land future front-line players. But the gaps between bonuses weren't nearly as big in the '70s as they would become in later decades. Moreover, many of the Expos' best picks would come from later rounds. What Bronfman did well, and did frequently, was sign stacks of rela-tively small checks, thus making a big impact overall.

Another example of Bronfman's generosity: When the Expos arrived in New York to play that first-ever regular-season series, Bronfman wasn't happy with the team hotel. No no, he said, this isn't good enough for us. So the team upped and left for the Waldorf Astoria. He would throw parties at his home in Palm Beach, Florida, inviting all the major league staff, minor league managers, coaches, and instructors. There is no evidence to suggest that athletes perform better after being draped in gold-plated terrycloth robes, or that a pitching coach can lop a half-run off his ace's ERA because he's had some champagne and a few pigs in a blanket. But it couldn't have hurt.

Incentives, on the other hand, *do* motivate people. In the spring of 1970, Bronfman gathered all of his minor league managers, coaches, and instructors, and his major league coaching staff in his home. He gave a heartfelt speech, then gave everyone a big raise, making them one of the highest-paid player development depart-ments in the league. It wasn't without precedent: Baltimore's Oriole Way of scouting and player development produced a caval-cade of stars over the years, from Brooks Robinson to Jim Palmer,

Eddie Murray to Cal Ripken Jr. The Dodger Way dated back to Rickey, with generation after generation finding their way to Dodgertown in Vero Beach, Florida, and eventually to the majors. Bronfman's largesse cultivated loyalty from his employees and attracted some of baseball's most-skilled teachers, which in turn made farm director Danny Menendez's job easier. For McHale, Fanning, Didier, and Menendez, the goal was simple.

"We had to have the best damn farm system in baseball," said Bronfman.

After those first four mostly fruitless drafts, one of the Expos' prime targets in 1972 was a high-school shortstop from California, a multi-sport star who'd gotten more than a hundred football scholarship offers. The Expos had scouted him since he was 16. Now, with the draft approaching, at least three other teams were also on his trail. Expos scout Bob Zuk got the order: run misdirection, bend the truth, lie if you must. Just get other teams off his scent. So Zuk spread the word. The prospect they were after was too keen on playing football. Besides, he was damaged goods, coming off a major knee injury. Oh, and if you wanted to sway him into choosing baseball as his vocation, the bidding would start at $100,000.

In retrospect, you could ask why other teams fell for all that subterfuge, rather than doing more due diligence and learning the truth. But the draft is a fickle and scary beast, a process so rife with failure that teams will pass on a premium prospect if they don't like the look on his face, let alone if he's an injury risk asking for a fortune. This time, the Expos' trickery worked. With their third-round pick, number 53 overall, they reeled in their man. They signed him for half what they claimed he'd demand, luring him away from a commitment to UCLA, where he'd signed a letter of intent to play quarterback.

Only thing was, they had other plans for their new find. Though he had spent only eight games behind the plate to that point, they intended to convert him to catcher. They would arm him with the best instruction to hone his defence, and nurture the power-hitting ability they felt would play at the highest level. After years of searching, they had found the player around whom they'd build the first winning teams in the franchise's history, the one who would eclipse Staub's performance and fame, and further the Expos' overriding mission: to turn fans' attention from stars on other teams to the stars of their own.

In the beginning, he was just a kid. But he would prove to be *The* Kid.

CHAPTER THREE

The Kid and the Kids (1974–1976)

T he Expos nearly ruined Gary Carter's career before his 19th birthday. And worse—Carter helped.

Though the team announced it planned to develop Carter as a catcher, at first they weren't ready to commit all the way. This made some sense, at least in theory. The Expos had drafted catcher Barry Foote third overall just two years before selecting Carter, and though they were bullish on Carter from the start, as the team headed south for spring training in 1973, it was still too soon to give up on Foote.

With Carter and Foote bound for Daytona Beach, the prudent move would have been to work with both as catchers. But while the Expos would eventually develop a reputation as a team with exemplary player-development skills, they could be just as impatient as everyone else. And with good reason: the novelty of a new franchise was starting to wear off, and attendance was waning. Entering their fifth season, the Expos still stunk. Moreover, their roster consisted mostly of dull players, retreads from other teams, or second-rate prospects who played only because the alternatives were grim. If Carter was going to be as good as everyone believed, why not get him on the field as soon as possible, through any means necessary?

Those means included giving Carter a spin in the outfield. The Expos organization would make many mistakes over the course of its existence, but the "Carter as outfielder" experiment proved to be one of the most spectacularly dunderheaded.

Not long after the players hit camp, Carter ran into his first setback. Which is to say, he ran into a wall. "Split his head open," recalled Steve Rogers, who'd make his major league debut a few months later. "Carter played outfield like a bull in a china shop. He almost killed himself out there."

This was typical for "The Kid," so named for his endless enthusiasm on the field. Though that enthusiasm sometimes bloomed into recklessness, even self-administered lobotomies couldn't deter Carter, or his employer. After getting his first big-league cup of coffee in '74, he broke into the lineup for good in '75 . . . and promptly cracked a rib while attacking Jarry Park's 5-foot outfield fence to make a catch.

Bored with merely injuring *himself*, Carter's next mishap was a twofer. Chasing after a flyball during a June 1976 game against the Braves, Carter crashed into centre fielder Pepe Mangual, a collision that knocked Mangual out of the lineup for six days. Carter got the worst of it, though, breaking his thumb and landing on the disabled list for a month and a half. Carter was already having a mediocre season at the time of the injury, and his performance tanked when he returned from the DL. The team's next big hope hit just .199 with two home runs over his final 47 games of the season.

Eventually, everyone got the hint. In 1977, Carter finally took over as the team's everyday catcher. He would later become one of the greatest power-hitting catchers of all time, an elite game-caller, and one of the league's most popular players with fans.

☞ STEVE ROGERS ON GARY CARTER ☜

Steve Rogers was both a great pitcher and one of the most brutally frank players the Expos ever had. That pull-no-punches approach lives on decades later, with Rogers now working for the MLB Players Association (MLBPA). Rogers and Carter eventually teamed up to form the greatest of all Expos batteries, as well as a fierce mutual admiration society. But while Carter came to be loved by Rogers and other teammates, he wasn't so warmly received at first. In a wide-ranging interview at MLBPA headquarters in New York, Rogers explained why.

"In '75, we didn't fare well. You had Gary Carter, Barry Foote, and . . . turmoil. Gary was the saviour of the Expos before he ever set foot in the major leagues. Early on, I was on the side of Barry Foote, because I knew Barry; I had gone to instructional league with Barry. Barry was a hell of a catcher. With Gary it was more that the organization had touted him before he ever made it to the major leagues. He was the guy that was going to turn it around.

"Then Gary's attitude when he came up was all this 'rah, rah' stuff and everything like that. There was this perception that he was a certain way, he was The Kid, he was just 19 years old. The one thing I can always say about Gary is he had a quarterback's arrogance. He had been offered that full scholarship to UCLA to be their quarterback, so he had that kind of vision, that 'I'm going to get it done' type of vision. And he had the cockiness that goes along with that. At the heart of all of that was that he truly wanted people to like him and he would do anything in the world to make it happen. Sometimes that combination rubbed people the wrong way.

"But the honest truth is I never had any feeling of malice toward Gary. By the time the transition took place and Barry had been traded and Gary was now behind the plate, my relationship with Gary had changed. Even though I liked Barry, Gary was a good catcher for me and we worked well together. By the end, I counted him as a friend and I don't have a bad thing to say about it.

"He developed into a great catcher. The last four or five years when I was throwing to him, we would both be thinking ahead, four or five pitches deep. In other words, he knew my entire repertoire, and how to use it. I threw a split-finger for a changeup; I might throw three in a game. It was always so great that I'm setting the ball in my glove, thinking about what to throw, and he's calling that split-changeup at exactly the right time. And Gary was a gamer. I've seen him go out there on one leg. He couldn't even stand on it. He'd be out there with an injured leg, in the middle of a pennant race, gutting it out. We were lucky to have him."

Of course, one player alone doesn't make a team. After whiffing repeatedly on draft picks in their first few seasons, the Expos finally started connecting on some singles and doubles—even a few homers.

In 1973, the Expos struck out in the primary June draft. At the time, though, the league had three different amateur drafts: one in January, and two in June. With the fifth pick of the secondary June draft, the Expos landed a player who would become one of the most memorable figures in franchise history, not only for his play on the field and his constant exuberance, but also for his contributions 20-plus years after his retirement.

Warren Cromartie holds the rare distinction of being drafted five times. He spurned offers from the Chicago White Sox (seventh round, June 1971); Minnesota Twins (third round, January '72); San Diego Padres (first round, June '72); and Oakland A's (first round, January '73) before finally signing with the Expos in the summer of '73. Drafted out of Miami-Dade Junior College, Cromartie jumped straight to Double-A, starting his career with the Quebec City Carnavales. It was a loaded club that surged to the Eastern League playoffs, led by three players who would go on to play big roles with the Expos. But Cromartie was already dreaming of playing in Montreal, two and a half hours away. He racked up big numbers in that '74 season (.336 batting average, 13 home runs, and 30 stolen bases), and when the Carnavales drove southwest from Quebec City toward Montreal, then turned away from Montreal and south over the border to play American teams, he'd catch a glimpse over his shoulder of what awaited him in the big leagues.

"Driving across the bridge, the city was so beautiful lit up," Cromartie said. "I'd heard so much about the Expos, about Montreal, and all the pretty girls there. What more could you ask for?"

He got his chance on September 6, 1974, making his major league debut against Pirates right-hander Dock Ellis, just 10 days before Gary Carter got his own call-up. Cromartie had 17 at-bats in the big leagues that year, then returned to the minors in 1975, spending the entire season with the Triple-A Memphis club. Two years later, he finally headed north for good with the big club out of spring training. Cromartie had drawn more attention in the draft than any of his core teammates on those Expos teams of the '70s and early '80s, yet never quite rose to All-Star status. Still, as a durable, better-than-average hitter who hit righties very well in his prime, he was an excellent supporting-cast member.

Another Florida native, born just six weeks after Cromartie, seemed to shadow Cro's every move as he climbed the ladder. Larry Parrish, undrafted, signed with the Expos in 1972. By age 20, he was Cromartie's teammate in Quebec City, manning third base and hitting with promise. When Cromartie got the call, Parrish was right there with him.

"We drove in from Quebec together, took the plane together, took a cab together, came through the tunnel together in Pittsburgh—we were almost crying," Cromartie said. "Before we went to the ballpark, we went to the hotel. 'Skip wants to see you,' we were told. So we go to Gene Mauch. 'Congratulations,' he says. Then the next thing we hear is, 'We lost your luggage!' Two rookies come to the big leagues, we got no fucking luggage! No gloves, no shoes, no bats. We borrowed other people's stuff. I had to borrow Steve Rogers' shoes. The problem was, they had a pitcher's toe plate on. My first big-league game, and I'm walking around pigeon-toed!"

Ill-fitting shoes notwithstanding, Cromartie and Parrish got through that first game just fine. It was Parrish, however, who progressed more quickly from there. While Cromartie headed back to the minors in 1975, Parrish claimed the starting third-base job in Montreal. He hit .274 with 10 home runs and played solid defence, holding his own as a 21-year-old rookie. Parrish was another player often remembered as much for his personality as his numbers: when the Expos eventually grew into contenders, many cited Parrish's intangibles—his ability and willingness to play hurt, his leadership—as key factors.

"When Parrish had his best year, he was playing with a wrist that he could barely move," said long-time Expos trainer Ron McClain. "Finally, the doctor had to put it in a cast. That was the only way to stop him from playing."

Not for long, though. Parrish sat for only six days before getting back in the lineup. In that peak 1979 season, even with that badly

injured wrist, he played 153 games, hit .307, and smacked 30 home runs. When Parrish's later departure coincided with a downturn in the Expos' fortunes, his ouster would become a big part of the narrative.

Andre Dawson was yet another Florida find, a Miami guy like Cromartie. But he didn't get nearly as much attention initially, partly because he was damaged goods. Playing football for Southwest Miami High School in 1971, Dawson severely injured his right knee after taking a direct shot from a teammate's helmet. He rolled on the ground in agony, and couldn't put any pressure on his leg. The team trainer said he only had a strained ligament, but Dawson felt something far worse.

Dawson went to the hospital the next day and learned that he'd torn both cartilage and ligaments, and required surgery on the damaged knee. Medical technology in the early '70s was nearly prehistoric compared to what it would become later, as was the advice proffered by doctors. After the surgery, Dawson got fitted for a brace and was told to just wait a couple weeks and see. No one prescribed any physical therapy, nor did Dawson pursue any. He tried to play on the knee in his senior year, but his mobility was shot. That injury helped drop him all the way to the 11th round before the Expos scooped him up.

When sportswriters talk about a player's work ethic, the tone can get hyperbolic in a hurry. We want to ascribe heroic traits to athletes, so we conjure up the most glowing descriptions imaginable: about how they worked out 22 hours a day in the snow, bench-pressing 18-wheelers while running to Bhutan and back. If a player is perceived as limited athletically, the gushing even escalates—as scribes vie to lionize the scrub who, through sheer force of will, made himself into a ballplayer.

Dawson was no scrub. He was a gifted athlete who would surely have generated a lot more buzz among scouts without the knee injury. But it's unlikely he would have wound up in the Hall of Fame if he hadn't pushed himself as hard as he did.

Not long after his surgery, Dawson started experiencing fluid buildup in his knee, and it only got worse from there. Doctors diagnosed the knee as arthritic. Another operation followed; cartilage was removed, leaving the knee as bone on bone. The diagnosis was grim.

"The docs said I'd be lucky if I played four years," Dawson said.

These weren't obstacles besetting an aging ballplayer at the twilight of his career. Dawson's knee was deteriorating—and his window to play seemingly shrinking—just as he was entering his early 20s. So he started attacking the problem as aggressively as he could.

The medical procedures were intense and never-ending. He'd get his knee drained three times a year: once at the end of spring training, once around the All-Star break, then again near the end of the season. He also got multiple cortisone shots every season, the number rising as his career progressed. The maintenance regimen was long, at times mind-numbing. Massages and icing, but also showing up before all his teammates for marathon stretching sessions. He'd get his knee taped before batting practice, then re-taped 45 minutes before the game. After the game came 20 minutes of additional icing, then a shower, after which the clubhouse was nearly empty. *Then* there were the workouts. Training with heavy weights was frowned upon in those days, with trainers suggesting that too much bulk hurt players' flexibility. So Dawson used Cybex machines to strengthen his quadriceps and hamstrings. Alongside those exercises were push-ups and sit-ups— too many to count. He'd often do all of that after 10 or 11 hours in the ballpark, having gone through all those warm-ups, played the actual game, and treated his knees afterwards. Made sense. There certainly weren't any lines for the machines that late at night.

Dawson's diligence kept him on the field and helped fuel some huge performances at every step. In his first year as a pro, he hit .330/.383/.553 at Lethbridge, Alberta, of the rookie-level Pioneer League. The next season, he hit .352/.413/.658 with 28 homers in just 114 games between Double-A Quebec City and the hitters' haven of Triple-A Denver. He made his major league debut on September 11, 1976, and became an everyday player in the big leagues the next season.

Numbers aside, Dawson's stone-faced resolve under the stress of searing pain quickly earned his teammates' respect and admiration.

"You'd see him laying quietly on the training table, getting his knees drained over and over—it was un-fucking-believable," said Bill Lee, the eccentric left-hander who would join the team in 1979 and become its most colourful character. "We would just go in and look at him. You knew how much it had to hurt, but he never showed it. I mean, his fucking knees looked like fucking Frankenstein's face."

It took a little longer to build a stable of dynamic young pitchers to complement the barrage of hitting talent emerging from the Expos system. Rogers got it started.

Montreal snagged Rogers with the fourth pick in the 1971 secondary draft. When the Expos took him, Rogers had 19 hours of senior-level classes left to complete his degree in petroleum engineering. He felt that if he didn't take those classes right then, he'd never earn his degree. An intellectual and a pragmatist as well as an athlete, Rogers wanted a fallback plan in case baseball didn't work out. So when he signed that first contract with the Expos, he made a pointed request: Don't send me to instructional league— let me finish my college education first. It took about 14 seconds from that point for the media to get on his case, a pattern that continued throughout what would become a long, illustrious, and outspoken career.

The argument over Rogers' desire to finish his degree wasn't his only immediate beef with the organization. When the three players drafted ahead of him in '71—the Senators' Pete Broberg, the Cubs' Burt Hooton, and the Brewers' Rob Ellis—all cracked the big leagues right away, Rogers expected the same.

"I went to Triple-A—and I thought I had been screwed," said Rogers. "I really felt like my talent hadn't been recognized enough."

Many elite athletes have that kind of arrogance as they climb the ladder toward professional success. It's often a healthy and necessary confidence that lets them shrug off failures and keep working toward their goals. Rogers was simply more candid than most about how good he was, and how his team should treat him accordingly. He did learn a little humility, though, and much sooner than he expected.

"I ran into the Rochester Red Wings, Baltimore's Triple-A team" while playing for the International League's Winnipeg Whips, he recalled. "They had [Don] Baylor, [Bobby] Grich, [Al] Bumbry, [Rich] Coggins, Terry Crowley . . . when you totalled all of the team's major league playing careers, they had just under 100 years of major league service. That team and those players pinned my ears back. They taught me that I had a lot to learn. So I learned that I needed to learn a whole lot before I could move up through the system. Which was a good lesson."

Rogers' minor league lessons were physical as well as mental. When he joined the organization, he threw only two pitches: fastball and curve. He showed some variety with the two offerings, sinking his fastball at times, then throwing another one that moved sideways rather than down. His curve also did a couple of things, one of them conventional and the other a slow bender (what Rogers called a changeup-curveball). In the fall of '72, though, Rogers learned two new pitches in instructional league.

One was the slider. In the early '70s, the slider hadn't yet become the ubiquitous pitch that hitters would see a decade or two later; for awhile, the Dodgers wouldn't let their pitchers throw sliders at all, just curveballs. As Rogers explained it, the Expos wanted him to learn the slider so he'd have another weapon against left-handed hitters.

The other pitch he learned was the cross-seam fastball, today more frequently called a four-seamer. It was (and is) less common for pitchers to start with a sinking two-seamer, then have to learn the straighter (and often slightly harder) four-seamer. Then again, Rogers was uncommon in many ways: he was a finesse pitcher with the swagger of a fireballer, smarter than many of his rivals, the kind of player who defied the notion that baseball was a reactionary game that ate deep thinkers alive . . . and was one of the most superstitious pitchers you'll ever see.

Scott Sanderson made his major league debut in 1978, and immediately noticed the staff ace's many rituals. Rogers' pre-start routine never wavered. He prided himself on recognizing mound conditions so he could be unfailingly consistent in planting and landing the same way on every pitch. These customs weren't so unusual for a successful starting pitcher. Rogers was just stricter about all of it, with fixations approaching kooky superstition. One of his loopier neuroses was to sit in exactly the same place between innings of every home start, on a towel a few inches from the rivets on the dugout's fibreglass benches. Prankster teammates would inevitably move the towel just enough to drive Rogers crazy.

Young and impressionable, Sanderson soaked up all of Rogers' habits and tics.

"Along with superstition comes discipline, attention to detail," Sanderson said. "A lot of it was routine and very important to him. I learned great lessons about preparation, routine, discipline. He took the game very seriously. I'm analytical by nature, so that kind of discipline and routine sat very well with me."

Rogers never seduced the baseball intelligentsia the way the more famous aces of his era did. But at his best, he could and did beat the best of his peers. He never did take home the award for the league's best pitcher, but he was always "Cy" to his team-mates—even though some members of the media tagged him as "Sigh" for his beefs with his managers, his periodic prickliness with writers, and his occasional tendency to get visibly upset when a fielder behind him failed to make a play.

The most damaging mark against Rogers would come when he was scapegoated for the most infamous moment in Expos history (more on that later). But those with the common sense to avoid reducing a pitcher's entire career to one pitch look past that moment. If we're dealing only with what pitchers did while playing with the Expos, Rogers was clearly the greatest pitcher the team ever had.

Rogers would soon gain ample support in the rotation from a quartet of young right-handers, all four drafted and developed by the Expos. And a few years later, once Carter, Cromartie, Parrish, Dawson, and Rogers had established themselves, a fresh batch of future All-Stars joined the fray. These players collectively formed one of the best groups of homegrown talent ever assembled on one team, including two Hall of Famers and another player, Tim Raines, who so obviously deserves that honour.

Yet ask any Expos player, coach, scout, or batboy from that period which player was the most talented, and there's a strong chance he'll rave about someone else. The player who generated the most excitement at the start of his career was taken in the same draft as Carter, one round before The Kid, in fact. He was a bundle of raw, fast-twitch talent, the player who came with the highest billing . . . and the one who became the biggest disappointment of the bunch.

Ellis Valentine was a 17-year-old hardware store full of tools when the Expos took him with their second-round pick in '72. Six-foot-four and strapping, he could hit the ball a mile. His excellent hand-eye coordination portended a future .300 hitter. He also ran exceptionally well for someone so big. Though still raw with his routes to flyballs, that speed promised superior outfield range.

Then there was his arm. Oh, that sweet, terrifying arm. It was so strong that when he was seven, he played against nine-year-olds. It was so powerful that his coaches immediately made him a pitcher, despite his other glaringly obvious skills. Valentine pitched all through high school, then got drafted as a pitcher and a first baseman. To their credit, the Expos quickly realized that the best fit for Valentine was as an outfielder, where he could put his combination of speed, power, and that mesmerizing arm to good use.

The typical course of action for a right fielder making a long throw is to aim for the cutoff man, who can then peg a relay throw to third or home and try to gun down the runner. Valentine had such a cannon for an arm that he could fire the ball home all the way from the warning track. Years later, the biggest stars of Valentine's day would still speak of his arm with reverence.

"They say that I can't throw like Ellis Valentine," said Pete Rose, the all-time hit king and one of the best to ever play the game. "Who can?!"

"He had the best throwing arm of anyone I played with or against," said Dawson, who was widely considered to have one of the best arms of his generation himself.

Valentine might've been a top-10 overall pick, but a ballplayer needs more than an arm: like Dawson, Valentine suffered a major leg injury. He broke it during the summer between his junior and senior years at Los Angeles's Crenshaw High School, an injury so severe that surgeon Dr. Robert Kerlan had to extend a metal rod from Valentine's knee to his ankle. That injury limited what Valentine, a multi-sport star, could do in his senior year. He didn't play any football, and he didn't pitch, either: instead, he spent that baseball season at first base.

Still, natural talent won out, at least enough for the Expos to take the plunge. Problem was, Valentine was so talented that he rarely experienced on-field setbacks, and never felt he had to work

hard for anything. Compared to Dawson and his hellacious work habits, Valentine's careless attitude looked even worse.

"I was very blessed, moved up the ladder quite quickly," Valentine said. "Even on the sandlot, I always played with older kids and had no problems, so that pushed me up a lot sooner. When I got drafted, I was just a child. But I still had that tremendous athletic ability, so I never had to struggle. I always knew I was going to be on a field somewhere, and kind of took that for granted. I didn't pay attention from a mental standpoint. Developmentally, that hurt."

If immaturity and poor work habits threatened Valentine's road to success, so too did adverse circumstances. Immediately after being drafted, Valentine got sent to the Expos' New York–Penn League affiliate in Jamestown, New York. Valentine was shipped there for purely logistical reasons—as a short-term stopover before being sent to play in Cocoa Beach, Florida—but just those few days in upstate New York underscored how emotionally fragile he was. Valentine had grown up in an all-black neighbourhood. Now, he was alone.

"Everything in Jamestown is white," he recalled. "The streets were white, the cars, even the grass seemed white. My second day there, I was depressed. I ventured out of the dorm where I was staying, went across the street to this bowling alley/café/pool hall. I go over to get a snack. I see this one guy shooting pool and he's black. I'm excited! I'm 17 years old, and I'm thinking, this guy is like me. Turns out this dude was from Puerto Rico. So my depression got worse. Now I'm *really* messed up."

A few days in Jamestown weren't going to have much lasting effect, of course; if anything, non-English-speaking players coming from different countries have it worse when thrown into small American towns as teenagers to play pro ball for the first time. But in the years to come, Valentine would demonstrate that emotional fragility was a constant, rather than something fleeting.

There'd be lasting effects from his busted leg too. The injured leg didn't heal properly, and set slightly shorter than the healthy one. The pain of the injury forced him to pound painkillers. But then, he couldn't stop. That first brush with addiction started Valentine down a self-destructive path that would eventually consume his career.

"Ellis, what I saw . . . he didn't want to grasp success," said Dawson. "He knew he was talented. But he didn't like the limelight, being the focus of attention. His problems got away from him; they took a toll on his talent and ability. It's too bad. His ceiling was unlimited."

Cultivating that new crop of talent was essential if the Expos were ever going to win. But change can be tumultuous for any team trying to claw its way to relevance. It certainly was for the Expos in the early-to-mid '70s.

One of the biggest visceral blows came when Rusty Staub was traded to the Mets right before the start of the 1972 season. Aside from being the team's best player, Staub's value as an ambassador for the ball club was sky-high by then. The winter before, Charles Bronfman had asked him to become head of the Young Expos Club. That group put on various promotions during the course of the season, including special days at the ballpark where kids could get in for 25 cents a head. The first year, the club signed 25,000 young fans to its rolls. In year two, 75,000. In year three, 155,000. The goal was to introduce Québécois kids to baseball, in the hopes that they might become the season-ticket holders of tomorrow.

On April 5, 1972, the Young Expos Club lost its pitchman.

"There was a players' strike going on at the time," Staub recalled. "I was at St. Ann's church in West Palm Beach—it was Easter Sunday. I saw [Mets manager] Gil Hodges there, the coaching staff, their trainer. I was just going to say hello to Gil. They ended up talking to me for like 10 minutes. I thought, 'Geez, Easter really brings out the best in people!'"

A surreal tragedy followed. The Mets coaching staff played golf right after church. Walking off the course, Hodges was asked what time he'd like to meet for dinner. "Seven thirty," he said, then keeled over. He died just minutes later of a heart attack.

Meanwhile, Staub didn't know he was about to become a Met, even though the deal was very nearly done. He flew up to Montreal and soon got a call from John McHale, who told Staub he'd been traded to the Mets for outfielder Ken Singleton, first baseman Mike Jorgensen, and shortstop Tim Foli. The move shocked everyone involved.

"Gerry Patterson was my agent," Staub said. "In his book [Behind the Superstars], the title of one of the chapters was, 'They'll Never Trade Rusty.' That's how I found out about the trade, from him.

"This was a young franchise, getting three young players, so I could see how it made sense for them. But then I found out how much Gil Hodges fought to make it happen, how much he wanted me to be a part of his ball club. That was one of the most disappointing things in my career, that I never got to play for him."

As painful as the deal might have been for many Expos fans, from a baseball standpoint, this was a good trade. Jorgensen, just 23, took over as the Expos' starting first baseman. It took a couple of years for his bat to get going, but once it did, he was an on-base machine. He hit .310 with a massive .444 on-base percentage in 1974 (albeit in only 366 plate appearances). Given more action the following year, he posted a strong .378 OBP. All told, Jorgensen spent five-plus seasons in Montreal, with those two seasons as the highlight.

Foli, by contrast, couldn't hit before he joined the Expos, during his time with the Expos, or after his time with the Expos. But during his prime in Montreal, he was one of the best defensive shortstops in the league. He grabbed the starting shortstop job at age 21, then sucked in groundballs behind Expos pitchers for five-plus seasons.

The best player of the three, however—and one of the best in the majors for much of the '70s—was Singleton. Though never much of a defender or base stealer, he could really hit. In 1973, Singleton's second season with the Expos, he played in all 162 games, hit .302, slugged 23 home runs, and led the league with a gaudy .425 on-base percentage. Buoyed by weak NL East competition that year, the Expos actually sat just a game out of first place as late as September 20, before finishing three games off the pace (despite ending the year with a sub-.500 record). In Singleton, the Expos had found a player three and a half years younger than Staub who in '73 surpassed anything Staub would do for the rest of his career.

Then they went and messed it up. In 1974, Singleton had a down year, hitting just nine home runs. He was still a useful player, though, batting .276 with an impressive .385 OBP. The Expos panicked anyway, shipping Singleton and pitcher Mike Torrez to Baltimore for pitcher Dave McNally, outfielder Rich Coggins, and minor leaguer Bill Kirkpatrick. Coggins played just 13 games for Montreal and played his final major league game just a year and a half after the trade. Kirkpatrick never even made the big leagues.

McNally was supposed to be the prize of the deal. The left-hander won 20-plus games four years in a row from 1968 through 1971, then 16 more in 1974, though with a below-average ERA and a strikeout rate that had cratered compared to his peak half a decade earlier. He made 12 starts with the Expos in '75, got hurt, and never pitched again in the majors. Aside from his success with the Orioles, McNally's claim to fame was playing out his option year in 1975, then getting convinced by Players Association leader Marvin Miller to file for free agency at year's end even though he had no intention of playing again. When arbitrator Peter Seitz ruled in favour of free-agency requests by McNally and fellow pitcher Andy Messersmith, MLB's reserve clause was effectively abolished, and baseball history was made.

Heady stuff, though not something that helped the Expos in any way.

Following his days in Montreal, Singleton made three All-Star Games, finished in the top 10 in MVP voting three times (twice in the top three), hit .300 twice, posted OBPs above .400 four times, and clubbed 20 or more home runs four times. Though Staub got all the accolades, it was trading away his replacement that ranks as one of the worst deals ever made by the Expos.

There were other damaging moves too. Trading Mike Marshall, one of the best and most rubber-armed relief pitchers in the game—then watching him win a Cy Young Award the next season with the Dodgers—didn't help either.

Then there was the manager situation. It's all well and good for people running an expansion team to preach patience, but eventually that patience wanes. Fans stop going to the ballpark. And the manager starts arguing with the front office about certain players and how to handle them. That was the rift that finally tore John McHale and Gene Mauch apart.

"They butted heads over personnel," said Dave Van Horne. "I think what didn't sit well with John especially was what happened at the end of the '75 season. It's September and we're fighting for every win we could get. They're discussing the call-ups in late August and one of the call-ups mentioned was a guy by the name of Gary Roenicke."

The Expos' first-round pick (eighth overall) in the 1973 June draft, Roenicke played well enough at Double-A in 1975 to earn Eastern League MVP honours. McHale felt that a September call-up could allow Roenicke to gain valuable major league experience, and maybe give a jolt to a losing team. McHale and others in the front office felt it was time for a youth movement that could be something to build on for the 1976 season.

"Mauch said no, he's not ready," Van Horne recalled. "'I don't need Roenicke, my outfield is fine,' he insists."

In the end, Mauch's desire to go with veterans won out, and Roenicke didn't make his major league debut until the following June. McHale, already frustrated by seven seasons of stagnation,

saw Mauch's stubbornness on *l'affaire Roenicke* as the last straw.
At season's end, McHale fired the team's first manager.

McHale would later tell confidants that it was one of his biggest
regrets; not just the firing per se, but that he didn't work harder to
resolve his differences with Mauch. With Mauch gone, McHale
huddled with Bronfman to find a replacement. The two men
agreed on their preferred candidate: Tommy Lasorda. A former
pitcher for the Montreal Royals, Lasorda appeared in just 26
games in the majors as a player. What he did do, however, was
impress observers with his managing skill while working in the
Dodgers organization. He then impressed Expos brass in face-to-
face meetings, enough for McHale to extend an offer for Lasorda's
first big-league managing job, in Montreal. Lasorda went back
to his bosses in L.A., leverage in hand—and not wanting to see a
bright, homegrown managerial prospect bolt, the Dodgers promised Lasorda he could have Walter Alston's major league managing
job as soon as the seven-time National League pennant winner
and four-time World Series winner retired. A year later, Lasorda
took over. Lasorda's Dodgers would become Expos' nemeses for
many years to come.

With Lasorda out of reach, the fallback plan was Karl Kuehl.
Though the results weren't yet evident in the Expos' win column,
the organization's well-run player-development system was starting to bear fruit. As manager of the Triple-A Memphis Blues,
Kuehl was considered a big part of the system's success, having
helped groom some of the Expos' brightest young prospects.

"He moulded Gary Carter," said Cromartie. "He'd work with
Carter every day, out early, out late, teaching him how to block
balls in the dirt. He made a big difference in turning Carter into
the ballplayer he became."

McHale hoped those teaching chops would translate well at the
big-league level, and that Kuehl could transform the Expos from

a team plagued by growing pains into a perennial contender. The gambit would fail miserably—spectacularly, even.

Trouble started almost immediately. After the McNally/Messersmith ruling, outraged owners fought to maintain their traditional dominion over players. They locked out the players for 17 days, interrupting spring training in 1976. When the lockout ended, Kuehl got into an argument with Foli, a silly dispute that foreshadowed bigger problems later that year. Under Mauch, players had been forbidden from wearing facial hair. When players returned from the lockout, Foli was one of several veterans sporting a mustache, even though McHale and Jim Fanning wanted to keep the facial hair ban going under the new skipper. As Foli got set to take the field, Kuehl confronted his shortstop.

Shave your mustache off, the manager said.

May I wait, Foli asked, to talk to McHale and Fanning first?

No. Do it now.

The conflict only escalated: pulled from the lineup late in one April game, Foli quarrelled with Kuehl in the dugout. After another clash during a late-May game against the Phillies, Kuehl benched Foli in favour of light-hitting backup Pepe Frias. Foli stewed on the bench for three games, the third of which was a 6–2 loss to the Cardinals in which Frias committed three errors. Rather than back the manager's play, Fanning told Kuehl to get Foli back on the field.

Things deteriorated from there. Players lamented Kuehl's poor communication skills. He didn't win any raves for his in-game tactics either. Kuehl was finally fired in August, and his interim replacement, Charlie Fox, closed out the season by managing 34 games. Then he, too, was finished.

As if bad trades, a bad manager, and the end of the team's postexpansion honeymoon period weren't enough, the Expos faced another, more esoteric challenge in their quest to become beloved contenders: volatile, and sometimes violent, politics.

The birth of the Expos coincided with the most chaotic period in the history of the Quebec sovereignty movement. In the early 1960s, the Front de libération du Québec (FLQ) began speaking out and acting out in favour of Quebec separation from the rest of Canada. Unlike community groups and political parties that supported Quebec's independence through peaceful means, the FLQ carried out numerous acts of violence. At first, the incidents were small in scale, including mailbox bombings in wealthy, mostly English-speaking neighbourhoods such as Westmount. Then, two months before the Expos played their first game, the FLQ bombed the Montreal Stock Exchange, injuring 27 people. The group's notoriety peaked in October 1970: over a span of a few weeks, the FLQ kidnapped British Trade Commissioner James Cross and Quebec Minister of Labour Pierre Laporte (whom the FLQ later killed); issued a list of demands that included the release of imprisoned FLQ members; and triggered the mobilization of army troops as well as the implementation of Canada's War Measures Act and a resulting suspension of *habeas corpus*.

The so-called October Crisis terrified many Montrealers, but it had little to no effect on the Expos, or anyone who played for, worked for, or followed the team at that time—at least if dozens of interviews for this book are to be believed. It took a legitimate, sovereignty-focused political movement for anyone involved with the Expos to become spooked.

By the mid-'70s, the Parti Québécois (PQ) had risen to prominence. The party's leader, René Lévesque, broached the possibility of a province-wide referendum to vote on Quebec separation. In 1976, the PQ gained enough support to mount a serious challenge to the incumbent Liberal Party in the Quebec general election.

For Bronfman, the rise of the PQ and the mere whisper of a chance that a referendum might get called triggered both denial and anger.

On the eve of the election, the Expos owner gave a talk to a Jewish community group. Unaware that there was a reporter in the room, and more strident than he should have been due to the uncertain political climate, Bronfman said a number of things that he quickly regretted.

"I ranted and raved and said that these guys were anti-Semitic, and if they got in I'd leave, I'd take my family out, I'd take [Seagram's] out," Bronfman said of the PQ.

At the time, Bronfman believed he had inside information from government sources, definitive proof that the PQ was going to lose. A *Montreal Star* reporter called him later that day to press him on the matter. If you're going to move your family in the event of a PQ victory, the reporter asked, what will you do with the Expos?

"I said, 'Well, under normal circumstances I'd sell it,'" Bronfman recalled. "'But who's gonna buy it in a separate Quebec? So I guess I have to take it with me.' Hello, headlines the next day! I was in deep doo-doo."

The doo-doo was deep indeed. The city's English media roasted Bronfman for threatening to move the team. French media painted him as intolerant. Months after the PQ won, Bronfman was still getting vitriolic letters egging him on, trying to call him on his threat and/or bluff. He'd see PQ ministers at ballgames and get into arguments with them when they wouldn't stand for "O Canada."

"It was war," he said. "It affected my everyday life, because I felt that I was being made a scapegoat."

Beyond Bronfman's own encounters, however, the effect of the owner's comments began seeping into everyday Expos business.

"We were at the Windsor Hotel in late '76," said long-time Expos public relations man Rich Griffin. "Dave Cash was brought into town, and we had a press conference at the Windsor. The media was gathered there, including this sports columnist for *La Presse* who was very political. Very PQ. The floor opened for questions. The columnist asks, 'Monsieur Bronfman, you promised you were going to move Seagram's if the PQ won. When is that going to happen?' Meanwhile, Dave Cash is just sitting there. He has no idea what's going on."

In the end, Bronfman's threats proved idle. His family stayed put. Seagram's didn't make any major changes; even if Bronfman had wanted to do something drastic, he would've had to battle a cavalcade of people to make it happen—including his brother Edgar, the president of the company. And the Expos remained in Montreal.

But Bronfman's tirade, while more candid (and wildly inappropriate) than what others might've offered, was—minus the accusations of anti-Semitism—not that far removed from what some Montreal-based business leaders were thinking.

The Royal Bank of Canada, the largest corporation in the country, kept its official headquarters in Montreal, but moved its operational head office to Toronto. Sun Life, the then-Montreal-based insurance and financial services giant, objected to the PQ-led passing of the Charter of the French language in 1977. More commonly known as Bill 101, the charter defined French as the official language of Quebec. For a huge company like Sun Life, one of the major frustrations came from a clause that required corporations to use French when communicating with French-speaking employees. By January 1978, Sun Life had shifted its headquarters to Toronto as well. And in a cruel twist of irony, another financial services giant kept only its titular headquarters in Montreal while moving its operational headquarters to Toronto. That company? The Bank of Montreal.

The PQ did go on to hold two referendums, one in 1980 and one in 1995. But despite a close call in '95, the province never separated. Today, Quebec remains a Canadian province in good standing.

Still, for many major companies, the perception that the Montreal business community could get hurt by a PQ election became a reality, although one that was largely self-inflicted. When Canada experienced rapid economic growth for much of the '80s and early '90s, Montreal, stripped of much of its corporate clout, lagged well behind. The erosion of the city's business community would eventually prove to be more harmful to the Expos' future than any one lopsided trade or disposable manager.

But those down times would come later. With the 1977 season approaching, the Expos were in fact about to launch a new era, backed by a sharp, combative, and colourful manager, in a new, gigantic ballpark. Despite the growing woes of its hometown, the most successful period in the franchise's history was about to start.

CHAPTER FOUR

That New Stadium Smell (1977–1979)

J ean Drapeau's promise of a new domed baseball stadium for the Expos became a bigger running joke with each passing year. The note he sent to the National League in 1968 pledging a new ballpark by Opening Day 1971 as part of the deal for an expansion franchise proved a farce. A few months later, the league granted an extension stretching to 1972; that deadline, too, came and went with no new park. A few weeks after the Expos played their first game, Charles Bronfman was asked when they could realistically expect a new stadium. "About 1973 . . . I should think." When Jim Fanning was asked in April '71 for a target date, he said he was confident the Expos could play in their new home by 1975. Probably. Maybe.

At the heart of the stadium discussion was a grander plan, however—one hatched by Drapeau back in 1963. It was the biggest of all his big dreams, one that the mayor felt would enhance his city's reputation around the world. He wanted to lure the Olympics to Montreal.

The city's first attempt to reel in the summer games ramped up in April 1966, when Montreal finished third behind Madrid and eventual winner Munich for the right to host the (ultimately tragic) '72 Olympics. Montreal again won the Canadian Olympic Association's nomination to represent Canada in bidding for the 1976 games. Drapeau's hope was to build a new stadium that could accommodate not only the Expos, but the Canadian Football League's Alouettes, concerts, and other events as well—while also serving as the main locale for the Olympics. The grandest plans projected a $124 million (Canadian) cost for a majestic, domed stadium that would include all the latest amenities for multiple uses. By comparison, Pittsburgh's Three Rivers Stadium broke ground in April 1968, was completed in July 1970, and cost less than half of Montreal's projected amount.

On May 12, 1970, votes were counted for the '76 Games. Round one of voting had been tight, with Montreal competing against Moscow and Los Angeles. In round two, a verdict was reached. Though Moscow and Los Angeles would host the games in 1980 and 1984, in 1976 the Olympics were coming to Montreal.

If the Olympics were Drapeau's baby, the stadium would be too—right down to its designer. The mayor had grown impressed with the work of French architect Roger Taillibert. In Paris, Taillibert had gained acclaim for designing the Parc des Princes soccer stadium and other venues. He was a reputable choice, but what was distressing was how Taillibert's hiring came to light. Drapeau struck a clandestine deal with Taillibert soon after the city won the Olympic rights, but the public didn't learn about it until reading a March 1972 piece in the *Montreal Gazette*. An editorial in the paper described the situation this way: "It is extraordinary that even in Montreal's municipal autocracy the mayor would keep such an important matter . . . a secret for so long."

Taillibert himself didn't help matters. Finishing on schedule and within the allotted budget, building a stadium that would be the right size and design to properly accommodate baseball—these factors took a back seat to Taillibert's own vision. Multiple delays plagued the project: construction crews staged a long strike, and brutal Montreal winters slowed progress to a crawl a third of the year. Spiralling costs for raw materials, especially the unfathomable amount of prefabricated concrete required to build this humongous edifice, forced stops and starts as the city kept scrounging for more money. These largely uncontrollable factors could be understood and forgiven. But Rory Costello, author of several Expos-related articles for the Society for American Baseball Research's (SABR's) BioProject, has detailed far more insidious happenings.

From the start, cronyism ran rampant. The problems began with the engineering firm in charge of the project, Régis Trudeau et Associes. Rather than solicit bids from multiple firms, City Hall went straight to Trudeau with the project. Turned out Drapeau's top advisor, Gérard Niding, steered the job to Trudeau after the company built his country house. This kind of mutual backscratching was certainly unethical, but nonetheless typical in Montreal, where legitimate construction-related businesses that received political favours still beat the many other outfits that landed fat contracts through mob ties. The bigger problem was that those in charge at Trudeau were flummoxed by the challenges of the job, including essential tasks such as moving the 40-ton concrete slabs that would form the backbone of the stadium.

Taillibert only made things worse when it came to containing costs. Believing the project to be more a living monument than a stadium, he refused to compromise on price for materials or labour, and even held sway over negotiations with contractors to ensure those hired could carry out his artistic vision. "What is money? Mere paper," he told *Montreal Gazette* columnist

Michael Farber in a 1986 interview. In the article, Farber added: "The bottom line, Taillibert said, will not be the figure some pencil pusher comes up with when the final bill is stamped 'paid' years from now, but what sort of heirloom Montreal will pass on to its children."

In August of '74, the province of Quebec finally stepped in and threw Taillibert off the project. Lavalin Inc. took over as project manager, while the Désourdy consortium became the general contractor. Both companies had ties to Quebec's Liberal Party, and the change in management read like a simple transfer of power from one group of cronies to another.

Despite all these setbacks and illicit connections, however, Drapeau remained confident that the Olympics—and Olympic Stadium—would be self-sustaining. At the very least, he talked a good game. "It is no more possible for the Montreal Olympics to lose money than it is for a man to get pregnant," the mayor vowed. As Costello recounted, Drapeau predicted not only massive revenue from Olympic tourists and baseball fans, but also "extraordinary revenue from commemorative coins, stamps, and souvenirs."

Unfortunately, Drapeau would be spectacularly wrong. While the rest of the world celebrated 14-year-old Romanian gymnast Nadia Comaneci's seven perfect 10.0 scores, the pageantry of the Opening and Closing Ceremonies, and other highlights, Montrealers and Quebeckers got punched in the face by skyrocketing costs, with Olympic Stadium delivering the most vicious uppercuts. The building's initial projected cost of $124 million spiked to $310 million, then to more than $600 million—about half the Olympics' total cost of $1.3 billion. Both ventures became gigantic money-losers for the city and its many male residents (who were now apparently with child).

In the short term, the Olympics were a disaster for the Expos. No one cared about baseball during the summer of '76, with the biggest sporting event in the world happening a few miles away. The ball club suffered through its worst season since the expansion year, going 55–107 while drawing a pitiful eight thousand fans a game. Some of the next-generation talent had arrived, with Gary Carter, Ellis Valentine, and Larry Parrish all claiming everyday jobs. But they were still too raw to make big contributions: none of the three were older than 22 on Opening Day.

The saving grace was that Montreal would finally have a permanent home for a major league team. When the Expos moved into Olympic Stadium to start the 1977 season, they found a sports facility unlike any that had ever been built. Though it had the same basic multi-use setup as cookie-cutter stadiums in Philadelphia, Pittsburgh, Cincinnati, and St. Louis, it looked completely different from the outside. The exterior of the building consisted of 34 giant, cantilevered concrete beams, meant to evoke huge hands with curved fingers. An attached tower, when completed, would be the largest angled, free-standing structure of its kind in the world. In architectural circles, the stadium was considered a grand accomplishment of modern design.

For less romantic baseball fans, the Big O looked completely different: a giant spaceship, far too large for a baseball game, dropped into the middle of a neighbourhood with little else around it except other Olympic Park venues and drab walk-up apartments.

"Not only did the ball club have no input about location, they had no input into the design, the construction, or configuration of the stadium," said Dave Van Horne. "None whatsoever."

As the Expos took the field for the '77 home opener, they found another major problem: the stadium wasn't close to finished, even after years of planning and construction. Both the Expos and visitors were stuck in temporary clubhouses. Front-office staff worked out of makeshift offices so cramped that several of them later became storage closets. The padding on the outfield walls was incredibly thin, injecting every dash to the warning track with the possibility of a season-ending injury. Ron McClain, the Expos' head trainer for 25 seasons, repeatedly warned the team about the wall and the damage it could do to the players. Management estimated the cost of replacing it at around $250,000, a pittance given the team's revenue stream, especially when the health of its core assets was involved. Still, nothing happened. Instead, several Expos outfielders got hurt smashing into it, including Andre Dawson, who suffered a broken bone in his knee.

More concerning for the players was the playing surface itself, a paper-thin layer of turf laid over another paper-thin layer of padding, perched on top of a thick layer of concrete. Here again, McClain warned his bosses what could happen. He was told the cost of replacing the turf would be around $1 million, a tougher financial burden to handle, but still a move that could save the team multiple times that, given the likelihood of games lost to injury. Again, no dice. The money would've had to come out of the city's pockets, and no bean counter at City Hall was particularly interested in projecting health outcomes for Warren Cromartie or Ellis Valentine. The rock-hard turf became so notorious around the league that players on visiting teams would leave the stadium to go run at a nearby park, for fear of wearing down their knees.

The lack of a roof only made things worse. When Drapeau had announced his grand plans for a new stadium, Bronfman kept insisting that it come with a roof to shield players from Montreal's often terrible weather. There was a roof, all right—it just didn't make it to Montreal for five more years, gathering dust in a warehouse in France for reasons ranging from cost overruns to design concerns to general incompetence from the stadium's operator, the Olympic Installations Board. It measured about 60,000 square feet of orange Kevlar, weighing 66 tons. In the meantime, players froze their asses off. Whenever there was moisture on any part of the field in early April or late September, there was a good chance those wet spots would freeze over, forcing infielders and outfielders to navigate big patches of ice. If there were ever a baseball field custom-designed to destroy the health of its players—especially its outfielders—this was that field. Though the Big O eventually got its cover, both the stadium and its woefully conceived roof would become giant albatrosses for the Expos, and the city, for decades to come.

For now, though, it was an upgrade over the minor league–caliber Jarry Park. And along with the introduction of Olympic Stadium, the Expos got another boost in 1977: Dick Williams.

Reeling in Williams was considered a coup of the highest order. In 1967, his first season as a major league manager, he had guided the Boston Red Sox to their first American League pennant in 21 years. The '67 Sox had talent, certainly: the great Carl Yastrzemski, Tony Conigliaro, George "Boomer" Scott, and pitcher Jim Lonborg all made headlines that season. But the Red Sox had won only 72 games in 1966, and so expectations heading into '67 were essentially non-existent. Sixth or seventh place, maybe.

Yaz was considered the only marquee player on the roster heading into the season, and only 8,324 fans made it to Fenway Park for the home opener. Moreover, this was an incredibly young team, with Yaz the only everyday player older than 25. The combination of the team's surprising success that year, as well as impressive breakouts for Conigliaro, Scott, Lonborg, and others cemented Williams' reputation for being unafraid to let talented young players play, develop, and thrive. In Boston, 1967 came to be known as the "Impossible Dream" season, and Williams earned a great deal of credit for making that dream possible, with the Red Sox going all the way to the World Series before losing to Bob Gibson and the St. Louis Cardinals.

Williams lasted less than two more years in Boston following that great season, however—more due to strained relations with ownership than any massive failures by the team. In 1969, the Sox stood in third place in September when owner Tom Yawkey tossed his manager overboard after Williams benched Yaz for a baserunning error.

Williams' next job in baseball came as third-base coach for none other than the Expos, working under Gene Mauch for a season. Those who remember that 1970 campaign gave generally positive reviews to Williams' time there. Still, he was ready to return to managing, which he did in 1971 with the Oakland A's. Williams was an immediate success in Oakland. The A's won 101 games that year, thanks to another young roster that included 25-year-old Reggie Jackson, 20-year-old Sal Bando, 25-year-old Catfish Hunter, 24-year-old Rollie Fingers, and 21-year-old lefty Vida Blue. The latter would garner Cy Young and MVP honours in 1971, while Jackson, Hunter, and Fingers were ultimately elected to the Hall of Fame.

Oakland fell short of the World Series that first year, but quickly broke through in '72 and again in '73, capturing back-to-back World Series titles. Williams showed excellent skill as a tactician with the A's, much of it stemming from his refusal to defer to veterans for reasons of seniority alone. In the '72 World Series, he started Gene Tenace, a young second-string catcher, over veteran Dave Duncan, figuring Tenace by then was the better player (Duncan was only a year older but he'd made his major league debut five years before Tenace). Tenace went completely bonkers, hitting .348 with four home runs and winning World Series MVP.

A cynic might argue that Williams benefited from killer talent in Oakland, and maybe caught a break or two in Boston as well. There's no question that Williams' early teams wouldn't have won if they didn't have guys who could play. But those who played for him saw Williams as more than just a caretaker.

"He's always joking about how he rode our coattails," said Vida Blue years later when Williams was inducted into the Hall of Fame. "But he's the one who taught us to play winning baseball. Dick Williams was that X-factor."

Once again, Williams clashed with a difficult owner, this time the mercurial, meddling, and money-hungry Charlie Finley. And once again, Williams had to leave a winning team. This time, leaving would backfire due to a woeful lack of talent in his new home. Williams took over as manager of the California Angels in 1974, guided his teams to just 147 wins against 194 losses, and was gone before the end of the 1976 season. But it was clear that Williams' reputation as a winner was well intact, with McHale and Fanning recognizing how difficult Yawkey and Finley could be, and how lousy the Angels' players were. Give Williams the exciting young talent he'd managed to such wonderful effect in Boston and Oakland, then surround him with supportive and sane bosses in the front office and owner's box—and the Expos too might win a championship.

"Dick Williams was not hired for a transition," said Jacques Doucet. "Because it was his second trip to Montreal, he knew a little bit about the situation here. And he knew that with the kids that we had, he and the team had a good chance of moving up. He was there to win."

To speed up the timetable, the Expos began aggressively courting free agents. Players newly blessed with the ability to shop their services to other teams understandably sought both big dollars and a chance to play for winners. Bronfman was prepared to bid against teams in bigger markets with deeper revenue streams, but convincing top free agents that the Expos could soon start winning was a harder sell. Williams was tasked with doing much of that selling. The Expos' first major target after the Williams hire was the single biggest fish in the free-agent pond, as well as one of Williams' former players. They were going after Reggie Jackson.

By the time he hit the open market after his 1976 season in Baltimore (where he was traded in advance of free agency), Jackson was a bona fide superstar. He'd played on five straight AL West–winning teams in Oakland. He'd been the American League's Most Valuable Player in 1973, and finished in the top five in MVP voting four times. He was a brash, magnetic, power-hitting machine who would put up numbers wherever he went, but would also pull fans into the ballpark and money into the till with his star power.

The Expos became one of three leading candidates for Jackson's services, along with the San Diego Padres (owned by McDonald's magnate Ray Kroc) and George Steinbrenner's New York Yankees. Jackson lived in Phoenix, Arizona, while Williams lived in southern California, close enough to warrant having the two men fly to Montreal together for the next stop on Jackson's free-agency tour. As Williams recounted in his autobiography *No More Mr. Nice Guy*, Jackson hated playing in Baltimore. He already had a good relationship with Williams, so it would be up to the Expos' higher-ups to convince Jackson of the city's charms. Bronfman threw a lavish party in Jackson's honour, and everyone in the city came over to the Bronfman house: the mayor, various dignitaries, "every hot shot I could think of," as Bronfman put it. While the glitterati gorged on hors d'oeuvres and sipped champagne, Bronfman learned there was a problem.

"A minor partner was a guy named Sydney Maislin," recalled Bronfman. "The Maislins were in the trucking business. His brother Sam got a call from customs, and they said, 'There's this guy named Reggie Jackson.' What about Reggie Jackson? 'Well, he just came through, and there's a problem. He's got some stuff in his suitcase.' What kind of stuff? 'Stuff.'"

John McHale's son Kevin raced to the airport, and along with Sam Maislin, helped pull Jackson out of the jam. Jackson showed up late to the party, pissed off that he'd been hassled by customs and lost his stash. The next day, the elder McHale met with Jackson and his agent to hammer out a deal. Even though Jackson was unhappy with the previous night's events, and even though the Expos were competing against the mighty Yankees for his services, the feeling among many in the baseball world was that the Expos had a legitimate shot.

"The feeling was, Bronfman could do this," said Van Horne. "He was just that powerful, that wealthy. He can make this happen if this person wants to come north of the border to play. You just assumed, 'Well, that will happen. We'll get him.'"

McHale talked with Jackson and his agent for an hour, without anything getting signed. Jackson instead signed with the Yankees soon afterwards, inking a five-year deal worth a hair less than $3 million. That whiff weighed heavily on Bronfman.

"I remember seeing a picture of Reggie and George Steinbrenner walking down Broadway or 5th Avenue or something," said Mitch Melnick, a broadcaster and radio personality for more than 30 years in Montreal, "and I went, 'Aw, fuck. It's not gonna happen.' I really thought he was going to sign here. New stadium, new manager, new era, big splash, best hitter available, Bronfman wasn't gonna be outbid. That was really the first taste of what made him, I think, a little bitter. He kept trying and failing [to sign big-ticket free agents]. Then he realized, 'Okay, let's pour it all into the farm system.'"

As great as Jackson had been in Oakland, he would gain his greatest measure of fame (and infamy) in New York. The Yankees had failed to make the playoffs in 11 straight years before his arrival, a painfully long run of failure for baseball's most decorated franchise. George Steinbrenner, like Bronfman, was a relatively new owner looking to make his mark with the advent of free agency. He'd lured Jackson's former teammate Catfish Hunter to New York with a lucrative contract two years earlier; in that race too, the Expos (and Padres) had been among the teams who tried to pull off the big signing. This time, Steinbrenner wanted to go even bigger. The '76 Yankees had lost the World Series, and Steinbrenner saw Jackson as the slugger who would help them win the next one. When Jackson finally signed on the dotted line, Steinbrenner couldn't resist crowing. Addressing the media, the Yankees owner said that Bronfman might have Seagram's, and Kroc might have McDonald's . . . "But I got the Big Apple."

With Jackson gone, the Expos began making alternate plans to build up their roster and supplement their stable of kids. To fill their gaping hole at second base, they signed free agent Dave Cash away from the Phillies. They traded away two players, Woodie Fryman and Rodney Scott, who would eventually return to the team and become important contributors. They also unloaded Andre Thornton, a first baseman who couldn't hit his weight in Montreal but would go on to become an All-Star in Cleveland. But the biggest name to pop up in an Expos transaction that winter was a seven-time All-Star with two World Series rings. Tony Perez was a pretty good consolation prize.

Perez was an integral member of Cincinnati's Big Red Machine dynasty. By the time the Expos traded for him he was 34, but he could still hit—and the price was still reasonable: soft-tossing reliever Dale Murray and Fryman, a 36-year-old. Perez quickly earned a reputation as a leader.

"Tony was a veteran you heard so much about, being part of the Big Red Machine," said Andre Dawson. "He filled a void at first base and provided that veteran leadership inside the clubhouse. He was a no-nonsense guy, a gamer. Wouldn't hesitate to pull you aside, talk about pros and cons of being in the big leagues to a young player. That made the transition that much easier."

Thus fortified, the Expos took a big step forward in 1977, their record jumping by 20 victories to 75–87. That still left them in fifth place, but the club's best homegrown prospects were starting to blossom.

At 23, Gary Carter enjoyed a colossal breakout, posting a .356 on-base percentage, slugging .525, and launching 31 homers, all while improving his pitch-receiving and pitcher-handling skills.

Fellow 23-year-old Larry Parrish struggled with injuries and luke-warm numbers, but further ensconced himself as the everyday third baseman. Warren Cromartie, also 23, hit .282 in 155 games and lashed 41 doubles in his first full major league season.

The Expos' two 22-year-old outfielders were the most exciting of the bunch. Andre Dawson hit .282 in his first full season, cracking 19 home runs, swiping 21 bases, and flashing impressive range and a rocket arm in centre. But Valentine was the one talent evaluators dreamed on the most. A five-tool player like Dawson, Valentine just *looked* a little better than his talented teammate, both in numbers and raw skills. He hit .293 in '77, smoking 25 homers and one-upping Dawson's impressive arm with an absolute cannon—so mesmerizing that many fans wouldn't leave their seats when opposing teams batted. The combination of Valentine, Dawson, and Cromartie was the best young outfield in baseball. Though they were brash, and they swung at too many pitches out of the strike zone, none of it seemed to bother Williams.

They were "the envy of the league," wrote Williams in *No More Mr. Nice Guy*. "I'll always mention Dawson first, because he was everyone's third choice. Of the three, he was always the slow learner, the one who'd need the most work and wouldn't go nearly as far." But he defied the odds and became the best of the three by a mile. Williams would have harsher words for Cromartie and Valentine later, after both players failed to live up to their full potential. Especially Valentine.

At the beginning, though, "he just let us go out and play," Dawson said of his former manager. "We were this young outfield, and he would just turn us loose. Pitchers, though, some of them had a problem with Dick. His patience, if it was tested, he would react to the pitchers, not to us."

Ah yes, the pitchers. While the lineup became flush with young stars, the Expos' efforts to develop front-line pitching lagged behind. Though Steve Rogers had by 1977 emerged as one of the best right-handed starters in the league, tossing a staggering 301⅔ innings that year with an ERA 23 percent better than league average, the next three starters behind him—Jackie Brown, Wayne Twitchell, and Stan Bahnsen—stank, teaming up to post a 4.50 ERA. Yet beginning the following year, and stretching over the next three seasons, their manager would save his nastiest barbs for his ace. Of all the player-manager feuds in Expos history, none topped Steve Rogers versus Dick Williams.

The title of Williams' autobiography captures the late manager's personality well. Even in his best moods, Williams wasn't likely to smother his players with warmth and kindness.

"Dick Williams used to think that in order to win, a good clubhouse fight would sort of get everybody energized," said Bronfman. "That was Dick's way of managing. Get everybody riled up and have a good fight."

Most players didn't seem to mind. Dawson and numerous other players described Williams as fair. Cromartie was one of many who later expressed regret that the Expos eventually let Williams go, lauding the skipper's abilities (and questioning those of his eventual successor). Williams was a big believer in depth and roster balance. For the bench, he sought out capable veterans willing and able to fill the role of ace pinch-hitter, rather than something larger. He loved hoarding speed on the bench, using pinch-runners in close-and-late situations whenever possible. Williams was every bit the tactician that Mauch was, only with less bunting, and was far less averse to using young players.

Rogers, too, lauded Williams' managing skill, despite their differences.

"Dick Williams was probably as good a manager as I ever played against, or with," said Rogers. "He ran the game extremely well. When he got there, that's when I started coming into my own. On managing the game, on never being taken by surprise in a game, he was always prepared, much like Gene Mauch. Very much so."

Rogers, though, saw another side to Williams: "He was one of the worst human beings I've ever been around."

The Williams-Rogers rift took root on August 28, 1978. The Expos had climbed into third place three weeks earlier and caught at least a whiff of contention, sitting 7½ games out with 48 games left to play. But the offence went ice cold over those next three weeks. In the middle of a 13-game road trip, Rogers took the mound at Dodger Stadium, and in typical fashion during that excellent season pitched well, tossing seven innings while giving up just two runs.

There were two problems with his performance, though. First, the offence again let him down, offering no run support in a 4–0 loss. Second, Rogers was in pain. Excruciating pain. From the early innings, his elbow was throbbing, to the point where he'd shake it vigorously every time he sat on the bench. Pitching coach Jim Brewer came over and told Rogers to stop messing with his arm. "Brew," said Rogers, "you cannot believe how bad it hurts." The next morning, he got up, took a shower, then raised his right arm to comb his hair. "CH-KK" came the horrifying sound from his elbow, which had locked into place. Rogers tried moving his arm, pressing on it to try and regain some motion, but nothing happened—other than more shooting pain every time he touched it. Already in L.A., Rogers went to see Los Angeles–based surgeon Dr. Frank Jobe, inventor of the Tommy John ligament replacement surgery. Jobe diagnosed a painful bone spur sitting right underneath Rogers' triceps tendon, and requiring surgery.

Even with the arrival of Tommy John surgery and other medical advances, 1978 was still a relatively primitive time for understanding and coping with injuries. But even by those standards, Rogers' manager was harsh. When Rogers missed the final month of the

1978 season, Williams fumed, then held it as a black mark against his number-one starter from there.

Williams wasn't the ace's only issue. After the surgery, Rogers was told to squeeze a ball to build the strength in his arm, then get a more detailed rehab regimen from Yvon Belanger, the team's trainer. Rogers explained the situation to Belanger, who said he'd call back shortly with a routine to follow. Only he never called, leaving Rogers to figure out his own rehab methods, with a little help from Brewer—but none from doctors or trainers. Having never suffered an injury like this before, Rogers didn't realize he'd also need to strengthen his shoulder during rehab, or else risk having his elbow heal while his shoulder weakened and became its own problem. In February of 1979, Rogers drove down to spring training, then headed to the airport to pick up his wife and sons, who were flying in to meet him. Arriving at the same time were Williams and the coaching staff. One of those coaches, Norm Sherry, asked Rogers how he was doing, if he was feeling better after going through all that pain, followed by surgery, followed by a long, arduous rehab.

"My elbow feels great, but my shoulder is killing me," Rogers told Sherry.

To which Williams replied: "Well, if you can't fuckin' pitch, then we'll get some-fuckin'-body else."

Rogers was ready to punch his manager, but was urged by Sherry to forget about it (especially since Williams had been drinking on the flight over). But the open sparring between the two men kept intensifying. Before one crucial game in 1979 that Rogers was due to pitch, Williams told beat writer Ted Blackman that he wished he could start one of his "good" pitchers instead. The disparaging comments would continue over the following two seasons.

Williams wasn't the only one with a reputation for being ornery: Rogers never hid his feelings on the field, and would sometimes let those behind him hear about it if they botched a play. He could also be smart to the point of arrogance, and was no master of diplomacy when he wasn't happy.

"It's all right to be smarter than somebody else," said long-time Montreal broadcaster Elliott Price. "But you don't have to let everybody know, all the time, that you're the smartest guy in the room."

Williams would later take much bigger swings at Rogers in *No More Mr. Nice Guy*. "I'm here to say Montreal's pitching emperor had no clothes. Steve Rogers was a fraud."

The manager described going out to the mound to talk to Rogers in big games only to find a pitcher who looked rattled, even had trouble breathing. "He didn't like the big situations. That would have been fine, except that in those situations an entire team and city and even nation were counting on him."

Okay, so Williams was a bit of hothead, carrying a grudge. And Rogers was a bit of a know-it-all who rubbed some people the wrong way. But the Expos still needed both of them as they took baby steps in their quest for relevance. Montreal won 76 games in 1978, just a one-game improvement over 1977, leaving the franchise with 10 straight sub-.500 seasons since joining the league. With the benefit of hindsight and a little statistical common sense, we now suspect that the '78 club was better than its record indicated: in 1978 the Expos scored 633 runs and allowed just 611, which if distributed evenly over the course of 162 games would yield an expected record of 84–78, eight games better than how the season ended in reality. There were actually 32 fewer runs scored in '78 than in '77, with Carter and Dawson among the players seeing sizable pullbacks in their offensive numbers. But the good news was that the pitching and defence finally came together, as the club allowed 125 fewer runs in 1978, finishing seventh in the majors with a 3.42 ERA.

Russ Hansen

Out of the owner's box and onto the mound: Charles Bronfman's uniform number 83 is in honour of the Seagram's whiskey.

Russ Hansen

The beloved grin of Gary Carter, "The Kid."

Russ Hansen

After winning the pennant with the Red Sox during their "Impossible Dream" season, and then two championships with the Athletics, Dick Williams managed two of the best teams in Expos history, only to get replaced near the end of the team's lone playoff season.

Shortstop Chris Speier slides home while teammates Tim Raines and Warren Cromartie look on.

Bon vivants in the dugout: Scott Sanderson, Pepe Frias, Larry Parrish, Ellis Valentine, Dan Schatzeder, and Sam Mejias.

The first Expo to enter the Hall of Fame, catcher Gary Carter was a force at the plate as well as behind it.

Ellis Valentine was one of the most talented players to put on an Expos uniform.

Long before T-shirt cannons: Larry Parrish takes part in a cow-milking contest.

The 1982 All-Star Game at Olympic Stadium was one of the high points in Montreal baseball history, with five Expos (Tim Raines, Andre Dawson, Gary Carter, Steve Rogers, and Al Oliver) representing the National League, and four of them (all except Oliver) in the starting lineup.

Russ Hansen

A Hall of Famer next to a should-be Hall of Famer: Andre Dawson and Tim Raines.

Jeff Reardon, nicknamed "The Terminator," briefly held Major League Baseball's all-time saves record, and is still seventh on that list, behind only Mariano Rivera, Trevor Hoffman, Lee Smith, Billy Wagner, John Franco, and Dennis Eckersley.

A young Tim Wallach, who would play thirteen seasons for the Expos, appearing in five All-Star Games and collecting three Gold Glove and two Silver Slugger awards.

The one and only Youppi! was the first mascot to be ejected from a Major League Baseball game. A true Montrealer, after the Expos moved to Washington, DC, Youppi! became the first official mascot of the National Hockey League's storied Montreal Canadiens.

Manager Felipe Alou, the Expos all-time wins leader, shares some wisdom with Andre Dawson, who ended his playing career with the Florida Marlins.

The last great Expo: Vladimir Guerrero.

The biggest difference on the mound that year was Ross Grimsley. The latest free-agent signing, the 27-year-old Grimsley was a slop-throwing left-hander who the Expos figured could at least eat a bunch of innings. The year before with Baltimore, Grimsley had tossed 218 of them but with middling results, posting a worse-than-league-average 3.96 ERA and walking more batters than he struck out. What happened next might be credited partly to Expos scouts, but mostly to sheer luck: in the 1978 season, Grimsley went 20–11, slashing his ERA to 3.05. He made his first (and only) All-Star team and finished seventh in Cy Young voting. This was the first time an Expos pitcher had ever won 20 games in a season—and the last, it turned out.

Grimsley probably benefited from joining the non-DH league. Though he did strike out more batters and walk fewer than he had in '77, he never dominated, not with just 84 punchouts (against 67 walks) in 263 innings. What he did well, however, was keep the ball in the ballpark and induce a lot of soft contact—allowing just 17 homers in 36 starts, plus a career-low .245 opponents' batting average on balls hit in play (league average that year was .280). He threw five different pitches, and was a master of painting the corners and changing speeds, going from slow to glacial. He was also well known for . . . shall we say, aiding the flight of the ball. Grimsley deployed the usual array of lubricants to get a couple inches of extra drop on his curveball. He also scuffed with the best of them, using everything at his disposal to create grooves on the ball that would cause pitches to swerve to one side or the other. Between the big numbers and the blatant cheating, he did a pretty great impression of future Hall of Famer Don Sutton, for that one season anyway.

Grimsley never came close to replicating that season thereafter, and got traded two years later. Still, he led a '78 staff stuffed with veterans who kept the team afloat while the kids continued to

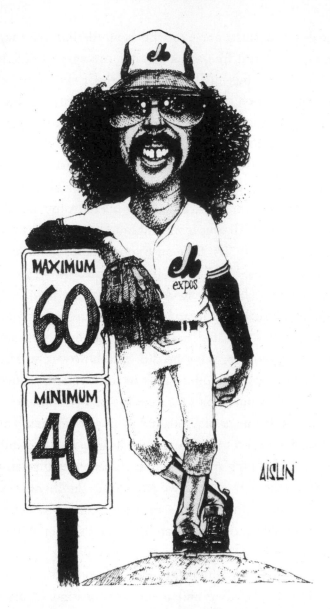

mature. Alongside Grimsley was Rudy May, the 33-year-old lefty acquired in a trade from the Orioles who posted the best strike-out-to-walk rate among any of the team's top five starters, logging 144 innings. Thirty-eight-year-old Woodie Fryman returned to the team in an early-June trade and pitched respectably, making

17 starts and putting up a 3.61 ERA that was right around league average. Meanwhile, Rogers' 2.47 ERA ranked second among all qualified National League starters.

Even better, some of the young guns started to arrive. In his first season as a rotation mainstay, 23-year-old lefty Dan Schatzeder flashed a 3.07 ERA and even hit well (for a pitcher). Twenty-year-old Scott Sanderson, a third-round pick just a year earlier, made his major league debut and shone, posting a 2.51 ERA over 61 innings mostly as a starter. David Palmer had come into the organization with less hype as a 21st-round pick in 1976, but by the time he cracked the big leagues as a 20-year-old two years later, he too was projected to be a big part of the team's future success.

When teams improve in certain statistical categories, it's instructive to figure out how and why it happened. In the case of the Expos' massive 125-run improvement in run prevention, you could pinpoint several factors. First, they ran out a more talented pitching staff. Grimsley's 20-win season might've been built with some degree of luck, but he was still a big upgrade over the likes of 1977 punching bags such as Jackie Brown. The addition of Grimsley, May, and Fryman, along with the emergence of some young homegrown pitchers, also nudged pitchers into roles for which they were better suited: Bahnsen shaved a run off his ERA after moving from a starter's role to the bullpen, for one. Furthermore, the team's defence was phenomenal behind them. The Expos turned 74 percent of balls hit in play into outs in 1978, the best mark in the National League. Those two variables pointed to real skill, encouraging signs as the Expos geared up for the 1979 season. But the Expos may have finally had some luck on their side, as well. For one thing, Expos pitchers simply stranded a greater percentage of runners they put on base, an MLB-best 75 percent in '78. While a few pitchers do show some ability to strand runners, a team-wide jump that big smacked of chance working in Montreal's favour. Furthermore, the Expos benefited from a league-wide drop in offence in '78; hitters batted .258/.323/.379 that year, compared to .264/.329/.401 in 1977.

Despite all this, however, the Expos were still losing.

The first big move in preparation for 1979 was to shore up the bullpen. Late-inning assassins like Goose Gossage and Bruce Sutter had begun springing up all over the league, ushering in a new era of relief aces. With the Expos well beyond their humble expansion beginnings and hoping to contend, finding a quality stopper made sense. With that goal in mind, they signed veteran free agent Elias Sosa. The 28-year-old right-hander had already pitched for five teams before landing in Montreal. But in '78, Sosa had posted a 2.64 ERA in 109 innings for Oakland, profiling as the sort of pitcher who could protect late-inning leads and throw multiple innings when needed.

In addition to strong relief pitching, a deep bench is a hallmark of competitive teams, which might explain why, for a full decade, the Expos had carried so many regrettable reserves. For 1979, though, Montreal acquired two players who'd been Expos earlier in their careers, nabbing Jerry White and Rodney Scott from the Cubs for fringe outfielder Sam Mejias. In his second stint with Montreal, White became a highly productive member of "the Bus Squad," the name given to the team's suddenly far more effective bench.

Initially ticketed for a part-time role, Rodney Scott instead beat Dave Cash out of the starting second-base spot. Cash had put up the worst numbers of his career in '78, with many observers blaming a lifestyle change that included Cash becoming a vegetarian, thus sapping him of his power. More likely it was simply a case of a high-contact, low-power hitter becoming unplayable once his bat speed slowed and he stopped hitting for high averages. Scott was no masher himself, hitting all three of his career home runs

in that 1979 season. But the man they called Cool Breeze drew a
ton of walks and possessed breathtaking speed, giving the Expos
the equivalent of a potential double whenever he came up. This
constituted a modest upgrade over Cash's limp bat.

"Dave Cash was a veteran free agent making a lot of money on
the bench all of '79, and Williams didn't care at all about that,"
said Melnick. "He wanted the better player in the lineup, and
Scott was it."

The biggest acquisition of the winter, however, proved not to
be a reliever or a hitter, but a starter: Bill Lee, the tall, junkballing,
rabble-rousing, wildly eccentric lefty. A few years earlier, acquiring Lee would've been a huge coup. From 1973 through 1975, he
averaged more than 275 innings per season, putting up impressive

numbers in Fenway Park, a stadium that could be tough on left-handers. By the time the Expos traded for him in December 1978, though, Lee's fastball was gone, wiped away by a shoulder injury suffered during a brawl at Yankee Stadium in 1976. Lee had come back as an extreme finesse pitcher, relying on guile and command to (sometimes) get hitters out. Though he'd posted a solid 3.46 ERA in 1978 with the Red Sox, he'd done so while walking more batters than he struck out, with just 44 Ks in 177 innings. If the Expos were going to hang their collective hats on this trade, they could latch on to two positives.

One, Lee's repertoire and stats column looked a lot like Grimsley's right before Ross the Boss had signed with Montreal, and that had worked out pretty damn well. And two, to get Lee, the Expos had to give up only a forgettable utility infielder named Stan Papi. The Red Sox believed that Lee's best days were long gone. He was also a pain in the ass by his final season in Boston, often calling Red Sox manager Don Zimmer "the gerbil" and publicly questioning his managing. "Zimmer wouldn't know a good pitcher if he came up and bit him in the ass," Lee told the local writers. After the Sox sold teammate Bernie Carbo to Cleveland for $15,000, Lee announced he was retiring from baseball and left the team, only to return a day later. He then pitched terribly toward the end of the year, erasing the memory of his strong first half. Meanwhile, Lee was closing in on 10 years in the big leagues, meaning he would soon have the right to veto a trade. The Sox wanted him gone, while Williams, who had managed Lee briefly in Boston and kept tabs on his career thereafter, wanted him as an Expo. The deal got done.

Lee was horrified.

"I cried, cried for about two days," he said. "Who wanted to go to the Expos? The team had never played above .500. Perennial losers."

Thirty-four years after it happened, Lee still remembered the exact date of the trade.

"It was December 7, 1978, Pearl Harbor Day."

Not to be dramatic.

"Not to be dramatic."

In fact, there was drama from the beginning. Lee spent the next few months living in remote Bellingham, Washington, doing lots of distance running, growing out his hair and beard, and living a mountain man's existence. When he showed up for the first day of spring training, stadium security detained him, thinking Lee was some kind of derelict trying to break in.

That was just one of several distractions generated by Lee, "The Spaceman." One Boston writer visited Expos camp to do a story on the ex-Red Sock, and Lee told the writer he'd been consuming marijuana in various forms for the previous 11 years. "I sprinkle it on my organic buckwheat pancakes in the morning," he explained. "It makes me impervious to bus fumes when I run." You could debate the science, sure. You might also argue (or not) with Lee's related points about the war on weed being misguided, with so many millions of people ingesting caffeine, alcohol, and nicotine without fear of legal reprisal.

Either way, adding a pot-smoking, House of David beard-wearing, say-whatever-the-hell-he-liked, anti-establishment type to the pitching staff was going to draw attention. But in Montreal— where free-spirited players came to be greeted by fans and most of the media with laissez-faire attitudes or even warm embraces—Lee fit right in. He might as well have been one of them, given how often he held court at Grumpy's. Hit the old downtown bar after a game and there was an excellent chance you'd find Lee, downing pints and spinning tales alongside buddies like famed editorial cartoonist Terry Mosher and journalist and raconteur Nick Auf der Maur. All of it preceded and followed by a few puffs in the Spaceman van.

Lee's *bon vivant* tendencies didn't always go over well with Williams, though, nor did the white lies Lee told to get out of jams. One day, Lee walked into the clubhouse, his legs covered in big gashes. Two versions of this story made the rounds afterwards, the first being that Lee had run into a fence while jogging at three a.m. The second also involved jogging at three a.m., only this time with a cat jumping out from behind the bushes and scratching him badly. In the end, the three a.m. part was true. The rest was not. In fact, Lee had been with a lady friend at her apartment when the woman's husband unexpectedly came home. Lee bolted out of the place, jumping off the second-story balcony onto a trellis, which he tried to use to climb down. The trellis broke, landing Lee on an iron fence, which messed up both his legs and his groin.

Still, Williams saw the value of putting up with Lee's foibles given what the left-hander could offer. Lee was as smart a pitcher as you would find, keenly aware of his limitations and able to squeeze as much value as possible out of a turf-burning sinker and wide array of breaking pitches. "He has a fantastic attitude," said pitching coach Jim Brewer in *The Year the Expos Almost Won the Pennant*. "If all the pitchers were like him, I'd be paid for doing nothing."

Finally, Williams had the team he wanted. The '79 Expos carried five right-handed pitchers and five southpaws. The team had supremely talented young players entering their prime years, a deep starting rotation and lots of options out of the bullpen, strong defence and a capable bench, plus power and speed—all blended with the kind of characters that could give other managers fits, but suited Williams and his just-show-up-and-play approach perfectly fine.

The Expos immediately proved they'd become a very different team than the losing bunch of the previous decade. Storming out of the gate, they won 15 of their first 20 games, capped by a perfect

7–0 homestand against the Padres, Giants, and Dodgers. Several pitchers caught fire from the start. Lee led the way, winning three of his first four starts, posting a 3.00 ERA and tossing a two-hit shutout against the Cubs. But what really stood out were the contributions of pitchers in lesser roles. Working mostly in long and middle relief in his first full big-league season, Palmer chewed up multiple innings at a time, pitching well in April en route to a 2.64 ERA over 123 frames. Schatzeder, the fifth starter and swingman, did everything from notching a four-inning save against the Phillies to pitching six innings of one-run, eight-strikeout relief against the Dodgers to putting up 10 innings of one-run ball in a crucial September game against the Cardinals. Sanderson formed the third leg of the team's excellent young trio, posting the best strikeout and strikeout-to-walk rates on the staff over 168 innings in his own first full major league season. Rogers, meanwhile, got off to a slow start in '79, finishing the year with very good but not quite elite numbers as he recovered from his elbow and shoulder problems. But the young guns—as well as relievers Sosa, May, Fryman, and Bahnsen—pitched well, allowing Williams to aggressively pinch-hit for tiring starters, keeping his front five fresh throughout the year. After ending their month of May with a 10–2 run, the Expos stood at 29–15, 3½ games up in the NL East. By July, they'd built a 6½-game lead, sitting on a 46–29 record.

Expos fans responded by . . . losing their damn minds.

Empty, the Big O was a dark, cold, forbidding place. It was massive, and far from the bosom of bustling downtown Montreal. It was, in the absence of a good and interesting team, a lousy place to see a baseball game. Management knew all of this. And with the club improving on the field, the front office got to work on the fan experience. For the many fans who travelled to Olympic Stadium by Metro, the entire walk-up experience became electric. Exiting at the Pie-IX stop (pronounced pee-neuf), you would walk shoulder-to-shoulder with thousands of fans from the subway car, through a tunnel, and up a ramp leading directly to the stadium entrance. The second you passed through the turnstiles, you found yourself in the middle of a big party, loud and raucous (but not too raucous) and inviting. Straight ahead was a beer garden, flanked by an Oompah band with the volume at 11. In a city that had French as its main language and English as number two, the whole setup surprisingly felt like Oktoberfest, right down to the music. You could count the number of people who knew *all* the words to "The Happy Wanderer" on one hand as you wandered to your seat after a beer or five, but every living soul in the ballpark knew the chorus. And whether it was pre-gaming in the concourse or celebrating a big Expos rally with the help of Fern Lapierre's booming organ, that chorus echoed through the building's cavernous expanse.

VALDERI

VALDERA

VALDERIIIIII

VALADER-A-HA-HA-HA-HA-HA

The combination of winning baseball and that festive environment drove attendance sky-high. A June series against the Phillies drew two crowds of 40,000-plus. An early-July weekend series against the Dodgers brought in 46,502 on Saturday, and 46,601 on Sunday. A late-May doubleheader against the Cardinals drew 52,539 crazies. A Friday night twin bill in July against the mighty Pirates beamed in 59,260 fans. That magical 1979 marked the first time the Expos drew two million fans in a season, a feat they repeated in three of the following four years—and it would've been five straight if not for the strike in 1981. Montreal finished second, third, or fourth in the league in attendance in each of those five seasons, outdrawing some of the biggest-name teams in the biggest cities. It sounds crazy now, but in '82 and '83, the quirky, goofy Expos even outdrew the big, bad New York Yankees.

"It was the most fun you could have at a Major League Baseball game," said Michael Farber. "This was before Wrigley Field became a theme park, and there was really nowhere else like it. You walked through that tunnel, you hear 'Valderi, Valdera' . . . this German song from this Oompah band . . . who does that?! The hat with three colours, we'd never seen that before. The scoreboard even had these cardboard-cutout chickens that went *bawk-bawk-bawk* every time an opposing pitcher threw over to first base.

"All of it might have seemed Mickey Mouse to the rest of the major leagues. But it was *our* Mickey Mouse. Montreal prides itself on being distinct, and the Expos were certainly distinct. Tom Boswell and I had this discussion once, about how *delightful* it was to be at the Big O in those days. It was utterly charming without being traditionally, basebally charming. It was *Montreal* charming."

It was especially charming when the young lineup was clicking, which happened in '79 far more often than ever before. Six of the Expos' eight starting position players were 25 or younger, and only one (Tony Perez) was older than 30. The hitting star that year was Larry Parrish. Shaking off the injuries that had limited him in the two previous seasons, Parrish batted .307 and set a team record by slugging .551, with 30 home runs and 39 doubles. Meanwhile, Gary Carter was an all-around terror, hitting .283 with 22 homers and cementing his status as one of the best defensive catchers of his generation. Dawson smacked 25 homers, stole 35 bases, and ran down everything in or near centre field, more than making up for his sometimes prodigious out-making at the plate. The bench also improved, as Williams had hoped. Ousted from his starting job, Cash turned around and hit .321 as a reserve. Veteran Tommy Hutton, the acknowledged leader of the Bus Squad, contributed a number of big pinch-hits. White was outstanding, hitting .297 with a sparkling .391 on-base percentage. Finally, Ken Macha batted only 36 times all year, but established himself as an unlikely team leader, with the kind of personality that would one day enable him to become a big-league manager.

"He didn't let any player that had status get away with anything," Lee now says about Macha. "He saw everything and he reported on it and questioned every athlete on his integrity. He was the kind of guy who could tell the king he's an asshole and get away with it."

The bench, and the team, still needed a little something extra for the stretch run, however. The Expos had fallen into a mini-slump heading into the All-Star break, losing five games off their first-place lead in just two weeks. With a lineup dominated by right-handed hitters (and several free swingers), a left-handed bat became management's top priority. On July 20, they landed the perfect player.

Rusty Staub, the one and only Grand Orange, was back in Montreal.

"I still remember Rusty Staub's first game back at the Big O," said Serge Touchette, who took over le Journal de Montreal's Expos beat in 1976 and covered the team for the rest of its existence. "They're playing Pittsburgh, eighth inning, down a run, runner on first. The PA announcer didn't even get to say Rusty's name. As soon as he touched the on-deck circle, people went nuts. Chuck Tanner changed pitchers. And the whole time, Rusty is standing there, waiting, and people were just losing their minds. This kept going and going, for several minutes. It was the greatest ovation I'd ever heard in my life."

Staub didn't come through with the big hit in that first game back home, but he did put up solid numbers over the final two months of the season. Meanwhile, the Expos went 15–11 in

August, shaking off their losing July. But the "We Are Family" Pirates were on fire, tacking on a 21–9 August to their 20–11 July, grabbing the division lead and threatening to put the season on ice.

Down 3½ games heading into Labour Day, the young and untested Expos refused to crack. First, they ripped through a 10-game winning streak, with one nail-biting victory after another. There was, Cromartie's walk-off base on balls in the bottom of the ninth against the Astros to start the streak, then an incredible comeback three days later in which the Expos tallied one in the seventh and two in the ninth to tie, followed by Rodney Scott's walk-off single in the bottom of the 10th to beat the Reds. Win number seven came on a Mets error, also in the bottom of the 10th. The final win of the streak was a classic. Promoted to the rotation late in the season, David Palmer tossed eight shutout innings against the Cubs on September 6, bagging the win after Carter homered in the top of the ninth for the game's only run. That outing capped a five-start stretch in which Palmer allowed just four runs, with three of those five starts resulting in nothing but goose eggs.

Still, the Pirates clung to a one game division lead, which widened to two games after a Montreal loss and a Pittsburgh win on September 7. Time for another streak, with the Expos ripping off seven in a row, the seventh win coming on a Scott walk-off single in the bottom of the 11th of a Saturday doubleheader that packed 48,459 fans into the Big O. Incredibly, frustratingly, the Pirates hung on to the NL East lead—even after 17 Expos wins in 18 games. What happened the very next day might've gone down as one of the greatest moments in franchise history, had the season ended differently. Playing yet another doubleheader against St. Louis, the Expos smashed the single-day attendance record they'd set in July, pulling in 59,282 fans. The game was 1–1 after two innings, but each side's pitchers allowed not a single run over the next seven frames. In the bottom of the 10th, the first two Expos went down quietly. Then Carter doubled and the hot-hitting White drew an intentional walk. With a chance to escape the inning, Cards second baseman Ken Oberkfell booted a groundball, loading the bases. And with the game on the line, the singles-hitting Cash—the man who'd lost his starting job, the guy who hadn't hit a home run all year—strode to the plate.

And blasted a walk-off grand slam over the left-field wall that sent a crowd the size of a small city into spasms of ecstasy.

"The Big O could be a nasty place," said Touchette. "It was cold and damp and windy. That stadium cost a fortune, you still had no roof, the turf was terrible, and the city didn't want to pay any more for it. You had to live with the problems. It was brand new, and it might have been the worst stadium. But in those years, at a moment like that, it sounded like the best place in the world to watch a baseball game."

As great as the atmosphere was in that first, heady winning season, the Expos caught some bad breaks too. Weather in Montreal that summer was terrible, with rainout after rainout forcing doubleheaders in September. From September 3 through September 16, the Expos played 17 games in 13 days, including four home doubleheaders (and twin bills on consecutive days that weekend against the Cardinals). They got no luck with their road schedule either, with rainstorms galore causing five more "away" doubleheaders to be scheduled for the season's final month: *nine* doubleheaders on the docket that month, all told. Somehow, some way, they plowed on. They swept back-to-back doubleheaders against the Mets at Shea Stadium September 19 and 20. More bad weather forced a third straight doubleheader on September 22, which the Expos split before taking the series finale the next day.

The team should've been running on fumes at that point. They'd lost their reliable shortstop when Chris Speier missed two weeks earlier in September. Rogers, coming off that painful bone-spur injury and surgery, had been advised by Dr. Jobe to throw about 160 innings for the year—190 at the most—and he'd run up 236⅔, getting lit up multiple times down the stretch and appearing totally spent. All the while, Carter's determination was nearly unfathomable. He played through a brutal ankle injury, refusing to take a seat and catching four games in those two days at Shea in absolute agony. He hit, too, banging out 14 hits in his final 31 at-bats of the season.

Unbelievably, through all that, the team rolled into Pittsburgh on September 24 leading the Bucs by half a game, about to start a four-game series that might decide the season. They began with another doubleheader, losing the opener to drop into second place. Trailing 6–3 after seven innings in the nightcap, the Expos rallied yet again, scoring three in the top of the eighth, then parlaying a Valentine RBI single in the top of the ninth into a thrilling 7–6 win.

And just like that, it all fell apart.

The Pirates clobbered the Expos 10–4 and 10–1 over the next two games, giving Pittsburgh a division lead it would never relinquish en route to a World Series title. Still, no one could possibly fault the Expos for coming up short. Carter didn't play again that season after the doubleheader in Pittsburgh. Rogers somehow gutted through eight innings of two-run ball in a last-ditch effort to salvage the year on September 30, only to get no run support in a heartbreaking 2–0 loss. The Expos ended up winning 23 of 34 games in September, a magnificent performance that might've been enough in nearly any other season, against nearly any other team.

There were regrets and what-ifs, of course. There was the late-August game in Atlanta in which the Expos built a big lead heading into the bottom of the fifth, in pouring rain. Schatzeder, ever the perfectionist, kept complaining to the umpires about the slippery pitching rubber, and kept cleaning his spikes between pitches.

That caused the umps to call the game right before the fifth inning could end and the game could become official, wiping out a near-certain win for the Expos that they never got back. Though it didn't show in their record until the very end, the doubleheaders took a toll as well, affecting everything from Carter's health to more routine elements that should've been easy but weren't—like travel, sleep, even meal times. They finished with 95 wins, enough to take either of the West divisions that season by a comfortable margin. It just wasn't enough to beat out the powerful Pirates.

"I think Williams did an amazing job, with the pitching staff especially," said Melnick. "The only thing wrong with the '79 team was the Pirates. They couldn't beat the Pirates."

No one could beat the Pirates. At 39, Willie Stargell was still terrorizing the Expos, launching balls once destined for Jarry Park's swimming pool into the Big O's upper deck instead. The Cobra, Dave Parker, was a five-tool player at the height of his powers. Bill Madlock and Bill Robinson, Phil Garner and John Milner: the whole damn team gave the Expos fits, taking eight of the final 10 games against Montreal that year. The pitching staff might not have been specifically designed to torment the Expos, but it seemed that way, with tough righty starters Bert Blyleven, Bruce Kison, and Don Robinson matching up against Carter, Dawson, Valentine, and Parrish, and submarining right-handed closer Kent Tekulve finishing up. At the end of a decade full of dynasties, the Pirates were worthy champions.

Though the Expos' season ended in disappointment, there was also great hope for the future. Their core players were all young, with yet another wave of talent coming. They hadn't quite made it over the top in the '70s. But with their farm system churning out new stars every year and the big club making huge strides, that hardly seemed to matter. At the dawn of the 1980s, incredibly, the Expos were the envy of the baseball world.

CHAPTER FIVE

Team of the '80s? (1980–1981)

I t was a note of optimism, a touch of bravado after a 95-win season that ended just two games short of a division title. With a scintillating but disappointing breakout 1979 season behind him, John McHale was asked by a reporter what to expect from the Expos in the future. Get ready, McHale replied, for "The Team of the '80s."

Looking over the Expos' roster heading into the 1980 season, it was tough to argue otherwise. Andre Dawson was entering his age-25 season that year. Gary Carter, Larry Parrish, Warren Cromartie, and Rodney Scott would all play the bulk of the 1980 campaign as 26-year-olds. On the pitching side, the Expos boasted a quartet of exceptionally young right-handers with big upside: 23-year-olds Scott Sanderson and Charlie Lea, 22-year-old David Palmer, and 21-year-old Bill Gullickson.

It would be two more years before baseball writer and statistician Bill James would emerge from obscurity with the first mass-produced *Bill James Baseball Abstract*, but that book contained a seminal James essay which argued that baseball players tend to peak around age 27. Even before that study came out, though, teams were keenly aware of the broader point: If you've got a handful of talented players in their early-to-mid 20s, you've got a chance to get better. If you had as many as the Expos had—plus up-and-coming younger players like Tony Bernazard, Tim Wallach, and Tim Raines just getting their feet wet—you had the makings of a dynasty.

"By the time the '79 season was over, maturity had set in," Carter told me in 2003. "We believed we had a great chance to win."

Still, young players always come with questions, and one in particular might have come with more questions than all the rest put together. With some solid numbers already on his resumé Ellis Valentine was considered the most talented player on the entire roster, but he hadn't yet become the superstar everyone expected. At 25, Valentine was entering his fifth full season in the majors, and though it wasn't difficult to imagine the Expos finally making that leap from pretenders to contenders to champions, it was a lot easier if you figured this would finally be Ellis Valentine's breakout season.

Problem was, any big performance gains from Valentine were going to come from talent, and talent alone. Like many athletes who make it all the way to the pros, Valentine was the best player at every level growing up, from sandlots as a kid to early organized ball, high school to the minors, all the way to the Show. Unlike many other elite athletes, Valentine coasted on those talents. Though sophisticated weight-training programs hadn't yet permeated the game, players were still jumping on Nautilus machines over the winter to improve their fitness; Valentine did not. To increase stamina and keep their legs in shape, many players stuck to running routines throughout the year; Valentine did not. Extra work in the cage, extra practice improving routes to flyballs, extra attention paid to nutrition and sleep patterns . . . Valentine did none of these things.

The side effects started adding up. Ron McClain took over as the Expos' head trainer in 1980, and he was hardly impressed by Valentine.

"He didn't try to work or stay in shape," McClain said. "By the time he got to me, he had gained 20 pounds. Then with me, in less than two years, he gained another 15."

Valentine's lack of work ethic and resulting weight gain were troubling enough. But there was a bigger problem. He was pissing away his career, and his life, on drugs and booze.

It started with his high-school leg injury, the one that resulted in one leg setting shorter than the other, and years of excruciating pain thereafter. That injury led to an addiction to painkillers. Olympic Stadium's rock-hard turf took a toll on his knees and ankles, ratcheting up the pain. When painkillers brought him down, Valentine went looking for mood-elevating drugs to stay on an even keel. Many players in those days popped amphetamines; you could find bowls full of greenies in many trainers' rooms, and no one made a fuss about it. Still, McClain never saw anyone throw down greenies more vigorously than did the ever-medicated Valentine.

Or as Bill Lee, no stranger to heavy alcohol and drug use himself, put it: "You take the greenies to get up for games. Then you have to kill the greenies with alcohol. Then you became alcohol-dependent. Then it became a vicious cycle."

Compounding all of these factors were the usual traps set for young, professional athletes. Drafted before his 18th birthday and in the majors just after his 21st, Valentine got everything a precocious and fancy-free ballplayer could want: tons of money, tons of adulation, and an army of friends and hangers-on who cared a lot more about having a great time (usually on Valentine's dime) than about his emotional, physical, and professional health.

Again, cash and cronies are commonplace for talented major leaguers. The ones with enough self-discipline know how to have fun while knowing when to say when. The next level up are the ballplayers who party excessively, have to sit out occasional games with mysterious cases of the "flu," and rely on greenies to help them overcome hangovers. Then there was Valentine, the womanizer who'd spill out of his apartment at the crack of noon with three companions on his arm, red-eyed and woozy. Valentine, who—and, granted, this was the height of baseball's cocaine era— did enough lines to get an elephant jacked up.

At first, Bronfman, McHale, and Williams tried to tell themselves that there was only recreational weed being used, away from the ballpark. Then one night, Expos coach Ozzie Virgil took a shortcut from the dugout to the bullpen, walking behind the stands, then back onto the field through the side door. En route, he spotted a small space underneath the box seats, with just enough room for a couple of guys to stand. Spread over the concrete floor was a towel, littered with stubbed out joints. Virgil told the manager. Though Williams would pick fights when angry and pick on certain players he didn't like, he usually gave his players tons of latitude. But seeing cleat marks on that towel, and realizing that players were sparking up in the stadium, in uniform? That freaked him out. Just not freaked out enough to do anything about it.

"I passed the buck," wrote Williams in *No More Mr. Nice Guy*. "After a sleepless night deciding that my job was to manage baseball games, I visited John McHale and told him about our discovery. Basically dumped it all in his lap. . . . Managers can't suspend players or call the cops without team presidents. Managers really don't have the authority to do anything but manage. So I gave the problem to McHale." A few chats between McHale and players suspected of smoking in the stadium went nowhere.

All of that was mild compared to Valentine's off-field pastimes. Rich Griffin, who handled public relations for more than two decades with the Expos before taking over as a columnist for the *Toronto Star* in 1995, can tell you stories. Like when the team flew to St. Louis on a road trip. Everyone gets off the bus. Waiting on the front steps of the hotel is an attractive blonde. Everyone recognizes her right away. She's a bartender at one of the clubs on Crescent Street, the go-to locale for anyone in Montreal who wants to party—ballplayers included. Now she's here, 1,100 miles away. She's waiting for Valentine. Given the non-stop coke-dealing happening on Crescent at the time, and how Valentine looked later that day, it doesn't take a genius to figure out what was going on: she's brought the stuff, and she's here to hook him up.

Or the West Coast trip immediately after the 1979 All-Star break. As talented as Valentine was, he made only a single All-Star team, and it was two years earlier. So for three days in July '79, while most players took it easy to marshal their strength for the second half, Valentine went on an all-time bender back home in Montreal. The break ended. And then . . .

"We're in L.A., getting ready to play the Dodgers," said Griffin. "It's mid-afternoon. A car wheels into the Dodger Stadium players' lot. The door opens, and they push Ellis out. Then the car pulls out and speeds away. He's out cold. So the first game after the All-Star break, they have to carry him from the parking lot to the training room. And he spends the whole game sleeping in the training room, on the floor. To me, that was Ellis."

Being likable and popular with teammates—that was Ellis too. Andre Dawson was as strait-laced a player as anyone on those Expos clubs, and he adored Valentine. "We had different character traits, but we fed off each other. All of us supported each other, looked after each other. He was a good friend."

Bill Lee said Valentine was "like a brother" to him, and vice versa.

As team trainer, McClain could render his professional opinion about Valentine's actions. But he wouldn't condemn his motives. "He was a great guy who just couldn't control himself."

Those outside the clubhouse raved about Valentine's charisma. As Dave Van Horne told Alain Usereau in *The Expos in Their Prime*, "He loved playing the game and he showed his happiness on the field with that great big smile and when he would come across home plate after a home run or after the team had won a game out on the field or after a terrific catch or a great throw, he would show that smile to the fans and that won them over."

That's what made all of his demons so frustrating. When sober(ish), Valentine would show flashes of absolute brilliance, hitting tape-measure home runs and showing off the best throwing arm the game had seen since Roberto Clemente. After awhile, Valentine threw out so many baserunners that a code emerged. "Someone would hit the ball to right field, and he'd just smile," said McClain. "They knew not to run on him."

Still, no one could deny that Valentine was hurting the team by failing to reach his full potential. Michael Farber recalls the time a pitcher threw to second to try to pick Valentine off, and he didn't even move: no dive back to the bag, just a glazed look in his eyes as the shortstop applied the easy tag. He'd also zone out on flyballs, missing catchable plays by five feet, then get booed by the locals. Thin-skinned, Valentine would occasionally ask out of the lineup to avoid the fans' ire. The 1979 season was a major disappointment in particular, with Valentine setting new career lows in batting average (.276) and on-base percentage (.303) while grounding into an ugly 23 double plays. With his speed waning and his weight rising, he was thrown out stealing nearly as often as he was safe. And his timing couldn't have been worse, given how close the Expos came to nabbing their first playoff berth. You couldn't necessarily draw a straight line between Valentine's addictions and Montreal losing the NL East title by two games. But you saw the Expos lose that game in L.A. with Valentine passed out on the floor. You saw Valentine looking listless down the stretch, hitting exactly zero homers in the final 34 games of the season, while teammates like Carter kept producing even with painful injuries. All of it made you wonder: What if?

After that season, the Expos went to the winter meetings and talked seriously about trading Valentine. It wasn't the first time they'd had that discussion, with Valentine's name first circulating in trade talks way back in 1977. McHale had grown increasingly worried that his right fielder was becoming a problem, and that Valentine's vices could negate his immense talent. Finally, the decision was made. They'd keep Valentine, and hope that becoming another year older would make him another year wiser.

Then they went and got Ron LeFlore.

Few players, then or ever, came with a more checkered past than did LeFlore. Born in Detroit, he grew up in a neighbourhood riddled by crime and poverty. He dropped out of school at an early age and steadily upped the ante on his vices, graduating from breaking into a local Stroh's factory to steal beer to shooting heroin as often as he could afford it. He earned his first arrest at age 15, and later got a 5-to-15-year sentence for armed robbery. Having never played organized baseball, LeFlore finally joined his first league while doing time at Jackson State Prison. What he lacked in experience he made up in jaw-dropping natural talent. Solidly built with big, strong legs, LeFlore was blindingly fast, stealing bases at will. Through a series of connections, one of his fellow inmates sent word to Tigers manager Billy Martin to come check out LeFlore.

If this sounds like an implausible idea, or an alternate take on Ricky "Wild Thing" Vaughn's rise in the movie *Major League*, keep in mind this was 1973, and scouting and organizational practices weren't nearly as well coordinated as they'd become 40 years later. Also, this was Billy Martin, a gunslinger of a manager who was known both for his fiery personality and his unorthodox tactics. LeFlore got permission to leave prison for a one-day tryout at Tiger Stadium. Detroit signed him in July of that year, and LeFlore made his major league debut the following summer at age 26. After six seasons with the Tigers, he signed a free-agent contract with the Expos. That's when the fun started.

Having curbed his drug use while playing in Detroit, he jumped right off the wagon in Montreal. LeFlore was quickly seduced by the city's party atmosphere, and found multiple willing accomplices on the Expos' roster. Rodney Scott, Rowland Office, Lee, and Valentine formed a clique with LeFlore that partied hard, resulting in many bleary-eyed mornings, constant late arrivals to the ballpark, and, with Valentine and LeFlore especially, many on-field mess-ups due to a perpetual cycle of cocaine and over-the-top drinking. Farber recalled one night when the Expos lost as LeFlore, clearly loaded, failed to make the play on what should've been an easily catchable flyball. When pressed on the error, LeFlore said he lost the ball in the lights. The next day, Dick Williams walked out to the spot where he believed LeFlore had been standing, then looked up into the lights. "Son of a bitch!" he cursed. Williams moved 10 feet. "Motherfucker!" LeFlore was, at the very least, stretching the truth.

Farber's wildest memory of LeFlore came from the final game of the 1980 season. Late in the game, Williams told LeFlore to be ready to pinch-run if Bobby Ramos reached base. Ramos led off the bottom of the eighth inning with a single, and with the Expos trailing the Phillies by a run, it was time for LeFlore to enter the game. Only he was nowhere to be found. Williams looked around, then spotted his speedy outfielder . . . walking out from the Phillies dugout. What the hell was he doing there? At the time, no one knew for sure. Trotting out from the wrong dugout wasn't even the craziest part. Once he'd figured out that he should be on first base and not chatting with the opposing team during a game, LeFlore actually regained his focus well enough to steal second base—and third base too—before scoring the tying run on a sacrifice fly.

LeFlore finally revealed the details of that incident in a 2013 interview with the *Toronto Sun*. "I was in the Phillies' locker room, talking with Pete Rose, and he said, 'Hey, you only need two more stolen bases to win the title.' So I ran out of their locker room, out of their dugout, across the backstop to our dugout. . . . I stole second base and Ozzie Virgil threw the ball into centre field. But I didn't keep running. I stayed at second base. Then I stole third. I ended up scoring and I won the stolen base title. Then I went back into the Phillies' clubhouse and drank some more champagne."

That was the amazing thing about LeFlore's one and only season as an Expo. Despite putting enough substances into his body to take out a small village, despite showing up unfathomably late all the time (four times just before the anthems), despite racking up enough transgressions to prompt many managers into benching him, suspending him, and tossing him into the nearest river, LeFlore played pretty well that year. Sure, he hit just .257—including one stretch in which he went 2 for 52—after batting an even .300 with the Tigers in '79. He managed just four home runs and slugged just .363. Despite his blazing speed, he played terrible defence after being moved from center field to left. But LeFlore was an absolute demon on the basepaths, stealing an incredible 97 bases while getting caught just 19 times. Prior to 1980, only two players in the 20th century had stolen more bases in a single season: Lou Brock and Maury Wills.

In a *Sports Illustrated* article on the speedy Expos that summer, LeFlore said he considered himself "more controlled now than before, when I used to just go with reckless abandon." Writer Douglas Looney described LeFlore's nefarious routine: "He studies pitchers and talks at length with them, liking nothing better than to get them gossiping about the foibles of other pitchers in the league."

Unfortunately, that base-stealing explosion wasn't enough to convince the Expos to keep LeFlore around. In *No More Mr. Nice Guy*, Williams ranted about LeFlore's "rabble-rousing in the clubhouse, his constant bitching about the food or the laundry or the managing. His late-night forays into strange parts of town, which wouldn't have been so bad if he hadn't taken the team's younger players with him."

Williams might've complained after the fact, but he didn't do anything about it that year, admitting, "I played him in every game he was eligible for."

The Expos hired McClain to be their new trainer with hopes that he could clean up the clubhouse culture of out-of-control drug use. He'd worked with Indiana University coaches Bobby Knight and Lee Corso, implementing stiff drug-testing policies for the school's basketball and football programs. But Major League Baseball's players union, then, as now, the strongest of all four major North American team sports' unions, lobbied to ensure that no such tests be allowed. That tied the hands of McClain, team physician Dr. Robert Broderick, and Dr. Larry Coughlin, the team orthopedist—all of whom knew better than most what was going on. The medical staff needed help from Williams to provide some disincentive for players to go on binges, be it through benchings, fines, or suspensions. No such help ever came.

"All you had to do was show up at the ballpark and you were in the lineup," McClain said. Under Williams' watch, there was "no discipline, no punishment for being late. The inmates were running the asylum."

Like LeFlore, Valentine showed remarkable on-field resilience even as he turned his insides into an elaborate chemistry experiment. Though he'd made some mistakes defensively and on the basepaths, he still hit well, sitting at .297 near the end of May and riding a 19-game stretch in which he'd hit .373.

Then, disaster. In the sixth inning of the game against St. Louis on May 30, 1980, Valentine came to bat against Cardinals righty relief pitcher Roy Thomas, with the Expos leading 7–2. Thomas reared back and fired a fastball. The pitch was up and in, and struck Valentine flush in the side of the face. It knocked him out, cracked his cheekbone in six places, and gave him a concussion, sending him to the disabled list for nearly six weeks during which he struggled with blurry vision. The incident had a profound effect on Valentine's psyche. He became afraid to face hard-throwing right-handed pitchers. He was mad at Thomas and mad at baseball—for what happened.

"MLB doesn't compensate you a damn for being a budding star, one of the top guys in the league for several years, then all of a sudden it's all stripped away by an injury," Valentine said. "That's fucked up. That's a bunch of crap. Pitchers do throw at you intentionally. I was very effective against the Cardinals and I do believe it was intentional."

Asked if he was under the influence when Thomas' pitch slammed into his face and if that affected his reaction time, Valentine wouldn't go into details. But more than three decades after that fastball to the head, he expressed regret for letting his addictions spiral out of control, and also frustration with the circumstances that led him to that point.

"I had no freaking clue, man," he said. "I had money in my pocket. I had fame. I had people treating me very well. I thought life was going to be like this forever. I was really a child. This is what baseball doesn't do. They don't grow these kids up as people. They just take advantage of them for the purpose of the game, putting people in the stands. What we have to do is learn some things. One problem for me was that there were very few mentors from a black perspective. A lot of guys don't want to talk about this but they might concur. A lot of us did struggle because we didn't have guys to talk to after the game like some of the white guys did."

What about coaches?

"This was the era after Jackie Robinson. You had black players, but no black coaches. I couldn't sit after the game and talk to a Larry Doby in the big leagues. One of the best years I ever had was in Memphis at Triple-A. Doby was the hitting coach. I had somebody to talk to, to mentor me. It was the most sane freaking year of my baseball career, even though I was only 19 years old. I could talk to him at games, go to breakfast, talk to him on the plane, on the bus. That meant a lot. Then I get up to the big leagues and I don't have that. All the questions and problems you had, drugs, alcohol, addictions, those were the coping mechanisms. It wasn't great, but it's all we had."

As frightening as that knockout pitch was, what's strange is how Valentine played afterwards. Despite his fears of facing right-handed pitching, Valentine absolutely raked upon his return from the disabled list. From the day he came off the DL until the end of the season, he hit .331 and slugged .571, producing a passel of big hits. Though he only played in 86 games that year due to the broken cheekbone and other injuries, Valentine still put up better numbers in 1980 on a per-game basis than in any other year that even came close to a full season.

The other good news was that the rest of the Expos were heating up. With Valentine on the DL, they went 21–16. LeFlore, Parrish, and other key performers also populated the disabled list as the summer wore on, yet the team kept winning. On June 8, the Expos swept a doubleheader at the Big O against the Cards. Those two wins, in front of 46,871 fired-up fans, launched the 'Spos into first place for the first time that season. On 31 of the next 32 days, Montreal was in first place. Areas that could've been weaknesses turned into strengths—like pitching. Two years after his 20-win season, Ross Grimsley was terrible, throwing just 41⅓ innings and delivering a hideous 6.31 ERA. Lee didn't make his first start until May 31 because of injuries, and pitched miserably when healthy, posting a 4.96 ERA. Plagued by injuries himself, David Palmer tossed just one inning between mid-July and mid-September, spending the rest of that time on the shelf.

But luckily for Montreal, the pitching cavalry had finally arrived. Bill Gullickson turned in one of the best seasons ever for an Expos rookie pitcher, posting a 3.00 ERA while flashing a superior strikeout rate. Though Palmer managed only 19 starts, he was great when he did pitch, posting a 2.98 ERA. Charlie Lea chipped in with 19 solid starts of his own. Those three young guns teamed with staff leaders Steve Rogers and Scott Sanderson to give the Expos' rotation the third-lowest ERA in the National League. Complementing that young rotation was a grizzled bullpen, led by 30-year-old Elias Sosa, 35-year-old Stan Bahnsen, and bionic 40-year-old lefty Woodie Fryman, who ranked among the top five relievers in the league.

The offence, meanwhile, ranked around the middle of the pack, with Parrish in particular having a big letdown season following his huge numbers in '79. Fortunately, the team had two superstars in Dawson and Carter. In a breakout season, Dawson hit .308 with 17 homers and 34 steals, winning both the Gold Glove and Silver Slugger awards and announcing himself as one of the best all-around players in the majors. Carter started 146 games behind the plate, appearing in 154 in all. He blasted 29 homers, knocked in 101 runs, and finished second in MVP voting. Most impressively, he started every game from September 1 through October 4 with the Expos in the midst of an airtight pennant race, hitting an off-the-charts .336/.414/.636 in those 31 games. All told, the Expos spent 67 days in first place in the NL East that season.

"I don't know why [the Expos] win," Phillies manager Dallas Green said in *Sports Illustrated*, "but they are pesky little devils."

On September 16, with less than three weeks to go in the season, the Expos led those Phillies by 2½ games. But Montreal then lost four of its next five to briefly fall out of first. Two head-to-head series figured to decide the race. First, the Expos took two out of three at Veterans Stadium, restoring their half-game lead—but only temporarily. The teams were tied heading into the final series of the season: Expos-Phillies, three games at the Big O, two out of three wins it.

The atmosphere was insane as more than 57,000 fans packed the park for the first game. Mike Schmidt, the MVP that year and one of the biggest Expos nemeses of all time, smacked a homer off Sanderson that provided the margin of victory in a 2–1 opener.

The Expos looked primed to even the series the next night in front of nearly 51,000 partisans, only to blow a one-run lead in the ninth. In the 11th, Schmidt came up against Bahnsen with a runner on first. The Phillies' all-world third baseman got ahead in the count 2–0, then got an absolute meatball of a pitch: fastball, thigh-high, dead straight, middle of the plate. In a career full of Expos-killing moments, this was the biggest, a two-run blast into the left-field bleachers that gave the Phillies a 6–4 lead, crushing Montreal's dreams for that first-ever NL East crown. For the second straight year, the Expos and their fans had their hearts broken in the cruellest of ways.

"That made it two years in a row going down to the last Saturday of the season, only to lose out to teams that went on to win the World Series," said Van Horne.

Once the sting from those losses wore off, however, optimism reigned. If coming that close once with that terrific core of young talent warranted good feelings for the future, having it happen twice got everyone predicting that the Expos would start winning pennants soon.

"These were pretty giddy days," Van Horne added. "You had two million–plus fans coming out, at a time when those were big numbers for a major league club. The support was terrific. By then, the radio network had 50-some stations. It was a great time to be an Expos fan. These were the halcyon days of the Expos."

If the third time was going to be the charm, the Expos would have to make it happen with the same core group of players. In typical John McHale style, Montreal didn't make any major moves in the offseason. Once again, the Expos badly needed left-handed power, with the lineup dominated by righty swingers Carter, Dawson, Parrish, and Valentine. Once again, they didn't have a viable starting second baseman. Once again, little was done to address these or other holes.

Actually, that's not entirely true. In an attempt to balance the lineup, the Expos signed lefty-swinging free-agent first baseman Willie Montanez. Unfortunately for them, Montanez was washed up by then, hitting just .177 in 62 at-bats in Montreal.

They also made a seemingly minor move that ended up biting them in the ass in a major way. At the time of the move, Rodney Scott had a big supporter in Dick Williams. "It will take tremendous play to beat Rodney out; I'm a big Rodney Scott man," the Expos skipper told Michael Farber in December 1980. Sure, Scott was the worst-hitting everyday second baseman in the league, threatening the Mendoza Line while hitting for absolutely zero power. "But you have to appreciate the speed," Williams said.

With the manager oddly committed to Scott, the Expos had no room for promising second-base prospect Tony Bernazard. So

Montreal shipped Bernazard to the White Sox for left-handed reliever Rich Wortham. In Wortham, the Expos were getting a pitcher coming off a 5.97 ERA the year before, but McHale wanted him anyway, for dubious reasons. "We were going to make him a number one or two draft choice when he came out of college," McHale said, ignoring the reality that Wortham had been drafted a long four and a half years earlier and had had a terrible time finding the strike zone since. Wortham never threw a single pitch for the Expos. Meanwhile, the 24-year-old Bernazard immediately became one of the best second basemen in the game. McHale had taken the team's biggest weakness and somehow made it worse.

The good news was that more reinforcements were arriving from the farm. In 1980, 20-year-old Tim Raines got promoted to the Triple-A Denver Bears. Any player that young who can even hold his own at the top minor league level typically projects as a good player in the big leagues—and Raines more than held his own. He led the league by hitting .354, led the American Association in triples, and set a new league record with 77 stolen bases (all in just 108 games). Raines got an assist playing in Denver's hitter-friendly conditions, but still the baseball world fell in love. Who wouldn't love a switch-hitter with a terrific batting eye, doubles and triples power, and ludicrous speed? At baseball's winter meetings following the 1980 season, 18 different teams asked McHale if Raines could be had in a trade. Eighteen times McHale said no—even when the Cubs offered Bruce Sutter, a dominant closer who would end up in the Hall of Fame.

That Denver team fielded other stars too, including Randy Bass (.333, 37 homers, 143 RBI) and Tim Wallach (.281-36-124). Though the mile-high altitude helped the team's offence, the Bears also got impressive contributions from several pitchers; 21-year-old Bill Gullickson was the best prospect of the bunch, putting up strong numbers in Denver before getting the call to the Show at the end of May. Led by those standouts, the Bears went 92–44, winning their division by 21½ games, and compiling the best record by any American Association team in the previous 60 years. In 2001, Minor League Baseball's website ranked the top 100 minor league teams of the 20th Century: the 1980 Denver Bears came in 37th.

Bass never lived up to his minor league hype (though he did become a star in Japan), and Wallach wouldn't make a significant impact in the majors until 1982. But Raines and Gullickson would play integral roles in the '81 Expos' success.

They got a taste of that success right out of the gate, winning 13 of their first 17 games. In their first rematch with the Phillies, the Expos swept their loaded division rivals, claiming sole possession of first place. The final win of that hot start was a thriller at home against the Dodgers. The Expos jumped out to a 5–0 lead against L.A., then watched that lead shrivel as the Dodgers scored three in the eighth to tie the score at 8–8, followed by the two teams failing to score until the bottom of the 13th. The Expos were so low on position players by that point that Bill Lee batted to start the inning. After Lee grounded out to first, Raines stepped to the plate.

To that point in his very young career, Raines had been absolutely incredible. He'd replaced Ron LeFlore as leadoff man and outdone his speedy predecessor. He was a little unpolished as the new everyday left fielder, having played second base in the minors (a position that didn't suit him well, else the Expos might've left him there). But he batted .348 to start the 1981 season, walking 13 times and striking out just five times. His most impressive feats, however, came with his feet. In his first 17 games in '81, Raines stole 19 bases.

Of all the kooky traditions the Expos had, none topped the scoreboard chickens. Every time an opposing pitcher threw over to first base, a supremely low-tech image of a chicken would flash on the screen, "Bawk-Bawk-BAWWWWWK" echoing through the stadium. I once saw Raines goad an opposing pitcher into 13 chickens during one turn on first. The first interview I ever did with Raines, I asked him, "Did you ever notice the scoreboard chickens?"

"Sure!" he replied. "We'd all compete to see who could get the most. I always won."

Raines wasn't just blazingly fast. He was also a student of base stealing. Being new to the league, he didn't yet have the mental database of pitchers that he'd rely on later in his career. Instead, he'd watch each pitcher intently from the dugout, studying all of their quirks: how they positioned their legs, little tics such as taking a deep breath before throwing to the plate (as opposed to a different habit when they threw to first). First-base coach Steve Boros lent a big hand, tracking and studying pitchers' moves to first as well their time to home, then huddling with Raines to exploit the most vulnerable. Those study habits showed: counting his brief call-ups in 1979 and 1980, Raines swiped 27 bags in the first 27 attempts of his career, a regular-season record that still stands. When the streak ended, it was a shock to all who witnessed it.

"There was rejoicing in the National League last Saturday. Baseball's Raines of Terror had ended," Jim Kaplan wrote in *Sports Illustrated*. "After stealing 27 consecutive bases over three seasons, just 11 short of the major league record, Montreal's Tim Raines was thrown out by Los Angeles catcher Mike Scioscia trying to steal third at Olympic Stadium. From New York to San Diego pitchers and catchers embraced, second basemen and shortstops cried for joy and managers began to breathe again, albeit nervously."

The one thing Raines hadn't done in his career leading up to that at-bat against the Dodgers in the bottom of the 13th, however, was hit a home run. That streak ended too, as Raines blasted a homer over the wall in right-centre, giving the Expos a 9–8 win and sending 28,179 fans home happy.

Then the losing started. Dropping three of four at home against the Giants in early May knocked the Expos out of first place. The one highlight of that series was a big one, though: a no-hitter by Charlie Lea, part of a terrific May in which the second-year pitcher went 4–0 with a 0.25 ERA and garnered National League Pitcher of the Month honours.

A subsequent trip to Los Angeles, San Francisco, and San Diego—the West Coast trip that had clobbered the Expos so many times over the years—proved no kinder in '81, with Montreal dropping six of nine games.

One of the biggest problems was a thin bullpen. Right-hander Steve Ratzer allowed that three-spot in the eighth against the Dodgers on May 1, with Raines' walk-off homer bailing him out. On May 14, Ratzer did a great job against the Dodgers, putting out an eighth-inning fire that set up a five-run, ninth-inning rally, but Woodie Fryman ruined it by allowing four runs in the bottom of the ninth for the blown save and the loss. The next day, the Expos again rallied in the ninth, tying the score 2–2. This time, Ratzer got the ninth-inning call . . . and served up a game-winning homer by Pedro Guerrero. Three days after that, a game against the Giants went to the 12th inning, with Lee loading the bases with one out. Ratzer came in and allowed a game-winning single. That would be the last pitch Ratzer would ever throw in the majors.

Coming off a good season in Denver, Ratzer had won a late-inning role with the Expos just a few games into his rookie season. It was a move by Dick Williams, born out of necessity, that back-fired far too many times. Left-handers Fryman and Lee fared well on most nights, but the Expos sorely lacked reliable right-handers out of the pen, hence the compulsion to throw an untested rookie into big spots. For the month of May, Montreal's bullpen posted a 4.58 ERA, second-worst in baseball.

The Expos needed help, and it wasn't coming from inside the organization—they needed to make a deal. At the end of May, they made a big trade with the New York Mets. Joining the Expos was right-handed relief pitcher Jeff Reardon, who'd racked up 110 innings with the Mets in 1980. McHale and Fanning had coveted Reardon for years, having drafted him out of high school way back in 1973 only to watch him head to college before eventually signing with the Mets. Now, he was about to become the Expos' top righty reliever (and a few years later, for a short time, the all-time leader in saves).

Reardon, however, was hardly the biggest name in the deal: Ellis Valentine was going to the Mets. McHale made the trade, and yet even he was crushed. McHale was there for the 1972 draft that ushered Valentine into the organization. He was there for all of Valentine's nine years with the franchise. When Roy Thomas' fastball smashed Valentine's face, McHale was one of the first people to rush to the right fielder's side at the hospital. But over the years, McHale came to realize that Valentine wasn't going to grow into the superstar everyone hoped he'd become. Given the toll that Valentine's various vices and injuries had taken on his body, he probably wasn't even going to last much longer in the majors. It was time to say goodbye.

"It was difficult," said McHale, talking to author Brodie Snyder in a 1981 interview. "We've had Ellis with us since he was 17 years old. I've often said he's like my seventh child. I love him and hope he does well."

Despite his best wishes, McHale's hunches were right; Valentine played just 256 more games after the trade, the equivalent of about a season and a half. After his career, Valentine went for drug and alcohol counselling, and has now been sober for 27 years. Today, he works as a counsellor for Harmony Community Development Corporation, a non-profit based in Dallas, helping rehabilitate people suffering from drug and alcohol addiction. His career didn't go as planned. But he did get his life back.

After that 13–4 start, the Expos won just 17 of their next 38 games. That left them with a 30–25 record, in third place and four games behind the front-running Phillies. That record was significant: a meagre 55 games marked the end of the season's first half in 1981. Major League Baseball's players were going on strike.

The reason for the strike was simple: MLB's owners had spent multiple lifetimes operating with players under their thumbs. When the reserve clause got repealed, players were granted the right to shop their services on the open market once they reached the point of free-agent eligibility. But if the owners couldn't stop free agency from happening, they hoped to at least curtail it. The plan they proposed demanded that teams receive major compensation for losing free agents to other teams. Under the proposal, a team that lost a free agent could pick a player from the signing club's roster, as long as that player wasn't one of 12 protected by the signing club. The players' union maintained that introducing compensation of that magnitude would make teams far more reluctant to sign free agents, thus restricting players' ability to seek full market value for their services. So though the work stoppage was a strike in the strictest sense of the word, there was no doubt that owner greed helped cause the walkout. While the players could have simply waited until after the season and negotiated then, they rightly figured that they had more leverage in June than they would in November. (This, of course, wouldn't be the last time an in-season strike would play a major role in Expos history.)

The impasse finally ended when the two sides reached a compromise where only teams losing a player deemed to be a premium free agent would be eligible for compensation, and the players made available in the offseason compensation draft would be less valuable than what the owners had proposed. In the end, the two months ripped out of the heart of the schedule proved to be much ado about very little. Only a few players ended up getting taken in the free-agent compensation draft, most of them of limited value. The compensation draft itself lasted just four years before being replaced by a new system in which teams could conditionally gain amateur draft picks as compensation instead.

Back to the 1981 season: on August 6, the owners agreed to split the season into two halves. This meant whichever teams were leading the four divisions before the strike had already claimed a playoff berth. The other four spots would be filled by the teams with the best records in the second half, once play resumed on August 10. There were several problems with this idea, starting with what would happen if a team won both the first- and second-half races in its division; the owners agreed that said team would face the second-half runner-up in a playoff series. There were also problems with teams having played an unequal number of games before the stoppage. First-half winners had little incentive to fight for every win in the second half, and it showed in their second-half records (just three games over .500, combined). The biggest potential source of unfairness loomed, however, if a team played well in both the first half *and* second half, but narrowly missed snagging the best record both times. Under that scenario, it was conceivable that the team with the best record in its division over the entire season could still miss the playoffs.

Fortunately for the Expos, the split-season rules gave them a reprieve. The team's erratic play in the first half was now forgotten. Put together a hot streak over the equivalent of one-third of a typical season, and they'd make the playoffs for the first time in franchise history.

When play resumed, Williams made rookie Tim "Eli" Wallach his new starting first baseman, replacing the struggling Montanez, who'd replaced Valentine in the lineup after the trade (with Cromartie moving from first base to right field). A few days later, the Expos traded Montanez to the Pirates for John Milner, another over-30 lefty first baseman, then gave Milner the first-base job, turning Wallach into a super-utility man. Milner showed a bit of pop and walked a bunch, but also hit .237 with no speed and poor defence. The season-long struggle to find a good every-day first baseman foreshadowed a major trade at season's end, and the team's continued inconsistent play amid all of Williams' lever-pulling irked McHale.

After splitting their first 12 games of the second half, the Expos won five in a row at home, setting up a potential homestand sweep against the Braves on August 30. With the score tied in the bottom of the 11th, Gary Carter walked with one out. Williams quickly summoned a pinch-runner: Steve Rogers, the staff ace who'd tossed a complete-game shutout just two days earlier. Cromartie hit a grounder to first, setting up a potential inning-ending double play. Instead, Rogers crashed into shortstop Rafael Ramirez, breaking up the play and causing a throwing error. It was a smart and aggressive play by Rogers, and also a highly questionable move by Williams to put his number-one starter in that spot in the first place. Right when the Expos needed him most, Rogers broke a rib and didn't pitch again for nearly two weeks.

Other factors contributed to McHale's growing disenchant-ment with the manager. Under Williams' watch, several players hadn't developed as hoped. Valentine was gone because of it, and Parrish, who'd been second in MVP voting two years earlier, had regressed badly and would finish 1981 hitting just .244 with eight home runs. Granted, injuries played major roles in both players' decline, but McHale had become less inclined to forgive given the expectations surrounding the Expos, compared to the disappoint-ing results. Losing the final weekend of the season to the eventual World Series champion was one thing. Finishing third in the first half of the '81 season, then limping along at 14–12 in the second half, a game and a half behind St. Louis with time running out, was harder to swallow.

On the morning of September 8, McHale called Williams to his suite at the Philadelphia hotel where the team was staying, and told him he'd been fired. Even with Williams' shortcomings, the firing seemed to happen quite suddenly—and at a strange time, with less than a month left in the season. McHale defended his decision to Brodie Snyder.

"We didn't feel we could win, the way we were playing, with a lack of direction and discipline and questionable tactics," he said. McHale defended Williams a bit, saying, "he has done a lot of good things for us. . . . He knew how to win." But since the strike ended, McHale said, Williams "seemed to have lost some of that."

Williams' firing sent shockwaves through the clubhouse. It was widely known that Williams and McHale had been talking about a new contract for the manager, and those talks had clearly gone nowhere. Though a small number of Expos, most notably Rogers, had grown tired of the manager's sometimes acerbic approach, the majority reaction was one of confusion.

"I don't know why they got rid of Dick Williams," Cromartie said 30 years after the fact. "It was the dumbest thing they ever did."

"The key to managing is to keep the five people that hate you away from the 20 that haven't made up their minds," said Lee. "That didn't happen this time."

If firing Williams that late in the season was confusing, hiring Jim Fanning to take his place seemed downright bizarre. Fanning had earned a strong reputation as a scout and talent evaluator with the Braves and then the Expos, but it had been nearly 20 years since Fanning had worn a uniform. Throwing him into the heat of a pennant race as the team's new manager was absolutely stupefying.

McHale ticked off the reasons for not choosing someone else. He didn't want to go outside the organization, because he feared that an outsider would need awhile to learn the Expos' culture, not to mention that hiring a big name would likely require a multi-year commitment, which the Expos weren't ready to hand out. Nor did McHale want to give the gig to one of the team's coaches, because he feared overmanaging from someone trying to earn the permanent job.

"I wanted somebody who would come in for a month without rocking the boat, who knew the players," McHale told Snyder at the time of the hire. "Jim was a natural choice. What this club needs is a custodian, not an advocate."

Others weren't nearly as charitable about Fanning's credentials. Michael Farber vividly remembered how the *Montreal Gazette* handled the hire.

"Jim was a terrific man, people called him 'Gentleman Jim,'" recalled Farber. "Loyal and selfless and tireless. Incredibly ill-suited to be the manager.

"Twenty-five minutes before his first game as manager, Jim is in uniform, first time in forever. And Jim says, 'I don't know, it's been so long . . . do the laces go under the flap, or over the flap?' I went upstairs and wrote, 'The Expos just hired a manager who doesn't know how to tie his shoes.' [Fellow *Gazette* writer] Ian McDonald had one of the best leads I've ever seen. 'Rain spoiled Expos manager Jim Fanning's debut last night. It stopped.'"

The Fanning experiment didn't start well. Montreal lost its next two games in Philly, giving up 21 runs in the process. The series opener against the Cubs made it three losses in a row, dropping the Expos' second-half record to 14–15. More and more, it looked like a third straight disappointing ending to a season was imminent.

But the Expos ended their slide by winning the final two games of the series against the Cubs. That set up a gigantic 15-game homestand, their longest of the year, and a welcome change from that September schedule two years earlier. The homestand didn't start well, though. Facing the Cardinals (the team they were chasing for the second-half crown), the Expos dropped three of five games, ending the series by splitting a pair of doubleheaders. Montreal was now just 18–18 in the second half, 3½ games behind St. Louis with just 17 left to play. The Expos continued to tread water at the start of another series against the Cubs, scoring an 11–0 blowout win only to lose a 2–1 nailbiter the next day.

That's when Montreal caught fire. Bill Gullickson started things off with one of the best pitching performances in team history. Facing Chicago, Gullickson spun a three-hit shutout, striking out 13 batters en route to a 4–0 win. The next night brought the opener of a two-game series against the Phillies. Starting for Philly was Steve Carlton, who'd won his third Cy Young Award a year earlier and again ranked among the league's most dominant pitchers. A classic game ensued: Carlton didn't allow a single run in nine innings, but Ray Burris, the veteran right-hander acquired by Montreal over the winter to solidify the back of the rotation, didn't either. It wasn't until the end of the 10th inning that both starters finally exited the game, with the score still tied 0–0. Reardon, who'd emerged as an excellent stopper and also someone capable of shutting down the opposition for multiple innings at a time, tossed three scoreless frames at the Phillies. The game went to the bottom of the 17th inning. With the bases loaded and one out, Dawson finally put the game to bed, slashing a single to centre to give the Expos a 1–0 victory.

That kind of huge hit was typical for Dawson in an outstanding 1981 campaign. In just 103 games, Dawson walloped 24 home runs, stole 26 bases, and hit .302/.365/.553, winning the Gold Glove and Silver Slugger awards for the second straight year, and finishing second in MVP voting. He did all of that while playing through loads of pain, his knees getting worse with every passing season on the Big O's unyielding cement turf. He'd have his knee drained three times a year, since it would build up 10 times as much fluid as the average player's; each procedure would get chased with a cortisone shot, which hurt like hell. His knees still throbbed every day, and wearing a brace would likely have limited the wear and tear, but Dawson insisted on having full mobility in centre field and on the basepaths. He fought through the pain, trusting his over-the-top workout regimen and the team's trainers and doctors to get him through the season. Ron McClain remembered those sessions well.

"When he would walk through the door," McClain said, "I'd tap whoever was on the table and say, 'Okay that's it, time for the Hawk.'"

For the brave souls in the stands who stayed the entire four hours and 28 minutes to see Dawson's game-winning hit, the win

was exhausting—but electrifying. It also typified a rising trend that no one would've expected: in hockey-mad Montreal, the surging Expos had become a hot commodity, maybe even hotter than the revered Canadiens.

The Habs had built a dynasty in the late '70s, winning four Stanley Cup titles in a row. This wasn't exactly shocking news—they'd also forged dynasties in the '50s and '60s, and won more championships than any other team in the big four North American team sports to that point (even more than the Yankees). But the Habs bowed out of the playoffs early in both 1980 and 1981, right as the Expos started taking off. The well-to-do crowd you'd normally see in the coveted red seats at the old Montreal Forum—men in three-piece suits, women in fur coats—started showing up in droves at Olympic Stadium.

"The Canadiens, for a short time, didn't block out the sun," said Farber. "There was an opening there. If the Canadiens weren't going to play firewagon hockey, the Expos could win people over by playing firewagon baseball."

"For a few years, the Expos were not only the top sports team in Montreal—they were the top sports team in Canada," said author Alain Usereau. "The Habs dynasty ended in the late '70s. The only Canadian hockey team during that period that went to the Cup final was the [Vancouver] Canucks, who were not that great and got swept by the Islanders. In Montreal, everything short of winning the Stanley Cup was a failure. Some people thought Montreal was entitled to win the Cup. 'Will you go to the parade this year?' 'Nah, I'll go next year.' Then the Habs got ousted three straight years in the first round.

"The Expos took their place. They had very colourful players at that time, who were perfectly suited to Quebec and to French Canadians. Sports fans here really like to watch a bum, to see how they would succeed. Here's an example: the Hilton Brothers were very popular boxers in Montreal, even though they'd be the last people you'd invite as guests to dinner. People identified with Bill Lee, Rodney Scott, Ron LeFlore. They identified with those teams."

"There was an aura," said Charles Bronfman. "One of the nice things was, a lot of corporate people would take people to the games. But don't forget, to fill up a stadium, you have to average 25, 30 thousand people. That can't just be corporate stuff. It really became the place to be for a hell of a lot of people. It was a tough place to get to. For people on the West Island, it was very difficult. But people kept coming anyway."

Of all the beautiful people who showed up to Olympic Stadium in that era, none was more recognizable than Donald Sutherland. The New Brunswick–born actor grew up a huge Expos fan. In 1972, he married French-Canadian actress Francine Racette and lived a bicoastal existence, working out of Hollywood and spending ample time in and around Montreal. He was to the Expos what Jack Nicholson is to the Lakers—the celebrity superfan with primo seats. Expos fans growing up in the '70s and '80s remember seeing Sutherland behind home plate—in a trench coat and hat, right in the centre-field camera shot—as surely as they remember watching Staub, Rogers, Carter, Dawson, and Raines.

Sutherland was a diehard fan, often driving three hours roundtrip from his home in the Eastern Townships outside Montreal to see home games. He showed up to one game in '81 with his arm in a sling, having injured himself on set; he was, of course, wearing an Expos patch on the sling. He became an ambassador for the team, doing voiceovers on Expos documentaries. He arranged to have friends in Montreal set the phone down next to the radio so he could listen to games, whether he was in L.A. or on a movie set thousands of miles away in Europe or Asia. Marcia Schnaar, a long-time Expos office assistant who worked for everyone from the team's general manager to the travelling secretary, remembers getting occasional, unusual calls from Sutherland.

"One time, he called from his cellphone," said Schnaar. "Nobody even knew about cellphones yet, but he had one. He was shooting a movie in Paris, and he's got just a minute before he needs to get back, but 'please, please, tell me what's going on in this game.' He needed to know."

Calls to the office or leaving phone lines open for three hours to listen to the game—these were just fallbacks. Whenever possible, Sutherland's agent would attach a clause to his movie contracts, stipulating that the studio must provide a radio and/or TV with satellite access on set. That way, if there was any way to pick up that day's Expos game, he'd be able to hear it or watch it, no matter where in the world he was shooting.

"Donald was a great fan of the game," said Van Horne. "He was good for the team—it was good for the franchise and for the city that he would be seen as a baseball fan. For all the years that he was supportive of the team, a lot of people associated Montreal with Donald Sutherland."

Sutherland and other Expos crazies were treated to a frenzied finish in 1981. Montreal led the second-half standings by 1½ games and headed to St. Louis for a two-game set, only to drop both games and fall a half-game behind with five to go in the season. First facing their '79 nemeses, the Pirates, the Expos swept that two-game series, getting strong starts from Gullickson and Burris. A Cardinals split during that same two-day stretch gave the Expos a half-game lead with just one three-game series remaining, in New York against the Mets.

That set the stage for Steve Rogers. Williams had never hesitated to question Rogers' courage under fire, complaining to anyone within earshot that the righty didn't have what it takes to win the big game. The criticism got to Rogers. Here was a chance to prove his old skipper wrong.

Facing a Mets lineup that included former teammates Staub and Valentine, Rogers was sublime, firing a two-hit shutout in which he faced just one batter more than the minimum for nine innings. Not normally a strikeout artist, Rogers struck out the side to end the game, giving him nine punchouts on the night, four of them against Mookie Wilson. That outing capped a season-ending stretch of 10 games in which Rogers posted a 1.72 ERA, including just three earned runs allowed in his last three starts of the regular season. Not bad for a supposed choker.

"This isn't pressure," he told Snyder after the game. "This is fun. When you're thinking about pressure, you can get pretty scared and hesitant about what you throw. This is fun because we're winning the way we know we can."

Pitching coach Galen Cisco was more succinct in his analysis. "He was mean," Cisco said of Rogers. "Mean!"

The Expos still needed one more win to clinch their first-ever playoff berth. They called on another homegrown player to get it done. Trailing 3–2 in the seventh with two on and one out, Fanning sent Wallace Johnson up to bat. Johnson wasn't a star like some of his fellow farm products: he had very little power, and merely decent speed. Brought up as a second baseman and playing a little first base later in his career, Johnson wasn't really equipped to play there or anywhere else on the diamond. He was, however, a very good pinch-hitter, working at-bats until he got a pitch he could handle. Added to the roster as a September call-up, Johnson was taking just the eighth at-bat of his major league career. The result sent the Expos faithful gathered around their TVs and radios into fits of delirium. A two-run triple to right put Montreal ahead 4–3 and blasted nearly everyone in the dugout off the bench and onto the field, pumping their fists and yelling at the unlikely rookie hero. The Expos took a 5–4 lead to the bottom of the ninth, giving Reardon a chance to slam the door against his former team. With two outs, Dave Kingman lifted a soft flyball to left. Terry Francona, another member of those early '80s Expos teams who went on to have a successful career as a major league manager, charged in and squeezed it for the final out.

The players' strike had done the Expos a huge favour. The St. Louis Cardinals in fact finished with the best record in the East over the entire season, as did the Reds in the NL West (as well as the entire National League). But neither St. Louis nor Cincinnati made the playoffs that year. In the East, the Cards finished a game and a half behind Philly in the first half, and a half-game behind Montreal in the second half, denying them a postseason spot. In their stead, for the first time ever, the Expos were headed to the playoffs.

"This is such a culmination of so much hard work, of individuals as a unit," said Chris Speier, in between gulps of champagne. "We have gone through so many changes together—the strike, personnel moves, the change of managers—this is the total release. No individual can hold you back. If you tried to keep your feelings inside, you'd go crazy. We can be six-year-olds. This is a kid's game anyway."

Amid the revelry in the clubhouse, there was one bittersweet sighting: Ellis Valentine. He didn't get a chance to celebrate the way he should have, as an Expo. But Valentine's old friends, the ones with whom he'd fought shoulder to shoulder through nearly a decade in the organization, did invite him in to share in the celebration.

"I'm really happy for them," he said. "A little of my heart is still there."

Montreal's opponent in the first round of the playoffs was first half-winning Philadelphia, the team that dashed their dreams a year earlier. The Expos offence was short-handed, as a broken thumb had knocked Tim Raines out of the lineup for the last three weeks of the regular season and would keep him out of the first round of playoffs as well. Montreal would make up for his absence with another round of lights-out starting pitching.

In Game 1 it was Rogers again, scattering 10 hits over 8⅔, then turning the game over to Reardon to nail down the final out in a 3–1 win. In notching the win, Rogers outduelled Carlton, no easy task after a season in which Lefty went 13–4 with a 2.42 ERA.

In Game 2, Gullickson was the hero. After an outstanding regular season in which he delivered a sparkling 2.80 ERA and led the staff with 115 strikeouts, Gully limited Philly to one run in 7⅔ innings. The Phillies had a chance for a big inning in the eighth, cranking out a single and two doubles to cut the Expos' lead to 3–1, setting up runners on second and third with two outs. But Fanning made two moves that helped save the inning, and the game. First, he pulled a tiring Gullickson, bringing in Reardon for his second straight save opportunity. Then, remembering the agony Mike Schmidt had inflicted on the Expos the year before (and pretty much from the moment he entered the league), Fanning ordered Reardon to walk Schmidt intentionally. Montreal's relief ace then got Gary Matthews to pop out and end the inning. A one-two-three ninth left the Expos just one victory away from the League Championship Series.

The series headed back to Philadelphia, where the Phillies fought back. In Game 3, they cruised to a 6–2 victory. Game 4, however, was a cliffhanger. Philly jumped out to a 4–0 lead, only to have the Expos come back to tie it at 5–5, sending the game to extra innings. In the bottom of the 10th, pinch-hitter George Vukovich hit a low fastball from Reardon over the fence for a game-winning home run, forcing a deciding fifth game.

In the scrum after the loss, a reporter asked Fanning about the prospect of having to beat the great Steve Carlton twice in one series. Fanning had his share of spats with various Expos players, but he trusted Rogers in a way that Williams did not. Locking eyes with the reporter, Fanning gave his reply. "They have to beat Steve Rogers in this series. So I'm not worried."

This would be the 14th matchup between Carlton and Rogers, with Rogers leading 6–5 with three no-decisions to that point. Carlton was red-hot right out of the gate this time, striking out the side to start the game. But Rogers matched zeroes with him, keeping the game scoreless into the fifth. Montreal then loaded the bases in that inning with one out, bringing Rogers himself to the plate. Carlton hung a slider, and Rogers connected, slapping a single up the middle to give the Expos a 2–0 lead. They added an insurance run in the sixth, and after that, it was the Steve Rogers Show. Here's Rogers escaping a two-on, none-out jam in the sixth. There's Rogers working around an error in the eighth. Finally, it's Rogers carving through the Phillies in the ninth, clinching the shutout, the win, and the Expos' trip to the NLCS on a lineout to Cromartie at first base.

It was time to celebrate, again. This time, with props.

"There was this set of twins, they were big fans," said Cromartie, his voice rising an octave as he recalled the post-game scene in Philadelphia. "They'd brought a big Canadian flag. I took the flag, I'm swinging the flag, sticking it right up Philly's ass. They had Carlton on the mound. 'How you gonna beat Lefty? How?!' We weren't even supposed to show up. I was proud. I was fucking proud. When I went up there and starting waving the flag, people went apeshit."

The next day, pictures of Cromartie waving the flag adorned newspapers all across the country. It wasn't a World Series or even a League Championship Series. But in the era of two TV channels—at a time when the door was wide open for a team to captivate the nation—the win and the waving of the flag resonated from coast to coast. The Expos were on a rocket ship, aimed at the World Series. All of Canada was coming along for the ride.

Blue Monday

T he first playoff berth in franchise history had been secured. The first playoff series in franchise history had been won. All that remained was a five-game series against the Los Angeles Dodgers, with the winner earning the National League pennant and a trip to the World Series. Ray Burris' five shutout innings in Game 2 sent the Expos back home to Montreal with the series tied 1–1. Jerry White decided Game 3 with a three-run homer in the sixth inning that turned the crowd at Olympic Stadium into a delirious mess. The Expos had a chance to clinch the series in Game 4, only for the Dodgers to score six runs over the final two innings en route to a 7–1 win. Now, with the League Championship Series tied 2–2, the Expos were a single victory away from advancing to their first World Series. What transpired next became one of the darkest moments in Expos history, one that would haunt the team for the rest of its existence and turn one man into a pariah for the rest of his career.

This is the story of Blue Monday.

Serge Touchette: "They won that first playoff series in Philadelphia. So they flew to L.A. They played two games there, split, *then* came back to Montreal. We came back around five o'clock in the morning. When we got out of the plane and got through customs, there were about two to three thousand people waiting for the team. I couldn't believe it. That's when I realized it was even bigger than I thought it would be. Even the players, they couldn't believe it. People were cheering like crazy.

"Then they played that first game in Montreal. One of the biggest moments ever in the history of the franchise happened in Game 3. Jerry Reuss was pitching for L.A., tied 1–1 in the 6th, Jerry White comes up . . . and hits a three-run homer. The reaction from the fans . . . it was like an explosion. Fifty thousand people stood up at the same time and went crazy. People were dreaming about the World Series."

Rick Monday: "This is before the roof at Olympic Stadium—it's cold, there's a threat of not only rain, but *snow*. Being from southern California, snow is a big deal when you're trying to play baseball. But we were reading in the papers how the boys from Hollywood won't be able to handle the cold weather. So Tommy Lasorda in his infinite wisdom before the first game up there said, 'We're going to show them how tough we are. They can't down-talk to us!'

"'I don't want anyone wearing their jackets!' Tommy told us. So, we're introduced, we don't have our jackets, we're on the third-base line and they proceed to introduce all but two people even in attendance for the game. They introduced everybody, and all the while the boys from Hollywood are standing there, shivering. And we're thinking, 'Whose great idea is this?! It's cold!'"

It only got worse from there. Game-time temperatures hit about 9 degrees Celsius (the high-40s) for Game 3 at the Big O.

They plunged to near freezing for Game 4, but the boys from Hollywood staved off elimination (and pneumonia) anyway, blowing out the Expos 7–1.

Game 5 was scheduled for the next day, a Sunday afternoon, with temperatures again diving toward zero. The Expos were expecting another packed house of 54,000-plus. Forecasters had predicted rain, sleet, or both, which combined with the cold prompted the umpires to postpone the deciding game until Monday afternoon. The predicted downpour wasn't as bad as feared, with some on hand that day believing the game could have been played—but the postponement did allow starter Ray Burris to pitch on a full four days' rest, after shutting out the Dodgers 3–0 in Game 2. It also reduced the Game 5 crowd to a shivering, tense gathering of 36,491. A tight, low-scoring game only raised the tension.

Steve Rogers: "Look at the first inning. We put runners at first and third with no outs against Fernando [Valenzuela]. Dawson's at the plate. Fernando usually throws the screwball. Instead he throws that little slider, jams Dawson right to the shortstop for a double play. A run scores. And that's it. That's our offence. Now, while nobody could say in the first inning that that's important, you look at how the game went on—that first inning was as critical as anything. They've already got someone warming up in the bullpen. If Hawk sees it better or gets a ball over the plate and drives it, we might be into the bullpen. One big hit and Fernando might be gone."

Mike Scioscia: "Fernando gave up that run in the first inning and then proceeded to pitch as well as you could ever imagine anyone pitching. You know, Fernando was young. He was only 20, but he understood the ramifications of what was going on out there. He was really focused on every pitch. We just didn't do much offensively to help him."

While Valenzuela dominated, Burris tossed another gem of his own, scattering five hits over eight innings. But the Dodgers pieced enough together in the fifth to tie the game. Monday and Pedro Guerrero led off the inning with back-to-back singles. After a Scioscia lineout, Burris uncorked a wild pitch, pushing runners to second and third. With Valenzuela up, the Expos brought the corners in, watching for a potential game-tying squeeze. Instead, Valenzuela swung away, slapping a grounder to second to score the tying run.

Both teams went down in order their next two times up. In the seventh, the Expos put two on, but didn't score. The Dodgers pushed Davey Lopes into scoring position in the eighth with an infield hit and a steal, but didn't score. On to the ninth the game went, with the score still tied 1–1. The Expos had pinch-hit Tim Wallach for Burris in the bottom of the eighth, meaning they'd need a new pitcher for the ninth. Jim Fanning now faced a big decision. Due up for the Dodgers was the heart of their order: right-handed hitters Steve Garvey and Ron Cey, and 35-year-old, lefty-swinging Rick Monday, who'd hit a ton in part-time duty that year and pushed the lighter-hitting Ken Landreaux out of the lineup.

The Expos' bullpen wasn't particularly deep that year, so even after their starter had given them eight innings, there were only two likely choices to start the ninth. Closer Jeff Reardon was battling a bad back, though he'd pitched in Game 1 of the series. The other most likely option was starting pitcher Steve Rogers.

Jim Fanning: "People don't remember that Jeff Reardon wasn't Jeff Reardon yet. He only had 10 saves in his career before coming to the Expos."

Steve Rogers: "Reardon had a bad back, but they sent him down there and he was ready to go for the ninth inning."

Serge Touchette: "They wanted to go with their best guy at the time, which was Rogers. Even if he wasn't a relief pitcher, if you're going to get beat, you want it to be your best guy. Rogers was the best pitcher in baseball at the time. He pitched well every time out down the stretch. He beat Steve Carlton twice in a week in the first playoff series. He threw a complete game against the Dodgers in Game 3. He would be pitching on two days' rest, but he was pitching so well. I thought it was a good move."

Tim Raines: "Rogers had to come in, but he had almost never pitched in relief in his career."

Jim Fanning: "Ask yourself who was the best pitcher in the National League the last five weeks of the season. Rogers. He'd given up two runs in the entire playoffs. After the rainout, he came to [pitching coach] Galen Cisco and me and said, 'It's my day to throw between starts anyway.' I told him if it came to that, I wouldn't have him relieve during an inning in progress. I said it'd be at the start of an inning. Burris was pitching a hell of a game, then he started to tire. We had an opportunity there to start the ninth, where it was not a save situation. So Steve Rogers came into the game."

Steve Rogers: "You know being brought in for that situation, it was not what had been discussed prior to the game. There were a lot of things that ebbed and flowed in that decision-making process. I was going to be the first guy out of the pen if Ray got into trouble and got knocked out early. It was always contemplated that I would be the first guy out of the bullpen before it got out of hand. Then he goes out and throws eight innings of one-run ball. Hell yeah, Ray was on his game.

"So they sent me down to warm up in a spot I wasn't necessarily expecting. I was fine physically, but my adrenaline was pumping too hard. I didn't control it and I was overthrowing the sinker. Mechanically, I lost the angle. I just took the bad mechanics from the bullpen out to the mound. I was going to have a throw day on either the second or third day, so I mean, I could have thrown five innings if they needed it. Physically and mentally at least, I was fine."

Garvey led off the inning with a first-pitch popout. Then Rogers got himself in trouble. Facing Cey, the Dodgers' fireplug third baseman, Rogers fell behind 3–1, then fired his trademark sinker. Instead of diving below the batter's knees as it had done so many times throughout Rogers' career, the pitch stayed up—a telltale sign that Rogers' mechanics weren't right, that he wasn't executing his pitches the way he normally did.

Cey took a huge swing and crushed the ball toward the left-field corner and the very reachable 325 sign. But he didn't quite get all of it. Hanging up in the cold October air, the ball died at the warning track, settling into Tim Raines' glove for the second out.

That brought Monday to the plate. The Dodgers' right fielder was a modest 5-for-22 without a single extra-base hit in the playoffs leading up to that at-bat. Fanning had left-handers Bill Lee and Woodie Fryman available. Lee had warmed up and was ready to go, though he'd pitched sparingly in the postseason to that point. Fryman had been torched for five runs in 2⅓ innings of work during the playoffs.

Bill Lee: "Reardon, Fanning would bring him in for the right-handers, but he's got to bring me in for the left-handers. When the inning started, I had warmed up on my own. I did it on my own, and I tapped my hat, and he brought in Rogers. He gets the first two guys, lefty's coming up, and Fanning leaves him in.

"Monday ain't gonna hit me. I'm gonna throw him a fastball, then he's gonna foul it off his foot. I'm gonna throw him another fastball, then he's gonna foul it off again. I'm gonna throw him a breaking ball away, he's gonna wave at it, inning over.

"He went with Rogers because that way he wouldn't have been criticized. That's the way he thinks, because, see, for Fanning, when you think, you hurt the ball club. Fanning, he can't pull the trigger. He has a really nice gun, but he's got no fuckin' bullets in it."

Jim Fanning: "Rogers was going to be the guy. It didn't matter if the guys coming up were left-handed or right-handed hitters."

Steve Rogers: "We wouldn't even be out there if I hadn't pitched so well leading up to that game. If I don't pitch that well, they don't even think of putting me out there. If I just scuffled in the third game and I come out after six innings, would they have looked at me [to pitch the ninth inning of Game 5]? No, it would have been Reardon from the get-go."

In 1981, we were still years away from widespread, batter-to-batter obsessions over righty-lefty matchups, to be sure. This also wasn't the first, or the last, time Lee and Fanning would emphatically disagree; one incident the following season would result in a near-fight, and a huge fallout for both men's careers.

Bottom line, Rogers wasn't coming out. But he was struggling, overthrowing and failing to locate his sinker. For the second straight time, he fell behind the batter 3–1.

Rick Monday: "I'm looking for a pitch I can drive. Very seldom does he get a ball above the knees, so you have to hit it whenever it is above the knees."

Steve Rogers: "You can make a case that the stretch of three starts leading into this game was the pinnacle of my career. But my mechanics just weren't there that day. Gary called sinker away, and I just threw it so badly that it just was one of those settling, nothing fastballs."

Serge Touchette: "'It was a BP fastball.' That's what he said afterwards."

Terry Francona: "It was a good swing. But it was so cold. I don't think anybody thought he hit it hard enough to go out."

Andre Dawson: "I didn't even think it would make the wall. It just seemed to carry and carry. I don't know what the wind was doing that particular day. I knew he hit it good, but I didn't think he hit it *that* good."

Rick Monday: "Here's the thing: it was so cold. There had already been balls that were hit hard that went nowhere—even in batting practice. You hit the bejeebers out of it and it goes nowhere. Steve had been so successful against us that year, and just a couple of days prior. And we knew we were probably not going to get a ball elevated at all.

"I finally do get one, and it's the only time in 19 years and 240-something home runs that I ever lost the flight of the ball. I knew it was hit hard, but I thought it was hit too high. Because I lost sight of the ball, I went down the first-base line and I'm watching Andre Dawson and he keeps going and keeps going and I'm thinking it's going to be too high—it's going to be caught. Then he kept going and I was like, 'Maybe it'll be off the fence, maybe it will be off the wall.' I was already past first base at the time. I was thinking, 'If it's off the wall I would be on second, maybe third base.'"

Tim Raines: "I'm in left field and I'm watching Andre go back to get the ball. He's running out of room."

Terry Francona: "It kept carrying and carrying. Next thing you know, he's going around the bases with his arm in the air."

The Monday homer felt like a crushing blow. But all was not yet lost. The Expos started a rally in the bottom of the ninth. After retiring Rodney Scott and the heavily slumping Dawson to start the inning, Valenzuela walked Gary Carter. Another walk, this one to Larry Parrish, knocked Valenzuela from the game. Lacking a true closer, Lasorda summoned Bob Welch from the pen to face Jerry White—the same Jerry White whose Game 3 homer might've ended up being the biggest in franchise history had the Expos made it to the World Series. On the first pitch, White slapped a slow roller into the hole between first and second. Lopes ranged far to his left, gathered it in and fired to first, where a fully outstretched Garvey snagged the throw an instant before White's foot hit the bag. Inning over, game over, season over, dream over.

Terry Francona: "It just deflated us. Nobody thought we were going to lose."

Tim Raines: "The Monday home run, it was probably one of the . . . I wouldn't say the worst thing that ever happened to me, but it was pretty hard to take. And then the last out was a groundball, bang-bang to first base. And I'll never forget this: Warren

Cromartie and myself were sitting on the bench, because every-body else had left. Just sitting there. 'What the hell, these guys beat us.' We sat on the bench after it was over and I was like, 'I can't believe we're not going.' I could not believe we weren't going to the World Series. We won [Game 3], all we needed was to win one game. We just couldn't win that one game.

"We probably had the best team in baseball. No, we *did* have the best team in baseball that year. We'd have kicked the Yankees' ass that year. If the Dodgers beat them, we'd have probably swept them. We had the team."

Mike Scioscia: "The Expos were a really talented club. You look at a lot of the players on the team, how their careers went, you can imagine how good they were. The guys that didn't have power could fly. The guys that couldn't run real well had unbelievable power. And then you had Andre Dawson or Tim Raines that could do both. You know, they had a deep lineup. They had great balance. They could steal a base. They could hit the ball out of the park. They all played terrific defence. So, that was really one of the best baseball teams I've ever played against."

Rick Monday: "You can't look past what a tremendous team the Expos had. I quite frankly don't think that the Montreal Expos of 1981 truly got the attention they deserved in terms of how good that ball club was and how good those players were. At that time, it was a ball club you looked at and said, they could beat you a lot of different ways. They could beat you with pitching, they could beat you with defence, they could beat you with offence, they could beat you with their speed—a lot of different areas. It's unfortunate we don't ask, 'Who else is on the podium?' It's, 'Who's holding the largest bouquet of flowers?'

"During that series, people were dancing in the aisles. It was really a tremendous, and I mean a tremendous, venue. In that series it was like a World's Fair, and the Olympics, and the World Series all at once. People were dancing and hollering, bundled up and having a good time. Every time the Expos did something really well, which they did often during that year, everyone would start singing, "Valderi Valdera." So now we win it, and we go back into the clubhouse and somebody started singing it in the locker room. It was finally our turn to sing. We had been hearing it over and over and over and over and over, and finally the crescendo was in our locker room. We found out later that some people got irritated, but we didn't do it as a disrespectful thing. It was blowing off steam; it was a magical moment. For us there was that extra incentive too, that little burr that was still under our saddle from '77 and '78. The World Series is going to start the next night. So it was a relatively short one-hour, 10-minute flight. Thank goodness it was not any longer. It was . . . let's say a very boisterous flight."

More than three decades later, some bitter Expos fans haven't forgiven those involved in the moment, when Monday smashed that hanging sinker over the 12-foot wall in centre, 400-plus feet from home plate. Some questioned Fanning's managerial inexperience, wondering if the Expos skipper should have used a different pitcher—Reardon at the start of the inning, or a left-hander against Monday after Cey's near-homer. Or when Rogers fell behind Monday 3–1, Fanning or Gary Carter could have suggested Rogers pitch around Monday to bring up Pedro Guerrero, who'd been awful throughout the postseason.

Others never forgave the two principals in the matchup, Rogers and Monday. Rogers won 158 games in his 13-year career, posting a career ERA of 3.17 (16 percent better than league average). He put up several big seasons, including his nearly unhittable stretch in September 1981, all the way through the playoffs with three lights-out starts against the Phillies and Dodgers—plus a huge year in 1982 right after giving up the infamous homer. Monday had been the first overall selection in the first-ever amateur draft in 1965. More famously, on April 25, 1976, he grabbed an American flag from two protesters just before they could set it on fire in the outfield at Dodger Stadium. His career numbers were pretty damn good too: 1,619 hits, 241 homers, 125 OPS+.

Still, fairly or not, mention either man's name in Montreal and many old-time Expos fans flash back to that fateful day.

Steve Rogers: "I talked to Monday about it after the fact. You know something? I've heard it and I understand what he's saying. He's saying, 'My career was more than just one pitch.' He said, 'I think I had a pretty damn good career.' He got paid to hit the kind of pitch I threw. He got paid to hit that ball hard. He did his job and I didn't do mine.

"The only thing I could say that has bothered me at times about Montrealers—and I understand it, so it hasn't bothered me in depth, it hasn't bothered me to the core—but when I've been up there a few times over the years, people come up to shake your hand, and go, 'Blue Monday.' Everybody does it. I've come to terms with that, and it's because that's the easiest way for them to relate to me. It's not meant to be negative. They know where they were when they were listening and the ball went over the wall. Every now and then it's said in a way that's not as nice. But I've come to grips with the fact that, for the most part, it's not malicious."

Jacques Doucet: "Steve Rogers was the main card of that team: the ace. People forget his great career. I was broadcasting a game for the Quebec Capitales [of the Can-Am League]. Bill Buckner's one of the managers in the league. He comes into town and I went to him and said, 'Mr. Buckner, you and Steve

Rogers have something in common. One play ruined your reputation.' I remember mostly when he was playing for the Dodgers and the Cubs, he was a really good hitter then and throughout his career—2,700 hits! Still, people come back to that one play. Same thing with Rogers."

Rick Monday: "The next year we go into Montreal, and Steve Yeager and I are going to dinner. We go in, we sit down, and we had ordered a beverage and we're at a table looking at the menu and this man comes up to us and goes, 'Gentlemen, I'm going to have to ask you to leave.' This was the general manager of the place. A nice restaurant. And we said, 'You're open, right?' This was a Sunday night, if I remember correctly. And he goes, 'We don't want any fights in here.' I was like, 'We're not going to fight. We just got off a plane, we're going to have dinner.' And he goes, 'Well, I'm not worried about you guys fighting, but there are six guys at this other table over here who want to kick your ass.' There were other things too. I would get so many phone calls that I'd finally have to put a block on the phone at the hotel. Some of them were humorous, some of them were very dark humour, some of them were no humour.

"A few years go by—I'm retired and now a broadcaster. It was the last year the Expos were going to be in Montreal. My wife joins me on the road trip and we bring my stepdaughter with us: she's a junior in high school at the time. So we're spending the afternoon in the old town and taking in the sights and my wife, Barbara Lee, says, 'Why don't we take Ashley to the restaurant we went to last year?' The restaurant has been there, I don't know, it must be 100 years old. As we were walking to the restaurant, Barbara Lee says, 'Why don't you tell Ashley about 1981, and what happened the following year when they asked you to leave a restaurant?' So I'm telling her the story. We open the door to the restaurant, and I was saying, 'You know they don't like me in this town.' We start to walk in, and this hostess runs toward us. 'You can't come in! You can't come in!' I turn to Ashley and say, 'See?! They really don't like me here.' It turned out they had an electrical fire in the kitchen and that's why we couldn't come in. But at that moment it was like, 'See?' So we had a good laugh about that.

"Talking about all of this . . . you're trying to get me shot in Montreal in case I ever return again, eh?"

Warren Cromartie: "I'm a big fan of Rick Monday, ever since he pulled that flag up. Always liked his style. He was a student of the game. Every now and again I wake up in a cold sweat thinking about that son of a bitch. And every time I see him, I want to punch his fucking lights out."

CHAPTER SIX

Coming Up Short (1982–1984)

O n July 13, 1982, a capacity crowd of 59,057 fans streamed into Olympic Stadium. Youppi!, the Expos' giant, orange, unknown genetic material fuzzball of a mascot, came decked out for the occasion, sporting a tuxedo. With the festivities about to begin, public address announcer Richard Morency called out the familiar names, his voice booming through the cavernous stadium.

"*Le voltigeur de gauche*, the left fielder . . . Tim Raines!"

"*Le voltigeur de centre*, the centre fielder . . . Andre Dawson!"

"*Le receveur*, the catcher . . . Gary Carter!"

"*Et le lanceur partant*, the starting pitcher . . . Steve Rogers!"

This wasn't just any game for the Expos, though. Sure, Raines, Dawson, Carter, and Rogers were all in the starting lineup. But on this day, they trotted onto the field not just as Montreal Expos, but also as National League All-Stars. As *starting* National League All-Stars. It didn't quite stack up to the six Yankees who started the 1939 Midsummer Classic at Yankee Stadium. But still, four players from the same team starting an All-Star Game played in their home stadium—in the post-expansion era? This had only happened one other time since 1969, when Dodgers fans elected four starters to the 1980 All-Star Game in L.A.

The Expos would have their fingerprints all over the game. Raines led off and stole a base. Carter knocked in the final run (in the sixth inning). Coming off the bench, the fifth Expos All-Star, Al Oliver, went 2 for 2 and scored a run. The winning pitcher was Rogers, the first pitcher to start an All-Star Game in his home park since Whitey Ford at Yankee Stadium way back in 1960. The '82 All-Star Game, a 4–1 NL victory, marked a coronation for the Expos and their hyper-productive farm system, a tribute to their elite status among the National League's best teams.

"It was a career highlight for me," said Raines. "It was awesome to have the game in Montreal, to have so many of us make it by getting voted in. That was the thing that really made me feel proud, because the fans had a big part of that; even though we deserved it, the fans had a big part. You probably had a lot of fans all over [America] that didn't give a crap about the Expos. They wanted to see their players there. But that one year, Canadian fans stepped up and became a really big part of the situation."

No one at the stadium could know it then, but baseball in Montreal peaked that night at the Big O.

The Expos' first strategic error had been bringing back their manager for the '82 season. As John McHale explained when he hired Jim Fanning to replace Dick Williams in the middle of the 1981 pennant race, McHale wanted someone who knew the Expos' culture and wouldn't require a big adjustment period. But Fanning had a steep learning curve anyway; he was, after all, a scout and front-office guy who hadn't worn a uniform in two decades. Furthermore, the excuse about maintaining continuity in the midst of the September stretch run no longer applied once the season was over. The Expos could have chosen from any available managerial candidate. They could have gone outside the organization and poached an up-and-coming leader stuck as some organization's third-base coach or Triple-A manager. They could have looked within their own organization and hired someone like Felipe Alou, who'd played a major role in the Expos' player-development success, and had years of managerial and coaching success on his resumé.

Instead, they chose Gentleman Jim, the universally respected baseball man who was ill-suited to manage a major league team.

"The right move was to thank Jim, acknowledge the great fun everyone had in the playoffs, but also that he's not a manager," said Michael Farber. When the Expos announced they were re-upping Fanning, Farber's first reaction was, "Big mistake. There's McHale up there at the press conference. He says, 'Today we're pleased to announce—if it's okay with you Mike—we're bringing back Jim Fanning.'"

The mainstream press, however, didn't much care who was managing the Expos heading into the '82 season. Montreal was the overwhelming pick to win the NL East that year, regardless. *Sports Illustrated* said the Expos would win. So did *Inside Sports*. *Baseball Digest* added, "The Expos' starting lineup may be the strongest in baseball." *The Sporting News* polled its 12 National League correspondents; 10 of them favoured the Expos to win the East.

Bill James went even further. "Let's face it, folks," the statistical guru wrote, "the Expos are without a doubt the best team in baseball today."

Finally there was Thomas Boswell, the esteemed author and *Washington Post* baseball writer. "The Montreal Expos will win the National League East this season," Boswell predicted. "They will win it again in 1983. Some things are simply ordained. Just as the Yankees and the Royals each made the playoffs five times from '76 through '81, so the Expos—who are by far the most misfortune-proof team in baseball—have already begun such a reign. Nothing stands between Montreal and greatness."

There wasn't much greatness to be found at the start of the year, though, as the Expos went just 12–12 through the first four weeks of the season. Meanwhile, another problem cropped up in the clubhouse as a rift emerged between Fanning and two of the team's veterans, Rodney Scott and Bill Lee. On May 7 in Montreal, the Expos lost their third straight game. A few days earlier, they'd sent reserve second baseman Wallace Johnson down to the minors. That position was now in total disarray: Johnson had proved unable to handle the defensive rigours, veteran Frank Taveras was poorly suited for anything but bench duties, and Scott, the starter for the previous three seasons, had been relegated to part-time work. A reporter asked Fanning if he might now move Tim Raines back to second base—the position he played for much of his minor league career—with young Terry Francona taking over the left-field job.

"We haven't got a timetable for it," Fanning said, "but it's fair to say that's part of the plan." The very next day, the Expos released Scott; a few hours later, Raines started at second base, Francona in left.

There were plenty of good reasons for booting Scott. A poor hitter even at his best, Scott's speed had made him a huge favourite of Dick Williams—but he'd gotten progressively worse in each of his seasons with the Expos and finally earned his release after hitting just .200 in 1982 (albeit in just 25 at-bats). He was also one of the last remaining members of the hard-partying clique that had once included Ron LeFlore (gone after the 1980 season), Ellis Valentine (traded in 1981 for Jeff Reardon), and Rowland Office (released three days before Scott). After years of ignoring and tolerating all manner of ill behaviour, McHale finally cut Scott loose.

This did not sit well with Lee, himself a known carouser and recreational drugs enthusiast. Thirty-five years old, nearing the end of his career, frustrated with Fanning from day one, and now enraged that his friend Scott had been turfed, Lee finally lost it. Wielding a bat and shouting obscenities, Lee lunged at Fanning, only to be stopped at the last second by Andre Dawson and Warren Cromartie. What happened next would be considered beyond the pale . . . for anyone except the Spaceman.

"I was in my uniform, the game was about to start, and I ran out of the ballpark," recalled Lee. "I was screaming and I ran into Terry Mosher. We were out in the vestibule outside of Olympic Stadium. He says, 'Come with me.' He grabs me and takes me down to Brasserie 77 on Hochelaga Street. The people in that bar still remember the day I was there in my uniform. I had four beers and I shot pool, and he calmed me down and the game was on and we were in a bad position late in the game when they needed a reliever. So I went back to the ballpark, went into the bullpen, and started getting loose."

Shockingly, Fanning did not use Lee in that night's game, a 10–8 Expos loss.

The Spaceman had pitched well in two of his three full seasons in Montreal, and he'd become a favourite with fans and writers— one of the franchise's all-time characters. But McHale had run out of patience with the eccentric left-hander. On May 9, Lee became the third Expo in five days to get released, with McHale tacking on a $5,000 fine on Lee's way out the door. McHale and Fanning weren't the only ones critical of Lee's circus act.

"Bill Lee and me are friends," said Woodie Fryman, quoted in *The Expos Inside Out*. "But we're both question marks at this stage of our careers. You don't do these things when you're a question mark."

Scott nabbed just 26 more at-bats in the big leagues, and Lee never pitched in the majors again. In purging LeFlore, Valentine, Office, Scott, and Lee over a span of a year and a half, McHale had also unloaded a group whose off-field offences ranged from smoking pot in uniform before games to, in some cases, all-night cocaine benders.

The rampant cocaine use, obviously, presented the much bigger problem. Expos brass didn't just worry that the biggest users' performances would suffer. The farther-reaching concern was that young, impressionable players on the roster would start developing coke habits of their own. Cocaine was becoming an epidemic across the major leagues, culminating in a series of high-profile drug trials three years later. Valentine's career had already been ruined by coke and other vices. The Expos could ill afford to have another potential star throw away his career.

Then the Tim Raines bombshell dropped.

In December 1982, Raines revealed publicly for the first time that he'd been using cocaine. In a revealing interview with Michael Farber for the *Montreal Gazette*, Raines admitted he'd spent $40,000 on coke in the first nine months of that year alone. "He snorted cocaine in his car before games at the Olympic Stadium parking lot," Farber wrote. "He snorted it after games in friends' apartments. He snorted it in washrooms on team airplanes. On a few occasions, he snorted cocaine in the Expos' clubhouse between innings."

Raines' $1,000-a-week habit hurt his numbers, which fell to .277/.353/.369 in 1982, down sharply from his .304/.391/.438 rookie campaign. He hit fewer home runs, struck out more often, and walked less often than he would in any other season as an everyday player.

"I could feel the effects," Raines told Farber. "I wasn't seeing good, and I wasn't eating well. I was juggling the ball in the outfield. I was misreading pitches."

Since no one knew about Raines' habit at first, the Expos chalked up his lackluster performance to a prolonged slump, or maybe a sophomore jinx. But these weren't just the usual struggles of a slumping player. One time, Fanning gave Raines the night off. When the skipper wanted his speedster to pinch-run late in the game, a teammate had to wake Raines up; he'd crashed hard from a post-cocaine letdown. Raines still stole 78 bases in '82, with an 83 percent success rate, but he was thrown out more often in 1982 than in any of his other first seven seasons as a starter. Several times, Raines got thrown out at second, then took several seconds to realize what had happened and that he needed to return to the dugout.

Most infamously, Raines slid headfirst every time he tried to steal. That in itself wasn't so conspicuous—plenty of other players did the same. But not many did so because they had a vial of coke in their back pocket. Thanks to his 5-foot-8, muscular frame, Raines had earned the nickname "Rock." After Farber's revelatory column, that nickname would take on a new, more damning meaning.

The good news was that Raines went into rehab, got clean, and kicked his destructive habit. Like Valentine before him, Raines had broken into the majors early, thrust into the starting lineup by his early 20s. Also like Valentine, Raines felt overwhelmed by the pressures of being a big leaguer and wished for a strong mentor. Unlike Valentine, Raines eventually found one.

"After everything that happened [in 1982] I went to Andre Dawson," Raines told me in 2011. "I said to him, 'Show me how to play.' He's not a guy who shares a lot of words. But to me it was just, 'Show me the way. You don't have to say anything. I'm never going to get in trouble again. I'm going to be a model citizen and I'm going to play the game the way you play the game. I'm going to come to the ballpark every day ready to play and play hard, just-like you.' And that's what I did."

AISLIN

Raines grew so close to Dawson that he often referred to him as his older brother. In 1983, Raines named his second son Andre—or "Little Hawk," a nod to the nickname of his godfather, Andre Dawson. Meanwhile, Raines' play rebounded that same year. He set career highs in runs scored (133) and stolen bases (90), and established himself as the team's third superstar player alongside Dawson and Carter. The trick for the Expos would be to build the right supporting cast to complement those stars.

For all of Raines' success later on, the Expos suffered for his off-year in '82. Given how good Raines was in his rookie year, then every season from 1983 through 1987, it's easy to imagine him winning two or three more games for the '82 club. Still, that wasn't the biggest problem for a Montreal team that was supposed to be starting a dynasty. Erratic play or no, the Expos couldn't keep Raines at second base as they intended after Scott's release, and the alternatives were collectively terrible.

Francona shattered his knee after colliding with an outfield wall in St. Louis, knocking the Expos' Plan B left fielder out for the year and forcing Raines back to the outfield. They tried Mike Gates at second for awhile, but he was Scott without the speed, hitting .231 with no power. On August 2, the Expos purchased Doug Flynn from the Rangers to plug the hole. Flynn couldn't hit either, batting just .244 with no power himself, and somehow drawing only four walks in 58 games. All told, the seven non-Raines players who patrolled second base in 1982 hit .216 with no home runs in 533 at-bats.

Not that this was anything new. From 1974 through 1984, no team put up weaker numbers at any position than the Expos did at second base:

Year	Player	AVG	OBP	SLG
1974	Jim Cox	.220	.288	.292
1975	Pete Mackanin	.225	.276	.375
1976	Pete Mackanin	.224	.256	.337
1977	Dave Cash	.289	.343	.375
1978	Dave Cash	.252	.291	.315
1979	Rodney Scott	.238	.319	.294
1980	Rodney Scott	.224	.307	.293
1981	Rodney Scott	.205	.308	.250
1982	Doug Flynn	.244	.256	.295
1983	Doug Flynn	.237	.267	.294
1984	Doug Flynn	.243	.267	.281

Put another way, during the eight-season span stretching from 1977 through 1984, the Expos' primary second basemen hit a total of six home runs; from 1980 through 1984, they hit exactly *zero*.

It's one thing for players with star potential to disappoint—
that happens all the time. But it defies belief that McHale,
Fanning, and the rest of the team's decision makers put up with
so much offensive incompetence for that long without fixing
the shortfall. The problem wasn't just one of neglect, however.
Though they would lose plenty of superior players over the
years, gift-wrapping second-base prospect Tony Bernazard to the
White Sox after the 1980 season for a fistful of dryer lint proved
to be—given both the timing and the alternatives left behind
at second—one of the most harmful trades in franchise history.
Trading fellow second-base prospect Tony Phillips for over-the-
hill first baseman Willie Montanez that same year didn't help
either, though Phillips didn't become a front-line player until
later. Given how often the Expos nearly won division titles in
the late '70s and early '80s, it's no stretch to say that finding even
average second basemen during that era might've changed the
course of Expos history.

It wasn't all bad for the Expos in '82, though. An off-season
trade that brought veteran first baseman Al Oliver from Texas
yielded immediate dividends, as the All-Star led or tied for the
National League lead in batting average, runs batted in, hits, and
doubles. Despite his "Scoop" nickname, however, Oliver's overall
defence was ugly—his shoulder so badly hurt that he had to shot-
put many of his throws, committing a staggering 19 errors in the
process. Still, after years of searching for a potent left-handed
bat to balance an overload of right-handed hitters, the Expos
fared better with Oliver than they'd dared hope; the 35-year-old
turned in the best offensive season of his long, impressive career.
Meanwhile, in his first season as an everyday player, third baseman
Tim Wallach blasted 28 homers, knocked in 97 runs, and played
solid defence. Carter was a monster as usual, launching 29 home
runs and winning his third straight Gold Glove. Jeff Reardon

thrived out of the bullpen, firing 109 innings with a 2.06 ERA. Finally, Steve Rogers delivered the best season of his brilliant career, leading the league with a 2.40 ERA over 277 innings, only to lose a Cy Young Award he deserved because Steve Carlton won four more games. (Three decades later, too many sportswriters still overrate the value of wins in these situations, failing to recognize how reliant wins are on teammates' performance, opponents' quality, and luck.)

Having been treated to three straight years of thrilling pennant races, fans showed up in droves: 2.3 million of them piled into Olympic Stadium that year, the third-highest mark among all National League teams and the highest total to that point in franchise history.

After their early-season difficulties, the Expos remained in contention, and on August 1, 1982, the Expos hosted the Cardinals for the final game of a four-game series. It was a key matchup at the end of a pivotal series, as Montreal and St. Louis were both in the playoff hunt, chasing first-place Philadelphia. I was seven years old, and this was my very first trip to a major league game. Even before the first pitch, I knew this would be the best day of my young life. As we walked through the turnstiles, a sonic boom whacked me in the face—the place was *loud*, with Oompah band horns and singing voices echoing through the concourse. After stopping for popcorn and ice cream, we shuffled through the passageway leading to our seats. That first look at the field, the din bouncing off the far reaches of the enormous stadium, the sight of that many people gathered in one place . . . it all overwhelmed the senses. That Sunday matinee against the Cards featured two of the top pitchers in the league, Steve Rogers and Joaquin Andujar, and 51,353 fans came to see it.

Neither Rogers nor Andujar pitched especially well that day, but Montreal scored three runs in the bottom of the seventh to take a 5–4 lead, one that would stand up for the win. That victory pulled the Expos to within four games of first place; by September 15, they'd cut the deficit to two games. But they could never quite break through, spending just four days in first place all season, and none later than June 24. In the end, it was the young and speedy Cardinals—not the aging, battle-tested Phillies—who won the East. The Expos actually played well against St. Louis in 1982, winning 10 of 18 games against the Cards. But in perhaps the biggest series of the year, an early-September three-game set in St. Louis, the Cards took two out of three, with both of those wins coming by 1–0 scores.

After holding off the Phillies and Expos to win the East, the Cardinals rolled from there, sweeping the Braves in the League Championship Series, then knocking off a loaded Brewers team in seven games to win their ninth World Series.

☞ EXPOS KILLERS ☜

There were plenty of Expos killers over the years: Willie Stargell got the pool at Jarry Park named after him, and Mike Schmidt's division-clinching homer in 1980 was one of many crushing blows he laid on Montreal. Still, getting smoked by future Hall of Famers was one thing. Letting Dane Iorg destroy you was quite another. The lefty-swinging outfielder, first baseman, and long-time Cardinal lasted 10 years in the big leagues, but was mostly a part-time player throughout his career.

Despite his light pedigree, he hit like Ty Cobb against the Expos. A career .276 hitter, Iorg batted .361 lifetime against Montreal, his best mark against any team. Asked about his mastery of the Expos, Iorg told of one game in 1981 when he went 3 for 3, all three of his hits off tough Expos righty Bill Gullickson, and all of them coming on broken bats. Iorg then absolutely crushed the Expos in '82, hitting .396 against them that year, with six doubles and a triple. But Gullickson wasn't Iorg's major victim. His voice rising, Iorg recalled faring well against one other Expos pitcher in particular.

"I *owned* Steve Rogers," he said. "I don't know why, but I owned him!"

The numbers bear that out. Though he was otherwise nearly unhittable in '82, Rogers faced the Cardinals four times that year, and Iorg banged out two hits in each of those games. When asked about Iorg, Rogers winced.

"He killed our whole right-handed staff," he said, shaking his head.

After years of Iorg terrorizing Expos pitchers, Rogers finally had enough by May 14, 1983, when Montreal travelled to St. Louis to face the Cards. Rogers' parents would drive up from

Springfield, Missouri, whenever the Expos came to St. Louis, and the right-hander confided in his dad, telling him he was going to hit Iorg the first time he came up in the hopes of making him less comfortable at the plate. The Cardinals opened the game with a 1–0 lead on a walk, an error, and an RBI double. Cardinals manager Whitey Herzog, knowing Iorg's history against the Expos and especially Rogers, had slotted their tormentor into the third spot in the lineup, meaning he was now striding to the plate. True to his word, Rogers reared back, fired a fastball, and drilled Iorg in the leg.

In 2,837²/₃ career innings, Rogers maintains this was the only time he ever deliberately tried to hit a batter.

"Dane had played with a lot of guys that have said, 'He's one of the nicest human beings ever,'" Rogers said of Iorg, a mild-mannered Mormon who was indeed held up as universally liked when I talked to others who knew him.

"I have no reason to doubt it. But I just couldn't take it anymore. The guy just killed me."

A year after Rogers plunked him, Iorg was sold to the Royals. After that, the two men never faced each other again in the big leagues. Considering the nightmares Iorg gave Rogers, other Expos pitchers, and every Expos fan during that era, this was a huge relief.

At the dawn of the 1983 season, the Expos were still a collection of stars and scrubs. A top-notch farm system had produced Carter, Dawson, Cromartie, Raines, and Wallach—plus Valentine and Parrish before them. The starting rotation ran deep, with Gullickson, Scott Sanderson, Charlie Lea, and others supporting the staff ace Rogers. But the roster remained plagued by major holes. There was the second base problem, of course. Then there was Chris Speier, who by 1983 had seen his defence slip and injuries start to mount, making a player whose bat was never all that good a clear weakness for a team with World Series dreams. Neither the bench nor the minors offered much help at those positions, nor did first base, where 36-year-old Al Oliver managed to hit .300 again in '83—but with little power, few walks, and more unsightly defence. From 1973 through 1981, five different Expos had finished first or second in Rookie of the Year voting. Now, the pipeline had run dry.

McHale reacted with complacency. Armed with a free-agency system that didn't exist when he ran the Tigers and later the Braves, the Expos GM barely touched the open market. From 1979 through 1983, with Montreal in contention every year and the need never higher to round out the roster with a few more jolts of talent, McHale signed: Ray Burris, the veteran right-hander who helped the rotation in '81 but didn't do much thereafter; Elias Sosa, a right-handed relief pitcher who pitched well for two years but was pretty much done by 1981 . . . and that was about it. The two biggest trades in that time were Valentine for Reardon (a big winner) and the Oliver deal, which looked great in '82 but less so thereafter, as the big name going the other way (Larry Parrish) enjoyed several more productive seasons in Texas. But the team's increasingly terrible middle infield remained unaddressed. Meanwhile, McHale and company failed to properly identify the rare quality young players they had in the system. In addition to giving away Bernazard and Phillips, the Expos also sold Ken Phelps to the Mariners, dumping a player who became a terrific hitter in Seattle (and later a punchline in a classic Frank Costanza rant on *Seinfeld*).

Even with the shortcomings, you can't have as much top-flight talent as the Expos did and not at least be in the mix. And the '83 squad did in fact contend for the NL East crown. They led the division for much of April, then again for a three-week stretch in late June and early July. They vaulted back into first on Labour Day and held that spot as late as September 13, after a 5–2 win over the Cubs. Through it all, fans again descended on Olympic Stadium, with the Expos' attendance setting a record that will forever stand as the highest mark in franchise history.

But yet again, an Expos season ended in disappointment. On September 14, the Expos lost both ends of a doubleheader to the Phillies, a team so old that—in a nod to the 1950 Philly team christened as "the Whiz Kids"—they were dubbed "the Wheeze Kids." That aging Philadelphia squad won just 90 games, but it was enough to take the East, and to put down the perpetually underachieving Expos.

"Woodie Fryman used to talk about how teams had a five-year window to win," said Farber. "This was the closing of that window."

From 1979 through '83, the Expos won more games than anybody else in the National League. Yet they reached the playoffs just once, and that lone post-season berth came with an asterisk due to the split-season format that allowed the Expos to sneak in.

"That was sort of the demise of the franchise," Carter said. "We didn't win those championships during the prime years, when we had a real chance."

So what went wrong?

There were the cocaine cases, of course. Beyond those off-field problems, though, some believed the Expos had the talent to win championships—but not the leadership. Parrish in particular had been well liked and respected in the clubhouse, and the trade that sent him to the Rangers got blamed for Montreal's leadership void.

"He was the heart and soul of those teams," said Dave Van Horne. "In the clubhouse, in the dugout, in the runway leading out before games. The team really missed Larry. Al Oliver was a terrific player, but Parrish was the one who could rally the troops."

At the end of the '82 season, Fanning returned to a front-office role, leaving the manager's job open. Here was another opportunity to hire a candidate who possessed both the experience and tactical acumen necessary for the role and the right temperament to lead the team. Once again, Felipe Alou was considered. Once again, the Expos brass went in a different direction. This time, the pick was Bill Virdon.

Having led three different teams to division titles or shares of division titles (the 1972 Pirates, 1980 Astros, plus the second-half crown for the '81 Astros), Virdon had the experience that Fanning didn't. He was also incredibly old-fashioned, a stickler for protocol who forbade drinking on flights during road trips. McHale hadn't realized the extent of the coke problem rippling through the roster until it was too late, and hiring a disciplinarian like Virdon was an attempt to instill order on a team in apparent disarray. With a lineup full of free-swinging hitters and a perpetually leaky defence that often featured players throwing to the wrong base, Virdon's strict approach seemed the perfect fit.

"He wasn't the easiest person to get to know, but when you took the time to get to know him, you found an interesting man, someone with a sense of humour," Terry Francona said in a 2013 interview. "He was the best outfield instructor I'd ever seen—he personally did it, himself, as manager. I've never been around somebody who made you work that hard, who paid attention to detail that much. It was hard. He was a taskmaster. But when he was there, that was the best outfield I ever played."

"He just commanded your respect," Tim Wallach told me in 2011. "Not because he was loud—he wasn't. You'd see him walk in and he had a way about him that got your attention. I just respected the heck out of the guy."

Francona himself went on to become a World Series–winning manager after his playing days, and in early 2014, Wallach was the

Dodgers' bench coach and a candidate for a future major league manager's job. Others, however, didn't see Virdon the way they did.

"Nobody liked the guy," said Cromartie. "It's a tough choice for me between Karl Kuehl and Bill Virdon, but I think Bill Virdon's got it. [Virdon] was a military-style guy. He was very uncommunicative. He liked to flex his muscles on top of the dugout steps. He thought he was a Marine guy."

To be fair to Fanning and Virdon, both men managed flawed rosters. McHale's overconfidence in his roster and/or reluctance to make impactful moves (depending on your perspective) led to inertia, and the Expos kept proving that what they had wasn't quite enough. Both the manager hirings and roster weaknesses fall primarily on McHale, who served as both team president and general manager from '79 through most of the 1984 season.

Even with all that, we can still chalk up a big part of their failure to far simpler factors: bad timing and bad luck. The Expos faced very tough competition for four years in a row. The Pirates knocked them out at the end of the 1979 season. Then came the Phillies in 1980, the Dodgers in the final inning of the deciding NLCS game in '81, and the Cardinals in September of '82. In each of those seasons, the Expos lost out to the team that would eventually win the World Series. If baseball had allowed four playoff teams per league in 1979 and 1980 the way it did after the introduction of the Wild Card format in the mid-'90s, and all else stayed the same, the Expos would've made the playoffs three years in a row.

But every other team faced the same challenges, and instead, the Expos reached the end of an era. After one more good season in '83, the bottom finally fell out for Rogers, who retired two years later. Cromartie signed with the Yomiuri Giants and didn't reappear in the majors until eight years down the road.

Entering the 1984 season, with yet another disappointing finish under their belt, Bronfman funded and McHale executed just one notable off-season pickup: an over-the-hill Pete Rose. The Expos knew him well from all those early-'80s battles with the Phillies. "Charlie Hustle" was expected to provide the leadership the team supposedly lacked, even if he was many years past his physical prime.

"I would characterize the Expos as a ship without a rudder [and] Pete Rose could be that rudder," Steve Rogers told *Sports Illustrated* writer Ron Fimrite. "He can bring another dimension. We have a strong nucleus, but nobody from that nucleus can assert himself as a leader. We're equals. You can't be a leader to your peers. Hell, we all grew up together. We're brothers. How can any of us be the dominant brother? We need somebody above that, a Pete Rose."

"Pete's the missing ingredient," Rose's former teammate turned Expos second baseman Doug Flynn added. "We need leadership, not so much on the field as on the bench and in the clubhouse. Our club has been too laid-back. Pete's not going to let anybody relax. I don't care if he hits .240, he can help us. He looks hungry and good. He has that look in his eye."

"He represents professionalism and enthusiasm and a winning attitude," said McHale. "We're betting that he has a breath or two left. Peer pressure, I think, is more effective than pressure from the manager or from management. Players respond more to it. As the crowds get bigger, the prizes larger and the races closer, we need someone to get up and say, 'Let's do it!'"

They did not do it. Rose hit .259 with no homers in 95 games before getting dealt to the Reds, and the Expos were never really in the hunt in '84. But the cruellest blow of all would come at the season's end . . . with the trade of an icon.

On Opening Day 1977, Gary Carter squatted behind the plate to catch Steve Rogers, then added a home run as the Expos went on to beat the Phillies 4–3. That was Carter's first season as the Expos' everyday catcher, rather than the injury-prone hybrid catcher/out-fielder he'd been. From 1977 through 1984, Carter was the best catcher in the game by a wide margin. Actually, that's underselling The Kid's value. Going by Wins Above Replacement—a stat that measures offense, defense, and baserunning, then adjusts for ball-park effects and the era in which a player played—Carter was the second-best player in baseball at *any* position over that eight-year span, trailing only the great Mike Schmidt.

More than just a superstar on the field, Carter was also the team's most popular player, the successor to Rusty Staub who embraced fans' rabid enthusiasm the way Le Grand Orange did. Carter took the time to learn some basic French, same as Staub. One of the most famous photos in team history is of Carter on Camera Day in 1983, being mobbed by delirious fans, most of them donning Expos gear, all of them either kids or teenagers.

"Gary was always available to the fans," recalled long-time Expos administrative assistant Marcia Schnaar. "His agent told him, 'These are the people who pay your salary; be there for them.' But I didn't see it as forced. It was genuine. He enjoyed talking to people. Especially all the little boys and girls who came to see him."

Carter was an invaluable asset for the Expos. Still, Charles Bronfman was about to trade him anyway.

The Expos' owner had grown frustrated by the team falling short of expectations year after year. During all those close calls, Carter had played well through injuries and come through in many big spots. But when he went 0 for 8 in a season-deciding home doubleheader against the Phillies in September 1983, Bronfman lost it. He accused Carter of choking—of not being worth the big money. That last part was the most germane. Even Babe Ruth had a few 0-fers in big games. But what started as a request for a $1 million investment in 1969 had become a major annual financial commitment for Bronfman. (And some of Carter's teammates felt underpaid by comparison, believing Carter's salary was augmented by his attention-grabbing personality.) Revenue streams were now falling behind players' salary requests. In 1984, the Expos finished below .500 for the first time in six years; attendance plunged 31 percent to just 1.6 million, the eighth-highest mark among the National League's 12 teams.

On April 13, 1984—just the ninth game of the season—Rose slapped his 4,000th hit a day before his 43rd birthday. It was a legendary individual achievement, but when that's the most notable highlight in a dull, mediocre season, you can understand why an owner would take things out on his highest-paid player. Even if Carter was worth every penny.

On December 10, 1984, it happened—the Expos traded Carter to the Mets. In the process, they unloaded the best, most beloved player in franchise history to that point.

"I was disappointed—I thought I'd be an organization guy, with the same team for my entire career," Carter said. "[But] by the time '84 came around, we were in fifth place. Bronfman took the same kind of approach with me that the Pirates did with Ralph Kiner: if the Expos can finish in fifth place with Gary Carter, they can do the same without him."

Today, a sub-.500 team with a thin farm system might ask for a package stuffed with top prospects in return for an established star in his prime like Carter. Montreal didn't do that. Instead, the deal revolved around players with big-league experience: Hubie Brooks, a 28-year-old third baseman with a decent bat who profiled as an offence-first shortstop for the Expos; Herm Winningham, a 23-year-old outfielder who'd shown no evidence he could hit (and never did); and Mike Fitzgerald, a 24-year-old catcher who was Carter's default replacement—but who surprised everyone a bit by having some decent years later on. The only player in the deal with exciting potential was Floyd Youmans, a 20-year-old flame-thrower who grew up with Mets phenom Dwight Gooden in the Tampa area, and who the Expos hoped would develop into a slightly lesser version of the spectacular Dr. K.

The Carter deal was reactive rather than proactive, a half-hearted attempt to stay semi-competitive rather than a well-conceived plan to build for the future. Though Brooks did put up some pretty good numbers in Montreal, the trade was made because of Bronfman's frustration with rising salaries, and his realization that the Expos were headed for financial trouble.

"When attendance declined, I remember saying that we weren't doing well, but Philadelphia wasn't either," said Bronfman. "Then I found out Philadelphia's season-ticket base was 20,000. Ours was 10,000."

"There was no question in my mind even then that we had a Hall of Fame–calibre catcher," said Van Horne. "Johnny Bench was the greatest catcher ever, and we had the heir to Johnny Bench's throne. The trade was a great disappointment because of Gary's charisma, his attachment to the community, and everything else. And also the bitterness that came out of all of that. I know it affected Charles [Bronfman]. He had perceived the Expos as one big family, and of course they were not. He realized it was all about business. In his mind, the players' attitude was that all the other things—the way they were treated, the way they had a good relationship [with the owner], all of that means nothing if the numbers on the contract are not to my liking. That was a bitter, bitter pill for Charles to swallow.

"He loved the feeling that these were his guys. And I think the Carter situation told him otherwise. They are only his boys if he is paying them what they think they should be paid—it all boiled down to money. This was not only happening in Montreal, this was happening throughout baseball. And if it affected different owners in different ways, it affected Charles deeply because what he viewed as a family enterprise wasn't any longer. It was all business. And he didn't like the way the business of baseball was going—the escalating salaries, the turmoil between the Players Association and the ownership group and so forth. All of that. I think the Carter deal was the one that iced it for Charles as far as getting out of the business."

Bronfman selling the team, and the resulting reckoning, were indeed on the way, with Carter the first big domino to fall. His trade was the first time an Expos owner ever cited finances as the overriding reason to let a star player go. The first, but certainly not the last.

CHAPTER SEVEN

Scrap Heap Darlings (1985–1989)

Toronto, like Montreal, had a rich baseball history of its own well before the big leagues arrived. The minor league Toronto Maple Leafs were founded in 1896 and played for 71 years, going from unaffiliated status all the way up to Triple-A. Also like Montreal, Toronto then went through nearly a decade without professional baseball. This made locals nostalgic for the sport, and made local politicians and businessmen want to do something about it.

By 1975, it looked like the city might finally get its wish. The San Francisco Giants were hemorrhaging money, and the league had seen enough. Baseball's inter-league committee, in charge of expansion and franchise moves, determined that Toronto could be a profitable landing spot for the Giants. By January 1976, an agreement in principle had been reached, with the Giants getting sold to a group led by Labatt Breweries for $13.25 million, then moving to Toronto to play at refurbished Exhibition Stadium. But a last-minute appeal by San Francisco's mayor earned the city a temporary restraining order from a judge, which gave the mayor time to locate a new local owner. The good news for Toronto, however, was that the inter-league committee's dual mandate was no accident; baseball's expansion moves, from the early '60s through the '90s, usually stemmed from failed relocation attempts. A few months after San Francisco got its reprieve, Toronto got its expansion team.

In a stance that seems unthinkable now, the biggest pro-Toronto advocate on the committee—the man who made the most aggressive push to bring a second major league team to Canada—was none other than Expos president John McHale.

"I'm fighting like hell to get a franchise for Toronto," McHale said in 1975, as talks for that city heated up. "It would be great for us up here [in Montreal]."

What McHale might've seen as an opportunity for a healthy rivalry, or a chance to further stoke baseball fervour in Canada to the benefit of the Expos, turned out to be something different altogether. The Blue Jays, in fact, would eventually help kill the Expos.

When the Expos were at their best, from 1979 through 1982, they were the toast of Canada. If they could surpass hockey's revered Canadiens during that time, it was a lock that they towered over the Blue Jays, an expansion baseball team that hadn't to that point even managed a winning season. The Expos also had an eight-year head start on the Jays, which had allowed them to build a national radio network and establish a national TV presence that fostered new fans throughout the country. During the Expos' glory years, stations in far-flung Canadian cities started carrying the pennant race games of August and September.

"It was, 'Oh, the Expos are in it again,'" said Rich Griffin, who got a close look at both sides of the rivalry over the years. "And then we'd get all the people from Toronto come to visit—that's where I met writers like Larry Millson and Allan Ryan. They would all come down and stay with the team for an entire home-stand. Some of them would go on the road for the final months. I think that probably pissed the Jays off because they have their own team and those writers were coming to us instead. There was not a lot of love lost between the two organizations."

Though they played their games 500 kilometres away (and in a different league), the Jays knew they were nonetheless competing with the Expos for fans and air time. Expos games were being broadcast in Ontario cities like Windsor and Belleville, which the Jays considered their home turf. But slowly, the balance of power began to shift. After six straight losing seasons, Toronto reeled off two straight 89-win campaigns starting in 1983. And the Expos' run of contending seasons ended with that ugly sub-.500 campaign in '84.

The time was right for the Jays to strike. They began lobbying Major League Baseball to punt the Expos out of the highly populous and lucrative southern Ontario broadcast region, making it exclusive Blue Jays territory. Charles Bronfman pleaded Montreal's case with the league.

"I spoke to [MLB Commissioner] Bowie Kuhn and said, 'Look, if you don't permit us to televise across the country—we're Canada's team right now—what you're going to do is, you're going to ghettoize us, and we'll become just the French team, and the Blue Jays will become the national team,'" Bronfman said. "'This is contrary to every goddamn reason I [agreed to own] the Expos. I did it to integrate Quebec into Canada. Now you're gonna ghettoize us, to separate Quebec?'"

Kuhn offered a compromise: the Expos could broadcast 15 games a year on TV in southern Ontario. Bronfman resisted, telling the commissioner that the Expos would get as many games as broadcast partners wanted to show on their airwaves. Kuhn shot back that they would do no such thing.

"I'm doing this in the best interests of baseball," Kuhn told Bronfman. He then reminded the Expos owner that Montreal, like every other team, wasn't allowed to bring legal action against the league to plead its case.

When Peter Ueberroth succeeded Kuhn as commissioner, Bronfman tried to lobby Ueberroth to change the terms of the agreement. Ueberroth replied that the Expos could have the 15 games Kuhn promised. After that, they'd have to pay for broadcast rights.

In other words, you can take your request and shove it. The Expos weren't going to pay for the privilege of having their games broadcast in an area they'd already had for the duration of their existence. And just like that, they were effectively shut out of the richest TV market in Canada. They'd been ghettoized as Bronfman feared, with open broadcast rights allowed only in Quebec and the relatively sparsely populated Maritime provinces. Toronto reaped the rewards, accelerating a power shift that would see the Jays ultimately replace the Expos as Canada's team.

The Expos could've protected their interests earlier by hammering out an agreement with the league establishing their broadcast rights throughout the country. But Charles Bronfman, John McHale, and company mistakenly perceived the Jays as an ally rather than a threat. McHale's stoic, old-fashioned business approach had blinded him to the cocaine epidemic ripping through his team's roster; Griffin, Dave Van Horne, Jacques Doucet, and others argue that it also prevented him from taking the kind of aggressive approach that might've prevented the Jays from muscling the Expos out of the country's most essential broadcast territory.

Chalk it up to the Jays' shrewdness, the Expos rolling over, an inevitable decision once Toronto got its own franchise, or all of the above. Whatever the case, Kuhn's decision ravaged the Expos franchise, causing more long-term harm, arguably, than Blue Monday or anything else that happened on the field.

While the Montreal metro area, then as now, ranked around middle of the pack in terms of major league cities' market size, the Expos would later face obstacles that other teams didn't have to overcome. The widening gap between the American and Canadian dollars became a problem, with the Expos collecting local revenue in Canadian dollars but paying the bulk of their expenses (most notably player salaries) in American funds. While the Expos remained mired at Olympic Stadium, the attendance and ticket price booms that rival teams got from building new ballparks widened the gap between Montreal and the rest of the league. The Big O's deteriorating condition and generally unappealing backdrop for baseball was one of several factors that drove fans away. These and many other poor business conditions would later make it impossible for the Expos to stay afloat (much less turn a profit or even break even) unless the team slashed payroll by trading away star players and letting them leave via free agency. Had those other problems not cropped up, sure, maybe the Expos could've subsisted on TV and radio revenue derived primarily from Quebec and the Maritime provinces. But with all those factors collectively working against them, they couldn't afford to lose the southern Ontario market.

"As soon as they lost access to southern Ontario, they lost the heart of the Canadian commercial business, corporate support, and sponsorship support," said Van Horne. "All of a sudden, the Montreal Expos were exactly that. They were Montreal's team. They were no longer Canada's team, and they couldn't survive just being Montreal's team. They couldn't get the rights for television feeds or sponsorships, because once you took away the southern Ontario market from the sponsors they weren't going to put money into it. They didn't need their gains in Fredericton and Sherbrooke and Quebec City. They needed to have both the Montreal and Toronto markets, and they didn't have that anymore. As we look back and see what happened after that, it really started a long, slow downward spiral."

The team on the field didn't look too hot either. The 1985 Expos contended in the first half of the season and even climbed to 14 games above .500 in late July. But they were no major threat to win—not with the Cardinals taking 101 games. By year's end, the Expos had allowed more runs than they scored, suggesting a team that probably got lucky in eking out 84 wins. Things got worse in '86, with Montreal managing just 78 wins, finishing 29½ games behind the eventual World Series Champions, the supercharged Mets.

Even more than sheer win-loss records, however, the mediocrity of those mid-'80s Expos teams was reflected in the makeup of their rosters. Years of poor drafts finally caught up to them, negating the successful player development in the '70s that built the contenders of the past. Few homegrown stars remained: instead, too many roster spots were filled by dull, unproductive players acquired from other teams.

As the rosters turned over, so too did the ranks of those in charge.

Near the end of the '84 season, McHale handed the general manager's reins to Murray Cook. If being battle-scarred was an important criterion for the job, the Expos had found the right man. Over a span of just 19 months in the Yankees organization, Cook went from director of player development to general manager to scouting director, with both his authority and job security challenged on a daily basis by George Steinbrenner during the mercurial owner's most unhinged days. Previously, Cook had worked for 21 years with the Pirates, including six years as scouting director.

Cook was thrust into a tough spot in Montreal. The day he got hired, he was told to trade Gary Carter, and he finally hammered out the deal in a stairwell of the Opryland Hotel during the '84 winter meetings with Mets execs Frank Cashen and Joe McIlvaine. (You wonder how Mets history might've been different if the Expos had accepted New York's offer of Mookie Wilson instead of Herm Winningham in the trade.) Cook got similar trade-him-now orders two years later with star closer Jeff Reardon. Meanwhile, the three years Cook spent as GM wasn't enough time for a new generation of homegrown products to develop as hoped.

Baseball even adopted a new rule thanks to a bad hand dealt to Cook. In the 1985 amateur draft, the Expos owned the eighth pick and nabbed Oklahoma State outfielder Pete Incaviglia. But Incaviglia wanted to play in Texas (and *not* Montreal). Five months after the draft, the Expos finally signed Incaviglia . . . and immediately traded him to the Rangers. Incensed, MLB later introduced the so-called "Incaviglia Rule," stipulating that no player taken in the amateur draft could be traded for at least one year.

Aside from the Carter trade, one of Cook's biggest immediate chores was finding a manager to replace Bill Virdon, who'd been dismissed after two disappointing seasons. Two notable names emerged in the hunt for his replacement. One was Felipe Alou, the long-time minor league manager and occasional major league coach who'd consistently impressed several higher-ups in the organization—just not enough to get hired as big league manager.

The other was Earl Weaver.

"That was John McHale's [idea]," recalled Cook. "We met with Earl at the airport in Miami. Meeting with him, it was obvious even to John that Earl was living in the past. John loved Earl Weaver. But Earl wouldn't have fit in Montreal. He just kept talking about the glory years in Baltimore."

The Expos instead chose Buck Rodgers. The former big-league catcher had managed parts of three seasons for the Brewers, losing his job 47 games into the 1982 campaign only for Milwaukee to reach the World Series under new manager Harvey Kuenn. Rodgers then managed in the Expos' farm system, guiding the Triple-A Indianapolis Indians to a championship and earning Minor League Manager of the Year honours.

A 180-degree flip from Virdon and his dour demeanour, Rodgers was "a real people person," said Jeff Blair, who covered the Expos for the *Montreal Gazette* during much of Rodgers' tenure as manager. Players gave Rodgers high marks for running a harmonious clubhouse. But nobody loved him more than the writers. Blair remembers many late nights spent in Rodgers' company closing down Grumpy's bar on Bishop Street. Like other newspapermen, Blair couldn't get enough of Rodgers and his stories, baseball-related or otherwise.

In addition to the new manager, the Expos' new scouting director was Gary Hughes. Mel Didier's departure after the 1975 season had taken its toll on the Expos' scouting pipeline, and though Montreal drafted some excellent players thereafter under Danny Menendez, not even the most ardent Expos die hard could deny that the team had lost its title as the model franchise for scouting and player development. Hughes had already worked as a scout and executive for the Giants, Mets, and Mariners—then worked with Cook in the Yankees organization—when he got called to come to Montreal. He replaced Fanning, who'd served as scouting director from 1983 through 1985, and got kicked back upstairs with Hughes' arrival. The first meeting of the two men left an immediate and major impression on Hughes.

"I got to the office at a quarter to nine, and the only person there was Jim," said Hughes. "He couldn't have been more gracious, he was so happy to have me here. I thought, 'Is this guy for real?' He was the most solid, gentle, genuine person I've ever met. We got rid of the scouts who cost him his job, so we started with a clean slate. They were dissatisfied with his drafts, which is funny— that year they had Incaviglia in the first round, they also got [future 13-year major league veteran starting pitcher] Mark Gardner in the eighth round, and they didn't do badly in the second round with Randy Johnson. I always say, 'Do you know what my first number-one pick did? Eight to thirteen in San Quentin.' That was Kevin Dean, our first-round pick in '86 who went to prison."

Though Hughes maintains a self-effacing view of the near half-century he's spent in the game, his track record in Montreal was exceptional. Hughes combined with farm directors Bob Gebhard, Dave Dombrowski, and John Boles to sign and develop 65 players over six years who went on to play in the big leagues. You could also measure the farm system's success by the high number of scouts and player-development people who went on to high-profile jobs with other teams later in their careers. That list included future big-league managers Mike Quade and Joe Kerrigan, future general manager Frank Wren, and a long list of future scouting directors.

But along with the new arrivals, there was a notable departure: McHale resigned as club president in 1986. From his thumbs-up for Montreal as an expansion city while serving as MLB deputy commissioner to his 17 years as Expos president and six years as GM during the most successful run the team ever saw, McHale's contributions were invaluable. From day one, he gave the upstart franchise an air of credibility. He oversaw the construction of a farm system that churned out two Hall of Fame players (as of 2014), turning a rag-tag roster into a perennial contender.

"John was highly respected throughout baseball," said Van Horne. "Charles' caveat on taking the franchise was based on McHale accepting the position of president. To give you an idea of his stature—had he not gotten involved with the Expos at the time, John probably would have become the commissioner. He would have been good at that job too."

Still, the time had come to step aside. At age 65, and 45 years after signing with the Tigers and starting his long journey through professional baseball, McHale was ready. Replacing him was someone with no experience running a baseball team, who nonetheless held Bronfman's trust, an ambitious Seagram's executive vice president named Claude Brochu. We'll get to his story a bit later.

Though the Expos won just four more games than they lost from 1986 through 1991, those six years with Hughes running the scouting department and all those savvy talent evaluators working with him laid the foundation for what would become the best team in franchise history. At the same time, Cook's knack for yanking quality players off the scrap heap proved highly valuable—especially considering what happened in the winter following the 1986 season. Dealing with an already depleted roster due to drafting and player-development failures and several key players going to other teams, the Expos now faced the prospect of losing their two remaining stars, Tim Raines and Andre Dawson.

Raines had established himself as one of the best players in the National League by that point, shaking off his drug-marred 1982 season and hitting .315 from 1983 through 1986. You could make a strong argument that Raines was in fact *the* best player in the NL over that stretch, having led the league in on-base percentage (.401), runs scored (445), stolen bases (305), and (as we can now see through the benefit of hindsight and advanced stats) Wins Above Replacement. He'd just turned 27, and had won the batting title, led the league in OBP, and made his sixth straight All-Star team in '86. Dawson by that point was no longer one of the team's two best players—not after years of knee injuries had eaten into his numbers and limited him to fewer than 140 games played in each of the previous three seasons. But even at age 32 with cranky knees, Dawson was still a valuable player and the last link to the crop of homegrown stars that came up with the team in the mid-to-late '70s. By all rights, Raines and Dawson should've been hotly pursued in a deep free-agency class that included other stars such as Jack Morris.

But these weren't ordinary times. At Commissioner Ueberroth's behest, every team agreed to a set of controls that would depress the price of free agents. Clubs would make every effort to avoid handing out multi-year contracts, and under no circumstances would they offer more than a three-year deal for a position player or two-year deal for a pitcher—no matter how good that player might be. With other teams showing little to no interest in free agents, players would be forced to crawl back to their own teams at a discounted rate.

Though collusion hadn't been proven yet, the players' union had already filed a grievance: everyone knew *something* was up. Moreover, Cook spoke publicly and loudly about Dawson's ailing knees, a move that figured to further depress the outfielder's already iffy market value. Understandably, Dawson was livid.

"The hurtful part about it was how Bronfman and McHale let it get to that point," Dawson told me in a 2013 interview. "I was a product of that farm system, I played 10 years for them in the big leagues. They knew I was committed to the organization, they knew I wanted to retire as an Expo; that it meant a lot to me, that I wasn't even being mindful of what that might mean to my career and [health] if I continued to play on that turf. But I could see that the writing was on the wall, that there was no sense of loyalty."

Fed up with his bosses in Montreal and finding no interest from other teams, Dawson and his agent Dick Moss showed up at Cubs spring training in Arizona with a signed blank contract in hand.

He'd take any offer Chicago would give him. Cubs GM Dallas Green offered a one-year, $500,000 deal, plus up to $250,000 in incentives if Dawson ticked off a list of accomplishments that included a highly unlikely National League MVP award. This was a serious lowball offer, even if you were pessimistic about Dawson's advancing age, and his knees. The Hawk accepted anyway, marking the end of his Expos career. That season, he blasted 49 homers, knocked in 137 runs—and won that MVP.

Raines, too, says he didn't want to leave. But he also grew angry at the Expos for their negotiating tactics, which included the seemingly self-defeating step of sharing information with other teams. As with Dawson, Raines couldn't find other suitors willing to negotiate fairly; the biggest offer he got from anyone else was a two-year proposal from the Astros for less than the $1.5 million he'd made in '86 alone.

"I really didn't want to leave, but I also wanted to be paid fairly for being an All-Star player," Raines said. When nothing close to that kind of offer came, Raines relented. "I went back to the Expos and said, 'Look, we can get this done.'"

Thanks to the league-wide collusion, those negotiations happened too late to bring Raines back for Opening Day the next season. (MLB's free-agency rules stipulated that teams had until early January to work out a deal with a player from the previous season; Raines' deadline to re-up with the Expos passed, meaning he'd have to wait until May 1.) The best player in the league was barred from participating in spring training, much less playing in games that counted in April. Instead, Raines spent the winter as well as the first month of MLB's regular season working out at a high school in Sarasota, Florida. He then muddled through a couple of games of rookie ball in a rushed effort to regain his timing. On May 1, just hours after being allowed to negotiate again, Raines signed a new three-year, $5 million deal to return to the Expos. The next day, Raines took the field for a Saturday matinee at Shea Stadium, coincidentally NBC's nationally broadcast Game of the Week, with Vin Scully and Joe Garagiola calling the action.

"They weren't sure if I was going to be ready to play," Raines recalled. "I was probably as nervous as I've ever been in my career. I go to batting practice, and I didn't hit one ball out of the cage—it was just like when I came up in '79 and couldn't hit anything. I'm like, 'What the hell is going on here?'"

What came next was, given the circumstances, the greatest performance by an Expos position player, ever.

With the team short of power hitters, Raines was installed in the lineup's third spot. On the first pitch he saw from David Cone, Raines crushed a triple off the right-field wall. In the third inning he drew a walk, then stole second and scored on a single. In the fifth, Raines smashed a groundball to the right side, a sure base hit if not for a terrific diving play by Mets second baseman Tim Teufel. Then, more hitting: a single to right in the sixth, an infield single and a run scored in the ninth, part of a two-run Expos rally that tied the game at 6–6. In the bottom of the 10th, the first three Montreal hitters reached base against tough Mets lefty Jesse Orosco. That brought Raines to the plate. The first pitch missed for ball one. Here's Scully and Garagiola on NBC:

> Scully: "High drive into left field, McReynolds watching . . . would you believe a GRAND SLAM for Tim Raines! That has to be one of the most incredible stories of the year in any sport. The first day back!"

> Garagiola: "That has to be one of those stories that if you wrote it for television, they'd say that's too corny. It'll never work! Can you imagine that? What a way to break in! [*whistles*]"

Shots of Raines being saluted at home plate by Reid Nichols, Casey Candaele, and Herm Winningham, followed by team- mates bowing to him from the dugout, then mobbing him as he arrives.

Scully: "So Tim Raines has a walk, two singles, a triple, a grand slam home run, *and* a stolen base."

Garagiola (referencing Mets fans' reaction to the grand slam): "Somebody's going to get hurt getting stuck in the gate leaving the park. They are just going in dro-o-o-o-ves!"

Raines' one-man onslaught launched what would become argu- ably his best season. Offence was up across the majors that year, but even adjusting for that league-wide surge, Raines' numbers stood out. In just 139 games, he scored a staggering 123 runs, best in the National League. He stole 50 bases in 55 tries, set a career high with 18 homers, hit .330, and set career highs in on-base percentage (.429) and slugging average (.526). Though Dawson won the MVP award that year thanks to voters' obsession with homers and RBI, Raines (as well as Tony Gwynn, Eric Davis, Dale Murphy, Jack Clark, and several other players) had a better overall season. And while the Dawson-infused Cubs finished last with their new slugger on board, the Expos won more games that year than in any other season in the '80s, contending down to the final days of the season.

Raines got pockets of support from some fellow lineup main- stays. Tim Wallach enjoyed his finest season, smacking 26 homers, leading the league with 42 doubles, and knocking in 123 runs. Venezuelan first baseman Andres Galarraga, one of the franchise's first homegrown stars from Latin America, hit .305 in his break- out year. Right fielder Mitch Webster, another buy-low find by

Cook thanks to a logjam in the Blue Jays outfield and a shrewd trade, batted .281, stole 33 bases, and banged out 53 extra-base hits. Still, Montreal struggled overall, ranking just ninth out of 12 National League teams in park-adjusted offence. The three least productive starters were Hubie Brooks, Mike Fitzgerald, and Herm Winningham, who had something in common: they were the three position players acquired in the Carter trade.

The pitching staff proved to be the team's saving grace, however, and Cook's biggest reclamation projects were the catalysts. One of those bargain-basement finds was, pound for pound, the most entertaining player in franchise history.

PASCUAL PEREZ

For an eighth-grade class of just 50 kids, we had vastly different spending habits. Some would run to the corner *dépanneur*, determined to blow their allowance in a frenzy of Garbage Pail Kids and Slush Puppies. The video-gamers would save for weeks at a time, then splurge on Nintendo's latest. The more fashion-conscious kids would use their allowances on clothes—Esprit, Jordache, Guess jeans.

Not me. The second I got my weekly pouch stuffed with loonies, I'd run to my pocket-sized Expos calendar, cross-reference it with the newspaper's probable pitchers section, then call my fellow baseball-crazy buddies. We were going to see Pascual Perez.

In his prime, Perez was a twitchy bundle of entertainment. He also owned a Hall of Fame-calibre Jheri curl, the kind that made you wonder if he owned a majority interest in Soul Glo Enterprises, and made him a prized find in any set of

'80s baseball cards. Rail-thin at 6-foot-2 and 162 pounds, he was a taunting beanpole, punctuating strikeouts by shooting finger-guns toward home plate. If he put a runner on, he'd peer through his legs to keep tabs on him. Successfully covering first base on a grounder hit to the right side often warranted a flurry of pelvic thrusts. If a strikeout ended a pressure-packed inning, you'd get the finger-gun, fist-pump, leap-off-the-mound shimmy-shake, followed by a sprint to the dugout.

Perez was a headhunter, too, jawing at batters who pissed him off, throwing at them on days when he was really on tilt. When Pedro Martinez came on the scene years later, rocking the Jheri curl and firing fastballs way inside, we saw the second coming of Pascual rather than the next Walter Johnson.

As eye-catching as Perez was on the mound, the greatest share of his notoriety came from a *Sports Illustrated* story detailing how Pascual earned the nickname "Perimeter Perez" in 1982—after he got lost just before a game while driving a borrowed car on the interstate that rings Atlanta. "There's a big radio and the merengue music was real loud," writer Franz Lidz quoted Pascual as saying. "I forgot my wallet, so I have no money and no license. I pass around the city two times easy, but the car so hot I stop at a gas station. I ask for $10 worth, and the guy say, 'You Pascual Perez? People been waiting for you at the stadium.'" Perez was 20 minutes away, and when he finally arrived he feared he'd be waived. Instead, Pascual was relieved when manager Joe Torre fined him—not one hundred dollars—but one hundred *pesos*.

To this day, Perez must be the only player to earn two different nicknames ("Perimeter Perez" and "I-285") *and* his own poster because of an off-field incident. You loved him because he embraced his own quirks and screw-ups. After the incident,

Perez could be seen wearing a jacket with "I-285" emblazoned in big characters.

There were other incidents too. Like the game in San Diego when Perez was called on to squeeze-bunt with lumbering catcher Nelson Santovenia on third.

"The squeeze is on . . . and Pascual swings away!" recalled Michael Farber. "Somehow, he fouls it off . . . miraculously, with Santovenia fearing for his life. They put the squeeze on again. He swings again. I asked Santovenia about it afterward. 'I'm screaming at him, in Spanish, SQUEEZE!' So I asked him, what's the Spanish word for squeeze. He looked and me and shook his head. 'Squeeze!'"

But when Perez was on, there were few better. In 1983 and '84, Perez made 63 starts, posting a strikeout-to-walk rate of nearly 3-to-1 and making the '83 All-Star Team. He kept that up despite the spectre of drug charges back home in the Dominican. His methods were unorthodox, but highly effective. Lacking a blazing fastball, Perez made up for it with a dizzying array of pitches thrown from a variety of angles. His signature offering was an eephus pitch: a huge, tantalizing looper sometimes called the "Pascual Pitch," or as Jacques Doucet and other French-language broadcasters dubbed it, "l'arc-en-ciel" (the rainbow).

Those Montreal years saved his career. Perez had gone only 1-13 with a 6.14 ERA for the Braves in 1985, was forced to the disabled list three times with shoulder pain, and was suspended for two weeks for disappearing after a loss in New York. He was out of organized ball in 1986, but the cash-strapped Expos signed him anyway. This was a typical move for a Montreal club that had blown up its dynamic core from the late '70s and early '80s and hadn't yet rebuilt its farm system.

Delayed several weeks due to visa problems, then a couple more months as he pitched his way into shape, Perez finally made it to Montreal for his Expos debut on August 22, 1987. What followed was a minor miracle: in 10 starts that year, Perez went 7-0 with a 2.30 ERA. This, despite not throwing a single pitch the year before and battling back from shoulder injuries and a lingering coke habit.

Expos employees from that era, including Rich Griffin, swear Perez drew an extra eight thousand fans per start in a city that rarely packed the park for specific starters the way fans do elsewhere. That's a debatable claim, but I can confirm that at least one 13-year-old lunatic would do everything in his power to see Perez in action. The Jordache kids might've looked sharper. The Nintendo kids were better at *Super Mario Brothers*. But if you were fortunate enough to see a Pascual Perez start in those days, you'd always come back with two things: a story to tell and a smile.

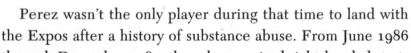

Perez wasn't the only player during that time to land with the Expos after a history of substance abuse. From June 1986 through December 1989, they also acquired right-handed starters Dennis Martinez and Oil Can Boyd, as well as outfielder Otis Nixon—all of whom had struggled with either alcohol or drug dependencies.

This should have seemed at least slightly crazy to just about everyone involved, since within recent memory the Expos had been compelled by common sense to excise multiple drug addicts and head cases from the roster. Yet now the front office was hoping that this new crop of addicts would find salvation in one of North America's most notorious party towns? With just about any substance of abuse available in unlimited quantities in just about any bar on Crescent Street? What on earth could the suits have been thinking?

It was all about the money. The club's roster, and especially the pitching staff, had been stricken by attrition, whether through injuries or skills erosion. The Expos needed someone—*anyone*—to soak up innings. They just had to be cheap.

"Take Martinez—we gave up almost nothing to get him," said Cook, pointing to the 1986 trade that cost Montreal light-hitting utility infielder Rene Gonzales for Martinez and cup-of-coffee catcher John Stefero. At that price, "what did you have to lose?"

Like Perez, Martinez's road back to big-league success was fraught with gigantic obstacles. When Martinez was born, the next-youngest of his six siblings was 10; his mother Emilia, 43. His father Edmundo was an alcoholic who left the family when Dennis was a small boy, and in Edmundo's absence, Emilia sold beans and rice in a small stall at the *mercado* while young Dennis kept the books. Still, the family barely got by. Dennis went most of his childhood without socks, and wore hand-me-down clothes with patches sewn into the seat of his tattered pants. He played baseball day and night, using socks stuffed with rocks as makeshift balls before graduating to organized play with real equipment. Problem was, he wasn't very good. Released by one of the worst teams in the Nicaraguan leagues, he signed with the Tiburones as a 120-pound third baseman at age 17. When manager Heberto Portobanco saw him messing around with curveballs in practice one day, he moved Martinez to the mound. That curveball, a pitch that often started at a hitter's eyes and ended at his knees, became Martinez's raison d'être.

"It was a natural pitch for me," said Martinez in a 2012 interview. When Martinez came of age as a pitcher, the slider was becoming the trendy secondary pitch to complement the fastball, since few could command a big, 12-to-6 curve. Martinez had no such problems. "I knew how to handle it from the get-go. All other pitches developed around my curveball."

Martinez's prospects shot up soon after his conversion to pitching. In 1973, he started in the gold-medal game of the Amateur World Series. He lost 1–0 to Team USA in 10 innings, but showed enough to impress Baltimore Orioles scouts Julio Blanco Herrera and Ray Poitevint, who signed him to a contract. Three years later, at 21, Martinez made the Show. Earl Weaver liked to ease young pitchers into the rotation gradually, and Martinez was no exception: in 1977, Martinez's first full year in the big leagues, he made 42 appearances, only 13 of them starts.

After that, however, he quickly developed into one of the most durable starters in baseball. Wielding four- and two-seam fastballs, a changeup, and his trademark curve, Martinez was a pitch-to-contact guy, which worked for him thanks to the perennially strong Orioles defence that was one of the pillars of Weaver's strategy. In 1979, just Martinez's second season as a full-time starter, he led the league in starts (39), complete games (18), and innings pitched.

Despite those achievements, though, Martinez felt underappreciated in Baltimore, pitching in the shadow of future Hall of Famer Jim Palmer and talented lefties Mike Flanagan and Scott McGregor. That insecurity formed a toxic mix with the same demon that haunted his father: the bottle. The day he lost that Amateur World Series heartbreaker, Martinez had been scheduled to meet with the O's scout. To calm his nerves, the captain of the Nicaraguan team slipped him a bottle of rum. Martinez took one shot, then a few more. That was the start of a 10-year battle, one that clouded Martinez's self-image and eventually wrecked his performance.

"I never got the credit I thought I deserved," Martinez said. "I looked at it like I was the scapegoat, the black sheep of the staff. Mainly because people didn't understand me. They called me a hard-headed boy, the guy who didn't listen. It's not an excuse, but sometimes having that resentment, that frustration—sooner or later it puts you in a bad situation, especially in the lifestyle we were in, to be pushed to drinking. I was one of the weak people. I avoided facing reality, that frustration I was going through."

In 1983, he finally checked himself into rehab. The Orioles won the World Series that year, without Martinez throwing a single pitch in the playoffs. The next three years, Martinez said, were all about his recovery, not his pitching. And it showed: he posted the worst numbers of his career from 1983 through '86, with a 29–42 record and an ERA over 5.00. A month past his 31st birthday, his last quality season four years gone, Martinez needed a second chance. He needed a desperate team.

Enter the '86 Expos. But despite their obvious needs, they didn't hand Martinez anything. Rather than toss him into the rotation, the Expos first used Martinez in relief. It was a complete disaster. The Pirates jumped on him immediately, piling up the runs, and Martinez kept looking back to the dugout, hoping for some sign from Buck Rodgers that the Expos skipper might let him off the hook. Nada. Martinez's final line that day: 3⅔ innings, nine hits, nine runs.

"They let me *wear* it, man," Martinez recalled, laughing a lot more 26 years later than he did then. "I was so miserable. I just let it all out, all the bad things, all the demons. After that, I started seeing the light at the end of the tunnel."

In his first meeting with Larry Bearnarth, the Expos' soft-spoken pitching coach told Martinez to forget his past struggles, that he should do what he'd always done and not worry about tinkering with his approach. Martinez made three relief outings, then joined the rotation in early July and pitched well enough the rest of the way—just 3–6, but with decent numbers otherwise—to merit another shot, somewhere. After an off-season in limbo due to his lousy four-year stretch, Martinez re-signed with Montreal, then got shuttled to Triple-A to start the 1987 season. On June

10, he finally got his first start back in the majors. Facing the same Pirates team that destroyed him a year earlier, Martinez threw seven strong innings, permitting just two runs and three hits. That start launched a huge comeback season in which Martinez went 11–4 with a 3.30 ERA in 22 starts. This was the beginning of the best six-year run of Martinez's career—even better than his heyday with the Orioles. Harnessing the location on his fastball to go with his knockout curve, Martinez made three All-Star teams in the next six seasons, four times posting ERAs below 3.00.

Led by Raines and Wallach, strong relief pitching from the tandem of Tim Burke and Andy McGaffigan, and the twin revivals of Perez and Martinez, the '87 Expos closed to within two games of first place with 15 to play . . . but got no closer. They finished the season 91–71, just four games behind the first-place Cardinals. They went 82–57 with Raines in the lineup, but just 9–14 without him. It might be a stretch to say that having Raines available in April would've swung the pennant race, but still, this was another what-if season for a franchise that just kept racking them up.

Meanwhile, after three seasons as GM, Cook was abruptly fired in August of '87. His dismissal wasn't due to poor performance by the Expos. Instead, it was over an affair he had with Pamela Brochu, team president Claude Brochu's wife. Bill Stoneman took over the general manager's job for a few months on an interim basis before giving way to farm director Dave Dombrowski in July 1988. The team obsessed with young talent on the field was now trying the same tack off the field: at 31 years old, Dombrowski became the youngest GM in baseball.

Dombrowski and company didn't have much to celebrate in '88. For starters, Opening Day was a bloodbath. The visiting Mets were a powerhouse, and this was one of their best performances. New York blasted six home runs at Olympic Stadium that day en route to a 10–6 win. The *coup de grâce* came in the seventh. With one out, Darryl Strawberry came to bat, facing reliever Randy St. Claire. Strawberry had already homered off Martinez. This time, he got a belt-high fastball out over the plate, and annihilated it.

It was Easter Monday, and I was there. Even though it was Opening Day and a packed house was expected, I didn't buy tickets in advance. Normally, that meant grabbing four or five buddies, buying cheap seats, then sneaking down to our preferred spot: section 117, first-base side, just past the base, 30 rows up. Since 55,412 others showed up that day, however, the best I could do were seats way down the line in left field in the upper deck, a nosebleed section of the stadium that in later years would be sealed off on account of apathy. This was so high up, it felt like you could reach out and touch the Big O's ugly orange roof. After Strawberry's blast, I could confirm that wasn't true. Because Straw took that batting-practice fastball and blasted it higher and farther than any ball I've ever seen, a majestic shot that carried and carried . . . and struck the concrete ring at the top of the stadium, just missing the vast expanse of orange Kevlar.

Mets fans and Expos fans still talk about that moonshot, about Strawberry, and about the worst omen a team could ever have on Opening Day.

By the third week of May, the Expos sat more than 10 games behind the division leader; by year's end they'd just managed a .500 record, falling 20 games short of the NL East–winning Mets. There were a few bright spots, though. Perez and Martinez continued their renaissances, and those two right-handers, along with the rest of the staff, got lots of support from a much stronger defensive middle infield. Tom Foley and especially Luis Rivera didn't hit much, but they were still big defensive improvements over Vance Law (gone via free agency) and Hubie Brooks (moved to right field, where he looked a lot better). Wallach won his second Gold Glove at third base while Galarraga earned his

"Big Cat" nickname as the most agile first baseman to ever play for the Expos. The additions of veteran castoffs Otis Nixon and Rex Hudler added 75 stolen bases from two part-time players. But the team just couldn't hit. Rookie Nelson Santovenia became the latest Expos catcher to make too many outs since Gary Carter's departure, and Wallach had a down year at the plate.

It was also time to accept that another prospect had flamed out. Though Brooks put up some pretty good numbers during his five seasons in Montreal, Floyd Youmans was supposed to be the gem of the Carter trade. Instead, he was a bust. In his one good season, 1986, the right-hander tossed 219 innings with a 3.53 ERA, but still led the league in walks. It all collapsed after that, in an all-too-familiar pattern. After an injury-plagued 1987 season, he checked into rehab, hoping to kick alcoholism. In '88, he managed just 13 starts, missing a huge chunk of the season after getting suspended for cocaine use. Then there were the terrible work habits that left him overweight and unable to harness the blazing fastball and promising secondary stuff that once portended future stardom.

Like Ellis Valentine, Youmans says he's a changed man now, having learned from a wasted youth. "I just had to grow up, man," Youmans told me in 2013. "I just had to understand. With my kids now, I teach them lessons, help them understand consequences. That it's not always about you, it's also other people. As a young person, when you're going through that, you have to think about who are you hurting." Unfortunately, Youmans' lessons came too late for the Expos, who traded him to Philadelphia after the 1988 season. He lasted just one more year in the big leagues, finished at 25.

If big-ticket free agents wouldn't come to Montreal, Dombrowski would find other ways to build a winning roster. While Murray Cook had gotten forced into a blockbuster trade due to owner disenchantment, and John McHale was usually too complacent to pull the trigger, Dombrowski showed he was willing to make aggressive deals to improve the team.

It started in December of '88, when Dombrowski flipped Youmans and Jeff Parrett to Philly for right-hander Kevin Gross. Parrett was coming off a big year in relief, having tossed 91⅔ innings with a 2.65 ERA that offered a great sell-high opportunity. Dombrowski figured the veteran Gross would soak up some innings, and that the bullpen was deep enough to overcome Parrett's loss. Two days later, Dombrowski upgraded the shortstop position, a problem for nearly every one of the Expos' first 20 seasons. The trade sent young right-handed starter John Dopson and punchless shortstop Luis Rivera to Boston for a hoped-for boost in veteran Spike Owen. Failing to find an elite second baseman to fill another historically weak position, the Expos GM instead signed veteran Damaso Garcia, then slotted him into a half-decent, low-cost platoon with incumbent Tom Foley. Add to that a centre-field platoon featuring Dave Martinez (acquired two years earlier, just nine days into Dombrowski's GM tenure) and Otis Nixon, and you had a team still short on stars, but more intelligently built, with more depth, than most Expos rosters before it.

Things didn't go quite as hoped to start the year, though. Expected to lean heavily on quality pitching, the Expos instead got the ugly version of Pascual Perez. First came a relapse of his cocaine habit, one that landed him in rehab in early February and left his status for the start of the season in doubt. Though he made it back in time for spring training, he went 0–7 with a 5.04 ERA to start the season, temporarily losing his spot in the rotation. Perez's seventh loss came against the Dodgers on May 20, the Expos' fifth straight defeat. It dropped them to two games under .500 and fourth place in the NL East. Another disappointing year seemed inevitable.

Charles Bronfman had other ideas. What started as an inkling to sell the team had grown into a full-blown notion, as Bronfman had grown increasingly bitter and disillusioned while wrestling with the cost of doing business, the sagging attendance, and the annual seven-figure losses. If he was getting out, though, Bronfman figured he should try to go out on top.

Word was getting around that the Mariners were willing to trade star lefty Mark Langston. Over the previous three seasons, only Roger Clemens had thrown more innings and struck out more batters than the 28-year-old Langston. When rumours started swirling that the Expos were not only interested but also a real threat to get him, no one could believe it. Trading for a high-priced star was something they'd never done—much less when that star was a few months away from free agency, and the price would be multiple premium prospects.

"The Mets were interested too," said Dombrowski in a 2012 interview. "We knew we'd have to give up a lot, and we didn't know if we'd be able to re-sign him. But we also knew we'd get two draft choices as compensation if we couldn't keep him. Really it came down to this: Charles wanted to win."

On May 25, the trade was made. Coming to the Expos were Langston and a player to be named later (Mike Campbell, a first-round pick who would never pitch for Montreal). Going to Seattle was a trio of high-quality pitching prospects. First was Gene Harris, a righty flamethrower whom the Expos considered the prize of the deal, then Brian Holman, a right-hander who projected as a number-four starter. The third was a gangly left-hander who threw harder than any other lefty in the game, but was so raw that half the time neither he nor the batter had any idea where his pitches were going. "No one knew," said Dombrowski, "that Randy Johnson would become that good."

Also, no one on the Expos roster that season cared. When word

spread that Montreal had made a go-for-it trade of that magnitude, the reaction was one of shock—and joy.

"I just thought, 'Oh man, we're going for it!'" said Dave
Martinez. "'This is *awesome.*'"

"I got back to my hotel room," said *le Journal de Montreal*
writer Serge Touchette. "Tim Wallach had called me. He'd asked
me if it was a joke. I called him back and said, 'No, Tim, it's true.'
He just started yelling into the phone."

The trade didn't just lift the team's spirits: it marked the start
of a big run. In the first series following the deal, the Expos took
two out of three in San Diego. Langston started the final game
of the set and absolutely bulldozed the Padres. In eight innings,
Montreal's new ace surrendered just one earned run on four hits,
striking out 12. A two-hour drive north brought the Expos to L.A.,
where they took two out of three from the Dodgers. And after a
long flight, they capped the road trip by sweeping three from the
Phillies. That series included Langston's second start as an Expo,
and it was another gem: eight innings, one run, five hits, nine punchouts. Throughout Expos history, West Coast swings had turned
into graveyards for the team's playoff chances. This time—counting the three-game set played just before the trade—it netted a
6–3 record. Throw in the sweep at Philly, and you had one of the
franchise's most successful road trips ever, one that left Montreal
just a game out of first place. Three weeks after that, in the middle
of what would become a six-game winning streak, they grabbed
sole possession of first place.

Time to double down. On July 2, Dombrowski flipped
three prospects to the Braves for lefty Zane Smith. Normally a
decent back-of-the-rotation starter, Smith couldn't find a spot
in Montreal's loaded starting five, not with Langston, Dennis
Martinez, Bryn Smith, Gross, and a rejuvenated Pascual Perez
healthy and producing. Instead, the Expos found a capable

left-handed relief pitcher who excelled for the rest of the season, tossing 48 innings with a 1.50 ERA as a bridge to Burke at the back of the bullpen. Two weeks after picking up Smith, Perez out-duelled Tom Glavine to beat Atlanta 5–2. That win improved the Expos' record to 53–39, good for a 3½-game division lead.

That wasn't even the most exciting part. After years sitting in a warehouse in France, then a few more years slapped onto the top of the stadium, the Big O's orange roof finally did what it was sup-posed to do. It was a miracle: the piece of crap finally opened.

I missed it all. Thanks to a class trip, I spent nine weeks that summer in Israel. Years before the proliferation of Internet and cellphones, with each long-distance call home costing a week's worth of pizza, my buddies and I searched for the tiniest scraps of Expos news wherever we could find them. Our parents mailed us clippings from the *Montreal Gazette* from notable games, so we could catch up on events of two or three weeks earlier. There was the 10-inning slugfest in Houston on July 7, won by a Tom Foley bloop single off Danny Darwin. The 12–4 rout of the Reds on July 23, in which Ken Griffey Sr.'s two home runs were answered by . . . two homers from *Mike Fitzgerald* in a five-RBI game that was probably the best of his career. Then there were the regular beatings laid on opponents by Langston—most notably the two-hit shutout with 10 strikeouts in Atlanta July 3, and the back-to-back complete games in late July against Cincinnati and Pittsburgh, in which Langston struck out 23 batters and allowed just one run.

Screaming crowds of 35,000, even 40,000-plus started showing up to the ballpark, toting armfuls of cardboard Ks to mark each Langston strikeout. The venerable Peter Gammons wrote a huge *Sports Illustrated* summer story on the Expos, in which he waxed optimistic on the team's chances ("After 20 years of disappoint-ment, the Expos are suddenly, well, maybe not America's Team, maybe not even Canada's Team, but they are a team that believes in itself and believes that it can win the National League East"). Gammons also quoted Bryn Smith complaining about Quebeckers serving gravy instead of ketchup with fries, and Smith's wife, Patti, lamenting her periodic drives across the U.S. border to buy Doritos (never mind that any proper *casse-croûte* had ketchup aplenty, and many *dépanneurs* carried Doritos). From nine thousand kilometres away, getting news of this first-place team in dribs and drabs, it all seemed like some kind of fever dream. But back home, people were starting to believe.

"As the season unfolded, there was a sense that the team had a chance to do something," said former Expos broadcaster Jerry Trupiano. "Expectations really went up after the Langston deal. Then they kept winning. [Legendary broadcaster] Jack Buck even said to me, 'You're going to get a ring this year.'"

On August 2 against the Pirates, Perez fired eight strong innings en route to a 3–1 victory. That marked the Expos' third straight win, moved them to a season-best 19 games over .500, and capped a seven-start stretch for the lanky Dominican in which he posted a 2.38 ERA with a 5-to-1 strikeout-to-walk rate. After that game, Montreal led the division by three games. The pitching-and-defence plan was working: the Mets were in the midst of a big dip following their huge 1988 season, and the rest of the NL East looked weak. The second Expos playoff berth in 21 years seemed ripe.

"I remember when we were supposed to be the team of the '80s, but then we didn't win and the place went dead," Raines told Gammons in that *SI* article. "Then [Gary] Carter and [Jeff] Reardon were traded, Andre [Dawson] left, and it looked like the franchise was dying. I know I wouldn't be here if collusion hadn't prevented me from going elsewhere. But I'm glad I didn't go. This is the most fun I've ever had. It used to be that all you ever heard around the clubhouse was how tough it is to play in a foreign city.

Now, all you hear about is how this is the happiest summer of everyone's baseball life."

Then the heartbreaking losses started.

The day after Perez's great start led to a win, Dennis Martinez's seven shutout innings weren't enough against the Pirates as mediocre right-hander Bob Walk dominated and the Expos finally lost in the 12th inning on a single by bench jockey Benny Distefano. Three days later, five Mets pitchers steamrolled the Expos lineup, leading to a 2–1, 14-inning loss on Kevin McReynolds' walk-off homer. From August 3 to August 23, the Expos went 0–3 in extra-inning games, 0–5 in one-run games, and dropped 14 of 20 overall.

The last of those losses might be the craziest game the Expos ever played. For sure, it was the craziest game I ever saw.

ᐳ TWENTY-TWO INNINGS ᐸ

We'd been back for a week from our summer-long trip when the Expos capped a 13-game home stand with a Wednesday night tilt against the Dodgers. Our team was no longer in first place, but still stood just two games out, very much in the race. After two months away from the Big O, it was time to go back. My buddy Bean and I met up at the du Collège Metro stop, and off we went.

Starting for the Expos was Perez, by now completely free of his early-season struggles and coming off a complete-game win over the Padres. Starting for the Dodgers was Orel Hershiser, the defending Cy Young Award winner. With two of the best pitchers in the league and a Dodgers team that didn't hit a lick all year, the ingredients were there for a low-scoring game. Nobody had any idea *how* low-scoring.

The Expos threatened in the early innings. They put a runner on third with two outs in the first but failed to score. Two singles in the second also netted nothing. The Dodgers didn't do anything at all until the fifth, when a leadoff single went nowhere. In the eighth, L.A. put runners on second and third with one out, then pinch-hit for Hershiser. But Perez struck out Mike Sharperson, then got Alfredo Griffin to line out, keeping the game scoreless.

Weird tactical moves started piling up. Rookie Larry Walker, playing in just his seventh major league game, was batting second. Manager Buck Rodgers apparently trusted Walker enough to bat that high in the order but not to swing away, and had ordered him to sacrifice in the bottom of the first after leadoff hitter Dave Martinez had gotten on with a single. In the bottom of the eighth, after ace pinch-hitter Wallace Johnson led off with a single, base-stealing machine Otis Nixon pinch-ran, but Rodgers ordered another bunt anyway. Again, the Expos didn't score.

The game stayed scoreless through the ninth and on into extra innings. The crowd of 21,742 started thinning out. Bean and I ditched the bleachers and snuck over to section 117. We ran into Brian (another one of the core group of diehards who bought walk-up bleacher seats 30 to 40 times a year) and his parents. They left after the 12th inning, the game still scoreless. Two guys two grades above us were downtown listening to the game, then drove over to the ballpark on a whim. They made it for the 13th, walked right in without paying, and ended up getting a full nine innings for their zero-dollar investment.

The game got more and more surreal as the innings ticked away. At one point we noticed a commotion from the Los Angeles dugout. Dodgers manager Tommy Lasorda was yelling about something; about what, we couldn't tell. Red-faced, he stomped over to home-plate umpire Greg Bonin, then unloaded a river of spittle in his face. A minute later, Bonin pointed to the top of the dugout. Turned out Lasorda had been kvetching about an unwelcome visitor. Youppi!, the Expos mascot, had been dancing on the heads of Lasorda and his players for the better part of two innings. When Youppi! pulled off his signature move, getting a running start then belly-flopping with a loud thud on the dugout to mimic a slide into second base, the Dodgers skipper snapped. He'd been nodding off in the dugout, and didn't appreciate being startled out of his nap. Bonin responded by doing something that had never been done in a major league game: he ejected the mascot.

For the few thousand fans still left in the ballpark, this was an outrage. In 1978, the Expos had introduced their first mascot, a freakish-looking cross between Mr. Met and Evel Knievel called Souki. He was a disaster, a sight so scary to kids that a father attacked him. Youppi! (French for "Yippee!") replaced Souki, and was an instant hit. Designed by Bonnie Erickson, creator of Miss Piggy and several other Muppets, Youppi! was a giant orange furball partly modelled after the Philly Phanatic, another Erickson creation. We all adored him as kids, posing for pictures with him, giggling

Souki, we hardly knew ye.

when he bopped his nose, a move that made his googly eyes bounce around (but was really just Youppi! repositioning his huge fuzzy head so he could see). We used to invent origin stories to explain his massive body and head-to-toe orange fur. The best theory we came up with was that he was a cat caught up on the Big O's roof, struck by lightning and transformed into the lovable creature who roamed the aisles and danced on the dugouts. The alternate theory was that Youppi! was Hubie Brooks in disguise. Whoever or whatever he was, an umpire tossing him from the game was a grave injustice. Tommy Lasorda would be on our shit list forever more.

The game only got nuttier from there. In the bottom of the 16th, the Expos looked like they were about to win it as a pair of singles and an intentional walk loaded the bases with nobody out. Wallach hit a flyball to centre, but not deep enough to drive in the winning run. Fitzgerald then hit a shallow flyball down the right-field line: Mickey Hatcher made the catch and threw home, but not in time to get Walker at the plate. Game over, Expos win.

Well, not quite. The Dodgers appealed at third base, arguing that Walker had left the bag too early. Bob Davidson agreed, calling Walker out and ending the inning. We were going to the 17th, still scoreless.

In the top of the 18th, it was the Expos' turn to catch a break. With a runner on first and two outs, Eddie Murray lined a ball all the way to the wall in right. Walker raced back after it and appeared to make a spectacular catch. Again, not quite. Replays later showed that he'd trapped the ball against the wall (MLB rules state that a ball must be caught in flight for an out). The initial ruling held. More baseball. More insanity.

In the meantime, Youppi! was allowed back into the game, on the condition that he stay on the Expos dugout and not venture over to the Dodgers' side. By game's end he was wearing Youppi!-sized pajamas, entertaining the three hundred of us crazy enough to stay the six hours and 14 minutes it would take to finish the game.

We reached that ending in the 22nd when the Dodgers' 25th man, backup catcher Rick Dempsey, came to the plate. Always a poor hitter (he batted .179 that year and .233 with just 96 homers in 1,766 career games), Dempsey was now almost 40 years old, hanging on as a little-used backup. Pitching for the Expos was Dennis Martinez. The team's number-two starter, Martinez hadn't pitched in relief in three years—but with the game going deep into the night, he lobbied Rodgers relentlessly to put him in the game.

"He kept yelling at Buck, 'Put me in the game, put me in the game, I want to save the game!'" recalled Dave Martinez.

He didn't save it. Instead, he left a pitch up, and Dempsey jumped all over it, jerking it down the left-field line for a home run no one expected. In the bottom of the 22nd, Dempsey would solidify his hero status. With two outs, Rex Hudler singled, then tried to steal second, only for Dempsey to gun him out. Game over. For real this time.

The only people happier than the players and umpires to go home that night were the broadcasters. "I could have kissed Rick Dempsey," said Trupiano, who handled play-by-play for all 22 innings.

At least Trup had broadcast partner Bobby Winkles with him. With Vin Scully and Don Drysdale away on other business, Dodgers play-by-play man Ross Porter called the entire 22-inning game by himself, the longest solo broadcast in major league history. "My wife, Lin, who was with me on the trip, sat next to me in the booth," Porter recounted 25 years later. "The game was scoreless for 15 innings. Lin asked me if she could get me a drink. I said no because there was no time to get to the restroom and back, if necessary."

As for the Expos, they never got any closer to first place after that game, somehow ending the season with just a .500 record following a September collapse. But hey, maybe we should have seen this coming, given the bad omen they'd received a few weeks earlier. The day after that glorious July night in which they got the retractable roof they'd been craving for 20 years to finally work, high winds prevented workers from closing it. When heavy rain followed and delayed the game for two hours, fans responded by running to the ticket office to ask for their money back. The retractable roof never worked properly for the rest of the Expos' existence.

Langston left at the end of the year, adding a cruel epilogue to a crueller season. Most people around the team—the players, the writers, Dombrowski, and especially Bronfman—stand by the trade, given the information available at the time. The one notable critic was Claude Brochu. Sure, the Expos president regretted parting with Randy Johnson, who went on to become a certain Hall of Famer. But to Brochu, the enduring lesson was that the cash-strapped Expos couldn't afford to take big risks.

"John McHale had said to me, 'When you get a chance to go for the brass ring, go for it,'" Brochu told me in a 2012 interview in Montreal. "I did it then. But after that year, I said, 'Nah, nah, nah. I'm not doing this again.' It's too risky for us."

That obsession with risk avoidance was about to become *the* story of the Expos. As much as the Expos had come to be known as a powerhouse of scouting and player development, their inability to pay for talent or even keep the players they had would become an equally enduring legacy.

CHAPTER EIGHT

Prelude to a Winner (1990–1993)

For 20 years, Charles Bronfman loved nothing better than to spend an evening at the ballpark. But one night in September 1989, things changed. Bronfman and his wife, Andy, had plans to join minority owner and long-time friend Hugh Hallward and his wife, Martha, at the Big O for a game. By that point, the Expos were all but eliminated from the NL East race, having blown a division lead that lasted for much of the summer. Still, Bronfman had been to countless games with nothing on the line, lived through plenty of disappointing seasons, and still shown up. Not this time. Just as they were about to leave for the ballpark, Charles called Hallward.

"I said, 'I know we're supposed to go to the game, but there's this nice Italian restaurant I've been hearing about,'" recalled Bronfman. "'Do you want to go there?' So we went to the restaurant and sat down. I looked Hugh in the eye and said, 'Hugh, do you know what this means?' He said, 'Yeah, I know what it means.' So we raised a glass, and said, 'Okay, we're for sale.'"

Bronfman didn't think his team would fetch a big sale price: this was years before franchise values took off, before massive national TV deals became the norm, and before a low-revenue team like the Expos could count on revenue sharing to make the club more financially viable. He figured he might be able to pull in $50 million; team president and Bronfman confidant Claude Brochu figured maybe $75 million. Bronfman was skeptical—both of the number and the idea that someone in Quebec would pay that price and keep the team in *la belle province*. But Bronfman liked Brochu's optimism and trusted his judgment. The Expos owner handed Brochu the task of finding a buyer.

Though Bronfman had made up his mind months before, he didn't actually announce his intention to sell the team until January 1990. American prospective buyers immediately began formulating their plans, and in August, a front-page story in the *Montreal Gazette* dropped a bombshell: a group of Miami investors had offered $135 million to move the Expos to South Florida. That figure threw everyone for a loop. Maybe Bronfman and Brochu had underestimated the growth potential for both the team and the sport? The good news for local fans was that Commissioner Fay Vincent threw his support behind Montreal, saying he didn't want the team to move. Still, finding a well-heeled local group that would pay up like the group in Miami was another story.

Before asking Brochu to start looking, Bronfman had approached Paul Desmarais, head of Power Corporation of Canada and one of the country's richest people, about becoming his partner and a minority Expos owner. Desmarais declined. Brochu's own early attempts to find investors also went nowhere.

"At the beginning, nobody on the private side wanted to touch this thing," Brochu said. "Baseball had labour problems, bad PR, salaries were out of control, spoiled players, drugs, all this stuff.

They all said, 'Geez, we don't want any of this.' So we needed to find another way to get the ball rolling."

To help his search, Brochu teamed up with Jacques Ménard, president of the Montreal Chamber of Commerce and head of Burns Fry, a company that specialized in mergers, acquisitions, and company financing. Both men agreed that getting blessings (and money) from various levels of government would be the best way to rope Canadian companies into the cause.

First, Brochu and Ménard approached Montreal mayor Jean Doré to gauge the city's interest. If the province gets on board, the mayor said, the city would too—so they went to Quebec premier Robert Bourassa. Though the premier wouldn't authorize direct subsidies, he green-lit the Société de développement industriel (an investment arm of the provincial government) to join the cause. Between the city and the province, Brochu and Ménard had secured a combined $33 million investment. This was a vital step in the process, especially north of the border.

"In the United States, governments play no role in the sale of a professional baseball team," Brochu wrote in his book, *My Turn at Bat*. "In Canada, particularly in Quebec, the situation is different. In the United States, the wealth is often long-standing and in the hands of individuals and private companies, while in Quebec— with a few exceptions—wealth is recent and institutional."

With those public-sector funds secure, Brochu and Ménard could circle back to the private sector for the rest. Again, they hit a brick wall. Desmarais told Brochu and Ménard that he knew nothing about baseball and "preferred hockey anyway." Jacques Francoeur of Unimédia said he was too old to get involved. Pharmacy magnate Jean Coutu found the $5 million buy-in for each investor too high. Pierre Péladeau, head of media conglomerate Quebecor, didn't see the ball club's profit potential. Bertin Nadeau, president of grocery store chain Provigo, wanted to "let others have the opportunity." Raymond Malenfant, who'd made a fortune in the hotel business, said "no Quebecker had the financial wherewithal to buy the Expos, except Charles Bronfman."

Even Bronfman's friend and co-owner Hallward didn't have much faith. He told his friends in the business community not to get involved since the Canadian dollar was only going to get weaker, making the team's problem of Canadian-dollar revenue and American-dollar expenditures even worse. He would prove to be right. If anything, he'd undersold the downside. The Canadian dollar didn't merely drop to 80 cents U.S.: it would plummet to *63 cents* in the early aughts—a freefall that would hurt the Expos' ability to do business. All the same, it wasn't what Brochu and Ménard wanted to hear in the middle of their buyer recruitment drive.

By July 1990, Brochu and Ménard still hadn't reeled in any major private-sector investors, so in order to speed up the process, they announced a September 1 deadline. Then they harangued two existing team sponsors, Labatt and Petro-Canada, into re-upping their sponsorship deals at higher rates (Labatt for five years and $35 million; Petro-Canada for four years and $16 million). Finally, the business community snapped into action. Canadian Pacific was in. So too were Quebec-based Desjardins Group (the largest association of credit unions in North America) and investment firm Nesbitt Burns. Brochu himself bought in: Bronfman had promised him a $500,000 sales commission for brokering the deal, but instead, Brochu asked for and got two $1 million loans from Bronfman (one of those interest-free), enabling him to take a $2 million stake in the team his soon-to-be former boss was selling.

Even with these and other commitments, the tally (combined with government contributions) didn't add up to the $100 million target price. So the next target became an investor willing to put up a chunk of cash while keeping the team in Montreal and remaining just a minority partner.

A New York art dealer expressed interest. Brochu and Ménard held several meetings with him. An avid baseball fan, he owned the Triple-A Oklahoma City team and dreamed of one day owning a major league club. Turned out he was a tough and stubborn negotiator, and wasn't interested in any arrangement other than his assuming controlling interest in the team. The two sides broke off talks, but it would not be the last time the Expos crossed paths with Jeffrey Loria.

Brochu and Ménard circled back to investors in Quebec, and as the list of committed minority partners grew, so too did the hope that this would work. Ultimately they'd be backed by some of the biggest and most respected businesses in Quebec—13 in all.

On November 29, 1990, the deal was done. The Expos had been saved, and would stay in Montreal.

Even so, the actions of a few partners foreshadowed future boardroom rancour. While Brochu and Ménard courted more buyers, two of those already on board—Claude Blanchet of the Fonds de solidarité des travailleurs du Quebec (the largest labour-backed investment fund in Canada) and Guy Langlois of Provigo—had tried to negotiate on the future consortium's behalf. They met privately with various existing Expos partners, including the Olympic Installations Board, in an effort to trim the Expos' operating costs and generate more revenue. Blanchet also complained to the media about Bronfman's total asking price— conveniently ignoring the much larger offer from the Miami group that had been turned down to keep the Expos in Montreal. Both groups would eventually fall into line, ponying up the $5 million investments and withdrawing their complaints. But partners taking team-related negotiations into their own hands—with one of them venting to reporters before a deal was even done—didn't bode well.

Another red flag came from Raymond Cyr of Bell Canada, a telecommunications and media juggernaut needed more for its clout than its $5 million investment (chump change for an entity that size). Brochu and Ménard had approached Cyr multiple times, only to walk away with nothing to show for it. This time, however, Cyr said yes. Brochu recounted the scene in *My Turn at Bat*:

"Cigar in his mouth, an amused look on his face, [Cyr] joked, 'Listen. I'm prepared to make a *donation*. Five million. But on one condition: that you never bother me about it again! Understood? *Never*.'"

As Brochu told it, everyone in the room burst out laughing. But Cyr's point lingered in the air like the blanket of smoke wafting from his cigar. *Never again*. No matter what happened to player salaries, no matter what kind of financial challenges the group might face in the coming years, under no circumstances could Brochu come back and ask for more money. Though the other partners didn't say so as explicitly, they would end up taking the same stance. Brochu had to hope that either revenue streams would soar or that the cost of running a baseball team would remain totally static after November 29, 1990. Because come hell or high water, few of Brochu's partners were going to chip in one additional penny to bail out the Expos.

Like every Expos squad but one before it, the 1990 team didn't win anything. That year's ball club did hold one special distinction, though: Delino DeShields, Marquis Grissom, and Larry Walker all were rookies. They laid the foundation for what would become the best team in franchise history.

A first-round pick out of Delaware's Seaford High School three years earlier, DeShields raced through the minor leagues, literally and figuratively. Nicknamed "Bop," he wasn't known for his pop, slugging just .379 during that time. He didn't hit for a high average either, batting just .252. But in two-and-a-half seasons on the farm, he swiped 142 bases and showed an excellent batting eye.

DeShields again turned on the jets in his rookie season. Appearing in 129 games, DeShields stole 42 bases, hitting .289 with a .375 on-base percentage while leading off for most of the year. His major league debut came on Opening Day in St. Louis, and it was a gem: four hits, two runs scored, three double plays turned—and yes, a stolen base. Fans like me loved the guy right away, so when the Expos returned to Montreal for their first homestand, my buddies and I came prepared. Terminally bored in high-school art class, we put our time to good use by making a gigantic sign. It was a simple message for our new favourite second baseman: Delino DeShields—DeRookie of DeYear.

Bop didn't quite win DeAward, but he did finish second behind Braves outfielder David Justice. He also made a big impression, not only on Expos fans but also on the rest of the league. DeShields credits his minor league coaches and instructors—a competitive advantage that the Expos enjoyed for most of their existence—for his ability to hit the ground running as a 21-year-old rookie.

"Extra groundballs and batting practice, all of that is a given," DeShields told me in 2012. "What accelerated my growth with the Expos were the guys instructing me. Jerry Manuel was in our organization as a coordinator; not only was he a good teacher, he also connected with kids. I played for [long-time major league superutilityman] Alan Bannister, who also understood what it took to be a big leaguer, and taught me how to get there."

Now a minor league manager himself, DeShields took those early coaching lessons to heart. "It's about getting between kids' ears," he said. "That's how you help good players become elite."

One of the other kids, and DeShields' running mate in both the minors and then the big leagues, was Marquis Grissom.

Grissom wasn't quite as prolific a thief in the minors as DeShields, swiping 64 bags in 206 games. But he wielded a broader set of skills. Like DeShields, Grissom leveraged his quickness and instincts into excellent defence, in his case as a centre fielder. He also hit just a tick below .300 in the minors and cranked 70 extra-base hits in those 206 games. He was older than Bop, having come out of Florida A&M like Andre Dawson, but was still considered a top young talent, having been named the 17th-best prospect by *Baseball America* before the start of the 1990 season.

Their teammate Larry Walker was cut from a different cloth. Walker grew up in Maple Ridge, British Columbia. He had raw talent as a baseball player, but he didn't project as someone who would make the big leagues—much less become a star. As a kid, Walker hadn't lived and died with baseball (instead playing more hockey), and he hadn't mastered the subtleties of the game because he hadn't played enough to do so. His motivation for signing with the Expos out of high school was pragmatic . . . and kind of hilarious.

"They offered me $1,500 U.S.—almost $2,000 Canadian! So that was pretty cool," Walker said in a 2013 interview.

Initially, Walker didn't understand the significance of signing, or the loneliness that would kick in when he left home for the first time to play in West Palm Beach, Florida. What he did understand was that his game needed lots of work. "At the beginning I sucked. The thought of actually playing in Montreal wasn't there. I had to learn the game. I played more fast-pitch [softball] than I did baseball for a little while there [as a teenager]. Americans grow up with baseball in high school, but I was slower to pick it up. I had a long way to go. Base running, fielding—that for me was fairly simple. My approach to hitting was, 'Guy throws the ball, I try to hit it. If I hit it, I run.' But the hard part was hitting something with a wrinkle in it. I had never seen a forkball before. Sliders and curves killed me."

Fortunately, Walker was supernaturally talented. DeShields remembered Walker dominating effortlessly at all kinds of games: golf, ping-pong, you name it. "Freaky hand-eye coordination," said Bop.

Walker was also one of the most fun-loving Expos of all time. The man they called "Booger" never took baseball—or himself—too seriously. He used a wide array of jokester gear: red clown shoes in his locker, plus diapers and a ballerina outfit that he'd make teammates wear (even when it wasn't officially hazing time). He was also a serial nap-taker. Any sliver of free time before the game, he jumped at the chance for some shut-eye, curling up on the floor in the corner of the clubhouse. He'd need someone to wake him for batting practice, or even the start of the game. When he woke, he was good to go—the type of hitter who could literally roll out of bed (or off the floor) and go 3 for 4.

Also, nothing could gross the guy out, whether he was belching out the entire alphabet, or performing various disgusting parlour tricks.

"I remember when we used to go to old Busch Stadium in St. Louis," said Darrin Fletcher, who joined the Expos after a trade with Philadelphia in December 1991. "There used to be a hot tub in the visitors' locker room. Larry would get in after the game and coax a few players into a bet: how long could he hold his breath under water. Younger players would say 45 seconds, tops. The veterans, we knew, so we'd put money on it. It'd be three, four minutes every time. Larry would duck his head under the water, then put his mouth on one of the jets that had an air pump, and breathe the air. Thinking of all the players who'd been in that hot tub after games, and I'm guessing how rarely they cleaned it . . . there's no way I would try it, let's put it that way. Didn't bother him one bit."

My idiot buddies and I loved Walker from the start. In another art class project, we made a giant sign honouring Walker's

hometown of Maple Ridge (and sending up the old country band the Oak Ridge Boys), declaring ourselves the Maple Ridge Boys. Though sneaking over to better seats remained our go-to move, we found ourselves staying put in the right-field bleachers more and more often, flashing our sign. A man of the people, Walker turned to the crowd and acknowledged us on multiple occasions. One night we weaseled our way down to the front row of the bleachers, sign in hand. During a pitching change, rather than going to talk with his fellow outfielders, Walker chatted with us for the next couple of minutes while the new pitcher warmed up. Small talk mostly: about the season, his fellow Maple Ridge native (and Boston Bruins sniper/Montreal Canadiens rival) Cam Neely, little stuff like that. If the pitching change had lasted long enough, he probably would have climbed into the seats and thrown down some poutine with us.

DeShields, Grissom, and Walker gave the team a boost in 1990, but they were by no means the whole story. On the mound, Dennis Martinez provided a bigger spark, firing 226 innings with a sparkling 2.95 ERA. In fact, the pitching staff as a whole was sharp that year. This was a big surprise, given the off-season losses of Mark Langston, Bryn Smith, and Pascual Perez to free agency. But strong contributions from reclamation project Oil Can Boyd (2.93 ERA), 1989 pickup Zane Smith (3.23 ERA), and an effective relief corps helped the Expos lead the National League in earned run average. One of those relievers won a special place in our hearts.

Every year, teams leave a certain number of players off their 40-man roster, making them eligible for other teams. The Rule 5 draft is the clearinghouse—the bastard stepchild of baseball drafts—where those unwanted players get chosen. It takes place every year at the end of the winter meetings, an afterthought to cap all the big trades and free-agent signings that went down over the previous four days. If a team is lucky, it might get a decent spare part out of the draft. More often, the acquired players never contribute, in many cases getting returned to their original teams for half their original measly cost.

But in very rare cases, a superior player emerges. The best Rule 5 pickup of all time is legendary Pirates slugger, Hall of Famer, and one-time Montreal Royal Roberto Clemente. Two-time Cy Young winner Johan Santana also emerged from Rule 5, as did future quality players like Darrell Evans, Bobby Bonilla, Jose Bautista, and Shane Victorino.

Then there was Bill Sampen. A fringe right-hander in the Pirates system, Sampen was acquired by the Expos as a Rule 5er after the 1989 season, a long-shot hedge against that winter's multiple pitching losses. Sampen made the team out of spring training in 1990, slotting in as a long man out of the bullpen. What followed was a surprisingly effective campaign as Sampen soaked up 90⅓ innings while posting a 2.99 ERA (strip out the four emergency spot starts he made that year and it drops to 2.59). His defining trait that year, though, was an uncanny knack for vulturing wins. Sampen won 12 games that year, an uncommonly high total for a reliever—and just *one* of the 12 came during those four spot starts. He was a nice little find for a Rule 5 pick.

And we were obsessed with him. Call it the work of hyperactive teenage minds, or just something to do during a long summer in the city. But no player on the 1990 Expos captured our imagination like Bill Sampen did. In fact, we were so smitten that we came up with a song, to the tune of "Mr. Sandman," that we sang every time a starting pitcher got in trouble that season.

Mr. Sampen (Yyyyyyeeeeeessss?!)
Bring us relief
We need a pitcher
Like you wouldn't believe
Bring us some strikes
And maybe some strikeouts
And send the Mets back to the dugout

My youth was definitely not wasted.

The 1990 season ended up going better than expected, with the Expos winning 85 games. But they still drew fewer than 17,000 fans a game, the second-worst attendance in 14 seasons at the Big O. A run of four straight decent-to-pretty-good seasons wasn't cutting it in Montreal.

Attendance woes be damned, all eyes were on the future. In August, with his team out of the race, Dombrowski pulled a kind of reverse Langston, flipping Zane Smith to the first-place Pirates for three prospects. While things worked out for the Pirates, as Smith's new club made the postseason (unlike Langston's Expos), Montreal got the best return of the two trades—headed by Moises Alou.

The son of Felipe Alou, Moises was wiry-strong like his dad. He had an unusual pigeon-toed stance without the big weight shift typical of power hitters, and attacked the ball instead with sinewy wrists and lightning-quick reaction time. He also eschewed batting gloves; in a notorious regimen to toughen up his hands, he *urinated* on them. Though he hadn't put up big minor league numbers, the Expos saw Moises as a five-tool talent who could improve with experience. But he also drew accolades for his *makeup*—the catch-all baseball term that defines a player's character and his ability to not only make the big leagues but also to thrive in them.

"Moises was one of the toughest players I've ever seen," Felipe Alou told me in 2013, referring partly to a gruesome leg injury his son would suffer in 1993. "He was a fearless individual, especially at the plate."

Take a father's pride with a grain of salt if you like, but Dombrowski and others saw the same character traits—one of the reasons they targeted him in that trade with the Pirates. Still, nobody predicted that Moises Alou would become a full-blown star, or that the other fruits of the deal would pay major dividends later on. After muddling along for several years with cast-off players and whatever remained of the early-'80s nucleus, things were starting to change. The Expos finally had something cooking.

It was just going to take awhile to see results. In 1991, the Expos lost more games and drew fewer fans than in any other season since 1976, their last at Jarry Park. They also bid goodbye to three huge links to the '80s, as the team's remodelling continued.

After limping to a 20–29 record, the Expos fired Buck Rodgers, ending his career in Montreal after six-plus seasons and 1,199 games. A rift had developed earlier between the team's general manager and its manager, and you could understand why: the Expos went from first place during much of the previous summer to a .500 record by season's end, despite Dombrowski's in-season trades for Langston, Zane Smith, veteran left-hander John Candelaria, and veteran pinch-hitter Jim Dwyer.

"He wanted to fire Buck after '89," said Mitch Melnick, the long-time local radio host. "He'd done everything he could, he got Langston, and it didn't work out. So he wanted to fire Buck, and Charles [Bronfman] told him, 'Listen, we've all made mistakes this year, including you. So don't rush. You can't fire him now. We got too close.' So, once Charles sold the team, it was obvious that Dombrowski was going to fire him. Aside from what happened in '89, Dombrowski didn't like Buck's methods. He wanted him at the ballpark more often, and that wasn't Buck's style."

It certainly wasn't. Like many Expos before him, Rodgers was a *bon vivant*, preferring to pound beers and tell stories during his downtime rather than spend day and night hunkered down in his office. This didn't sit well with Dombrowski, who jettisoned Rodgers in favour of the more strait-laced Tom Runnells.

When a team fires a manager in the middle of the season, its options are limited, and promoting one of the coaches (as the Expos did with Runnells) makes sense. Like Rodgers, Runnells had led the Indianapolis Indians to an American Association title. But in hiring him, the Expos had somehow again bypassed Felipe Alou—for a *fifth* time. It wouldn't take long for the Expos to realize that they should have hired Alou in the first (or fifth) place.

The wasted opportunity was magnified when Dombrowski himself stepped down as GM just three months after making the change. A year after Miami investors had tried to poach the Expos, a different Miami group led by Wayne Huizenga landed an expansion franchise for South Florida. The opportunity to build a new franchise from scratch was a tough offer for Dombrowski to turn down. He still might've stayed in Montreal, but for one gnawing concern.

"Between the language, the taxes, and everything else, they always had a hard time attracting other organizations' best talent via free agency," Dombrowski said. "But they could always combat that by being aggressive in scouting and player development. Near the end of my time in Montreal, we had that regime change, and with it came a change of philosophies. The new group wanted to cut back in expenditures, even in scouting and player development. I knew that would hurt in the long run, and I knew I didn't want to see that happen."

Rodgers was gone; now so was Dombrowski. But the biggest departure had to be Tim Raines. Like Carter and Dawson, Rock was more than a ballplayer to the people of Montreal. He was an icon who stamped lifelong impressions on kids growing up in the '80s. He connected with the community in a way that transcended what he did on the field.

One of these connections was the Grand Slam Baseball School, run for more than 20 years by Johnny Elias, first in Montreal's Town of Mount Royal suburb, then a few kilometres away in Côte Saint-Luc. The list of graduates from the summer baseball camp includes former major league pitcher Derek Aucoin and current big-league catcher Russell Martin. But most of the kids had no aspirations of playing at the highest levels—they just loved baseball. Those afternoons in the summer sun were made even brighter by the constant presence of Expos players. A few of them would show up to teach baseball skills and talk to campers for $100, maybe $200 for a couple hours; most of them did it for free. Raines was one of them. The campers sure as hell remember.

"I was six, maybe seven years old, and I remember Raines being there," said Brian Benjamin, who along with Elan Satov, Eric Kligman, and Andrew "Bean" Kensley formed the core of the Maple Ridge Boys, the group of classmates who accompanied me to hundreds of games at the Big O growing up. "He was hitting balls out of the park, onto the street, and I just stood there in awe watching. Then he came over and talked to us for a long time. I mean, I *loved* Tim Raines."

Unfortunately, and unfairly, the voting members of the Baseball Writers' Association of America haven't loved Raines as much.

☞ TIM RAINES' HALL OF FAME CASE ☜

At this writing, Raines has come up for Hall of Fame induction seven times, and been rejected seven times. This is ridiculous.

From 1981 through 1990 with the Expos, Raines hit .302 and posted a .391 on-base percentage (second-best in the NL). During that time he drew 769 walks, just 17 behind the first-place Dale Murphy among National League players in those 10 seasons. Raines stole a league-leading 626 bases, more than Cardinals speedster Vince Coleman, and nearly twice as many as the number-three player on the list, Coleman's teammate Ozzie Smith. Raines' 926 runs scored ranked first, as did his 81 triples. His 273 doubles placed him third, behind only long-time teammates Tim Wallach and Andre Dawson. And by Wins Above Replacement, Raines was number one. In other words, the best player in the entire National League from 1981 through 1990—10 full seasons—was Tim Raines.

Never in baseball history, other than in cases of steroids use (and that's a whole other hornet's nest), has a player who was the best in his league for an entire decade been denied induction into the Hall of Fame. Raines' detractors argued that he was a lesser player after leaving the Expos, and they're right. He struggled with injuries and played in 100 games or more just four more times after the 1992 season. But Raines still put up fine numbers, with on-base percentages of .401, .365, .374, .383, .403, and .395 from 1993 through 1998—playing key part-time roles on two World Series–winning teams in New York. He stole 808 bases in his career, the fifth-highest total of all time (with all four players above him in the Hall of Fame), and Raines' 84.7 percent career success rate is the highest ever for anyone with nearly as many attempts.

Voters' obsession with round numbers—and only *certain* round numbers—has clouded their judgment. Tony Gwynn made the Hall of Fame on the first ballot with 97.6 percent of the vote. That always struck me as funny, and not because Gwynn wasn't a great player; he certainly was. But Gwynn posted a career .388 on-base percentage and 763 extra-base hits in 9,288 at-bats; compared to Raines' .385 OBP and 713 extra-base hits in 8,872 at-bats—with Raines stealing 489 more bases. The two started their careers and retired at almost exactly the same time, and the numbers add up to basically identical career value. But because Gwynn made his living slapping singles, while Raines was a master of drawing walks, Gwynn and his 3,141 hits sailed into the Hall, while Raines and his 2,605 hits are still on the outside looking in. Raines, by the way, also reached base more times in his career than Hall of Famers Honus Wagner, Roberto Clemente, Lou Brock, Richie Ashburn . . . and yes, Tony Gwynn.

Try this exercise: replace 600 of Raines' 1,330 career walks with 400 bunt singles and 200 strikeouts. You're left with an inferior player who'd have been enshrined in Cooperstown years ago: this because the voters are obsessed with hits and don't count walks—and because humans happen to have 10 fingers and are thus obsessed with counting by increments of 10, 100, and 1,000.

It comes down to this: Tim Raines kicked ass, and too many people missed it. Induct the guy into Cooperstown already and let's end this nonsense.

Though Raines was irreplaceable, the player tabbed to fill his shoes as the Expos' biggest star was certainly memorable: another Jheri curl–rocking showman, a three buttons–unbuttoned, gold chain–wearing, diamond earring–sporting, 45-second-home-run-trot-producing character named Ivan Calderon. His first season with the Expos ended up being the second-best of his entire career, as he slugged 19 homers, stole 31 bases, and hit an even .300. Unfortunately, the good times with Calderon didn't last. He played in just 48 games the following season, and was out of baseball at 31.

What was effectively Calderon's last hurrah was wasted, as little else went right for the '91 Expos. The rest of the lineup was a disaster, with DeShields taking a huge step back after an excellent rookie season, and Grissom struggling in his first season-long run with a full-time job. The most perplexing numbers, however, came from the two stalwarts at the infield corners. In his third straight drop-off from a terrific 1988 season, Andres Galarraga hit just .219 with nine home runs, striking out four times more often than he walked. The Big Cat got traded to St. Louis at year's end (then went on to have a huge second half to his career that few could have expected). Across the diamond, after nine straight good (or better) seasons, Tim Wallach hit a wall, batting just .225. Once a dazzling defender at third base, his range had shrunk too, and at 34 it seemed clear that he was on the downside of his career. Wallach would get shipped to the Dodgers before the 1993 season.

Meanwhile, the problems in 1991 weren't restricted to the field: the stadium itself literally fell apart. First, a portion of the always cranky orange roof tore open in June. Repair crews managed to fix that problem quickly. They could do no such thing with the next mishap: a 55-ton beam fell from the facade of the stadium and crashed onto a walkway near one of the outside entrances. Luckily, no one got hurt. But the Expos were forced to play their final 26 games of the year on the road, as 13 home dates were cancelled. With fewer than 14,000 fans per game filing into the Big O that year, the cold, cavernous, terribly located stadium's reputation already under fire, and the team swooning, this latest calamity seemed likely to strangle future attendance.

About the only highlights in '91 came from the pitchers. And really, you could boil down all the good tidings to one weekend in L.A.

On July 26, 1991, Mark Gardner took the mound against the Dodgers. He'd been decent to that point, posting a 3.30 ERA even though he sometimes struggled with control. He was certainly sharp that night in Dodger Stadium. Through the first seven innings, Gardner didn't allow a single hit, with a two-out walk to Eddie Murray as his only blemish. In the bottom of the eighth, the Dodgers got a leadoff walk from Kal Daniels, but a botched bunt attempt and a double play quickly squelched that potential rally. Gardner breezed through the first two hitters in the ninth, getting Alfredo Griffin on an infield popout, then striking out Chris Gwynn on three pitches. On his fifth pitch against leadoff hitter Brett Butler, the Expos' starter induced a groundout to second base. Gardner had thrown a no-hitter.

Well, sort of. True, Gardner had fired nine no-hit innings. But the record books only count that as a no-no when your team actually *scores*. The Expos didn't do that. They managed just a single hit through the first eight innings, advancing just one runner into scoring position but failing to cash him in. They got a walk and a single in the top of the ninth, but again failed to score, as a Calderon flyball sailed to the warning track before dying in Darryl Strawberry's glove.

You knew what was coming next. Dodger Lenny Harris opened the bottom of the 10th with a high chopper over Gardner's head. Spike Owen charged, tried to field the ball . . . and dropped it. A frustrating misplay, but with the ball hit that slowly, Owen would've had no chance to get Harris either way—it was an infield hit, busting the no-hitter. At least there was still a chance for the win. But two batters later, Strawberry slapped a game-winning single, giving the Dodgers a 1–0 victory, and leaving Gardner with nothing. (Freaking Strawberry never failed to drive us crazy. The fact that about 15 of us spent most of that game in the Orange Julep parking lot—refusing to move with a no-hitter on—didn't help.)

"I had a great game, but I don't feel good about it," Gardner said later that night. "It's still a loss. It was a great accomplishment but it's still a loss."

Not just a loss: no-hitters don't come around that often, and the Expos had only three, despite Bill Stoneman bagging two in the team's first four seasons. Somehow, only two days later, the Expos found redemption.

When Dennis Martinez took the mound for the final game of the series, it was a scorching 95-degree afternoon at Chavez Ravine.

Though he couldn't explain why, Martinez said he came out feeling a little different than usual—a little more confident. Odd, since the Dodgers led the NL West by six games at the time and were riding a five-game winning streak. They'd shut out Montreal in each of the first two games of the series. And through the first five innings of Sunday's game, Dodgers starter Mike Morgan didn't allow a single baserunner.

Like Gardner, Martinez plowed through the Dodgers with ease. But while Martinez didn't allow any hits, he didn't allow any baserunners, either. Through five, six, seven, and eight innings, not a single Dodger reached base. Martinez said he didn't even feel a sweat until the ninth, given how quickly he and Morgan were mowing down hitters—heat be damned. Though there weren't advanced pitch-tracking systems back then to break down every Martinez offering that day, you'd swear he threw 50 of those trade-mark knee-buckling curveballs. He was so unhittable, only five Dodgers even got the ball out of the infield. And unlike Gardner's start, the Expos actually scored in the seventh, with a pair of runs against Morgan.

Then, the ninth.

"I ran back out to the mound, I could hear the crowd applauding me," Martinez recalled. "That's when it hit me, and my legs all of a sudden got real heavy, like I could barely move."

Mike Scioscia went down quietly with a weak flyout to left, then Stan Javier struck out swinging. That brought up the Dodgers' best pinch-hitter, Chris Gwynn.

"I got ahead 1 and 2, then tried to go inside and tie him up. The ball came back toward the middle of the plate. The good thing was it was a little high. He got the barrel of the bat on it—if he could have extended his arms, it would have been out of the stadium. But he didn't. I knew he hit it well, then I looked to Marquis Grissom. I'm watching the ball, I see Grissom running, then I see him separate his arms and yell 'I got it.' The whole time I'm yelling, 'Come on Grissom! Come on Grissom! Come on Grissom!'"

The Expos' centre fielder squeezed the final out, and Dennis Martinez had done it. For just the 13th time in major league history, a pitcher had thrown a perfect game.

The reactions were unforgettable. Martinez raised his arms in triumph, pounded his glove, then got swarmed on the mound—with the longest-tenured Expo, Wallach, the first to embrace him. The kid who'd grown up in a broken, poverty-stricken home in Nicaragua, who nearly pissed away his career and his life with booze only to return with a flourish in Montreal, had just done what only a dozen men before him ever had. Overcome with emotion, Martinez cried in Wallach's arms, his shoulders shaking. A huge Sunday crowd of 45,560 rained cheers down on the man who'd just turned their team's hitters into rubble.

In the clubhouse afterwards, Walker showered Martinez with beer, and the conquering hero carefully wiped it off his face. Later that night, teammates and friends toasted him with champagne; Martinez raised his glass, then set it down without taking a sip.

For many Expos fans, Dave Van Horne's reaction to that final out remains the enduring memory from that day. Channelling Martinez's nickname, the Expos' play-by-play man had the perfect call for the moment, one that remains the most famous call in Expos history.

"El Presidente, El Perfecto!"

———

If Dave Dombrowski had been looking for a law-and-order guy when he fired Buck Rodgers, he sure as hell found one in Tom Runnells. The Expos were a young team, and Runnells felt that his players needed rules. Lots of rules. Rules that would even include strict curfews—complete with frequent bed checks—on the road. The kind of stuff a manager would enforce on a high-school team, but certainly not in the majors.

So on the first day of workouts in spring training 1992, Runnells decided to have some fun with his hard-nosed reputation. Greeting his full squad for the first time, he showed up wearing army fatigues, wielding a bullhorn.

The media skewered him for the move, writing a stack of critical columns. Serge Touchette nicknamed him "T-ball," because he felt the fatigues were a bush league move. Though the General Schwarzkopf impression got all the headlines, most of the players got the joke.

"He was doing a spoof on his hard-ass routine," said Fletcher. "I think he was trying to do a *Saturday Night Live* skit, to make light of it."

Runnells spent a good chunk of that spring trying to loosen the team up. Playing against type was certainly a goal. But so too was raising morale for a team that had been through a truly miserable 1991 season.

"We had a long-drive [golf] competition out on one of the back fields," Runnells recalled in a 2012 interview. "You should have seen Walker and some of the other guys just rippin' away. Some of the Latin guys [who hadn't golfed before] taking full swings and the ball just barely dribbling off the tee. Everybody just hootin' and hollerin'."

Those who defended Runnells felt that he meant well, but also that he was in over his head. He was just 36 years old, and lacked the experience and gravitas to command the respect and attention of his players.

As the season started and the losing resumed, everyone got tight, coming down with a case of what Fletcher called "bootylock." Furthermore, the long list of rules posted in every locker like the Ten Commandments, treating the players like high-school kids, and the puzzling player moves (such as shifting the Gold Glover Wallach to first base in order to shoehorn inexperienced second-base prospect Bret Barberie into the lineup) proved too much for the players to take. It wasn't long before they declared a mutiny.

"We're in San Diego, this is early 1992," said Elliott Price, who was doing play-by-play for the West Coast swing. "And L.A.'s burning, because of the Rodney King riots. So the games got cancelled, and we didn't go. We stayed in San Diego. So Runnells schedules an early-morning practice at Jack Murphy Stadium before the flight home. I'm having this wonderful crab sandwich at Horton Plaza, sitting there by myself reading the paper. Next thing I know, Tom Foley, Spike Owen, and Rick Cerone are sitting at the table with me, and I know that the manager's gone. Because they've had it. He's done. They had made up their mind that this guy was not going to manage the team anymore."

Dan Duquette had taken over as GM in September 1991 when Dombrowski left for Miami. He wasn't a big Runnells fan, agreeing with the consensus that Dombrowski had rushed Runnells into the job. On May 22, the hammer fell. The man who fired Runnells and the man who replaced him were about to engineer a gigantic turnaround.

Duquette's background was in player development, having served for four years as head of that department. During that time, he worked alongside an all-star team of up-and-coming managerial talent. Jerry Manuel had also worked as a minor league instructor, honing the skills of the Expos' many great prospects; he later landed his own major league managing job. Neal Huntington parlayed his minor league experience into a future GM job. Kevin Malone replaced Gary Hughes as scouting director in '92, and would later rise to the position of general manager.

Those men, along with Frank Wren (who'd been hired during the Hughes era and served as assistant farm director and assistant scouting director before going on to become GM in Baltimore, then later, Atlanta), helped influence Duquette's decision making, guiding his views on everything from how to value young players in trades to knowing when to call a prospect up to the big leagues.

Duquette had also been impressed by the long-time West Palm Beach manager who'd then coached on Runnells' staff—despite having had more success than Runnells in player development. Passed over repeatedly for the big chair, Felipe Alou and his six winter league championships finally found an ally in Duquette, who was willing to give him a shot. So it was that at age 57, Alou became the Expos' new manager, and Major League Baseball's first Dominican-born skipper.

The Expos didn't start off well under Alou, though, losing eight of their first 13 games. Then they caught fire. From June 7 to July 30, Montreal won 31 of 51 games, and even pulled into a tie for first place. Players—especially the team's younger members—responded to Alou's leadership. DeShields returned to the solid form of his rookie season, while Grissom started to show off the power/speed combination he'd shown in the minors; the top two batters in the Expos lineup combined to steal 124 bases that year. Walker, now entering his prime and four years removed from the major knee injury that cost him the entire 1988 season, hit .301 with 23 homers. Felipe's son Moises, given a crack at the starting left-fielder's job thanks to a Calderon injury, hit .282 and smacked 28 doubles in 115 games.

Thirty-eight-year-old Dennis Martinez was still the staff ace, making the fifth of what would be six straight Opening Day starts, flashing a 2.47 ERA, and making his third straight All-Star Game that season. Some young stars were emerging on the pitching side, too.

Mel Rojas had been signed as a teenager out of the Dominican Republic seven years earlier. Given his first heavy workload in his third big-league season, he was a monster, firing 100⅔ innings, allowing just two home runs all year, and delivering a 1.43 ERA. Rojas always had good raw stuff, including a split-fingered fastball that could be devastating with two strikes. The problem was that he didn't get ahead of hitters often enough during much of his minor league and early major league careers. But under Alou, Rojas harnessed his command, issuing just 26 unintentional walks and fanning 70 batters—many of those with the splitter. Like Moises, Rojas had good genes; he was Felipe's nephew. And like Moises, Grissom, Walker, and other improving young players, he benefited from Felipe's guidance.

"He had a way about him," said Fletcher about the new manager. "He had a good sense of whether his players could do it or not. That ought to have been his forte, having spent so much time with younger players, having all that experience in the minors and in winter leagues. But it was more than that. He had a calming effect too. Guys played well under him."

"He put us in the right situations," said DeShields. "There was never any doubt about what was going on between the lines when he was managing. Plus he had the ability to connect with players, and still give them space. I never saw him in the locker room, never saw him invading anyone's space. If you came to him, sure, he'd talk to you. But he never crossed that line."

The Expos couldn't hold on to first place in 1992. But they still won 87 games, finishing second in the East behind the Barry Bonds–led Pirates and improving by 16 games from the year before. Alou's Expos also re-energized the fans. After suffering through that catastrophic 1991 season—even worrying about their safety as the ballpark started to crumble—Expos supporters stormed back to the Big O in '92. They averaged 30,000 fans a game for a mid-July series with the Padres, then drew huge crowds of 41,935 and 46,620 for two weekend games against the Dodgers a few days later. This was nearly sold-out territory in the early '90s, when the Expos closed off several thousand seats in the stadium's highest reaches, dropping capacity from just under 60,000 to the mid-to-high 40s. By year's end, they'd lifted attendance to 20,607 a game, a 50 percent jump compared to 1991 levels.

For the final home game of the season, 41,802 filed into Olympic Stadium. The Expos were out of the race—but the fans came to say goodbye to a legend.

On November 15, 1991, Montreal had reacquired an old friend, plucking Gary Carter off waivers from the Dodgers. Thirty-seven years old and nearing the end of his career, Carter would serve as a veteran leader and goodwill ambassador. Reduced to part-time catching duties, he played in 95 games and hit just .218 in 1992. No one cared. Just as fans feted Rusty Staub's return in '79, they were eager to welcome Carter back for a final season.

Carter started in that final home game, batting fifth behind Walker. He went hitless in his first two at-bats, which was no big surprise given the tenor of the game: a 0–0 tie through six innings, as Expos right-hander Kent Bottenfield traded zeroes with Mike Morgan (the well-travelled veteran who a year earlier had gone toe-to-toe with Martinez during his perfecto). With two outs in the seventh, Larry Walker drew a walk, bringing Carter to the plate.

The crowd erupted, greeting Carter with a long standing ovation. They kept right on cheering throughout the at-bat, even as Morgan got ahead in the count 0–2. Carter stepped out of the box, adjusted his batting gloves, then did his trademark tug of the left sleeve. He stepped back in, tapped home plate and waggled his bat twice, then set up in his classic stance, bat held high. Cubs catcher Rick Wilkins set a target down and away. Morgan kicked and delivered. It was a fastball that caught more of the plate than the Cubs pitcher wanted. Carter slashed the pitch deep to right field. It carried and carried, over the right-fielder's head. It took one hop off the wall, giving Walker enough time to scamper home with the go-ahead run—the only run of the game, it would turn out, in a dramatic 1–0 Expos victory.

The reaction was deafening. An explosion of sound, every man, woman, and child in the ballpark standing and saluting The Kid. Carter's ear-to-ear smile lit up the scoreboard. He pulled off his batting helmet and waved it at the crowd. Pumped his fist. Jogged off the field as Tim Laker came in to run for him, pointing his helmet skyward again. A dugout full of hugs. Then, after what would turn out to be the final at-bat of his Hall of Fame career, one last curtain call. For every scorching-hot game Carter squatted in, every knee injury he fought through, every day game after night game he played long after the Expos had fallen out of contention . . . Montreal fans gave it all back with their appreciation that day.

There was one last little postscript on that final at-bat. As Carter's line drive carried out to right, it looked for a moment like the ball might be caught. But the right fielder was just three months younger than Carter himself, not quite at the end of his career, but in his 17th major league season. If Carter's swan song was going to mark the end of an era for the Expos, it seemed only fitting that his final hit would land just inches beyond Andre Dawson's reach.

If the 1993 Expos needed an extra source of motivation, they got one five hours down the road in Toronto. In the fall of '92, the Blue Jays became the first Canadian team to make it to the World Series. The first two games were played in Atlanta, home of the National League champion Braves. Before Game 3—the first World Series game ever played outside the United States—Jays president Paul

Beeston had to decide who he'd ask to throw out the first pitch for this momentous occasion. Beeston chose the man who made baseball in Canada a reality in the first place: Charles Bronfman.

"I told him yes, of course," recalled Bronfman. "That was probably the craziest and most wonderful 24 hours of my life. I threw out the first pitch at that game, then I went the next day with my family to Ottawa, where I was made a member of Her Majesty's Privy Council for Canada. Then later that day, I became a Companion of the Order of Canada. I remember the governor general [Ray Hnatyshyn], he put this thing around my neck, and I said, 'Well, today was a doubleheader.' And he said, 'No, it was a tripleheader. I was at the ballgame last night.'"

It was a thoughtful gesture, one that touched the Expos' long-time owner. It also rang a bit hollow for many Expos fans, given the Jays' muscling Montreal out of the Southern Ontario broadcast market (a defensible if ruthless business move . . . but a much nastier manoeuvre was coming in the years ahead).

If the Expos were going to challenge the Jays' claim to Canadian baseball supremacy, they'd have to do it with a day-care lineup. Montreal position players averaged just 25.7 years old in '93, the second-youngest group in franchise history behind only the 107-loss disaster of 1976. Among the eight batters with the most plate appearances that year, none were older than 27. Even so, with players like DeShields, Grissom, and Walker by now established as lineup mainstays, the time was right to hand Felipe Alou a new crop of prospects on which to work his magic.

The youngest everyday player was Puerto Rico native Wil Cordero. He'd earned his first taste of the big leagues in '92, hitting .302 in 45 games. Spike Owen leaving via free agency had opened the door for Cordero to take over at shortstop. As with Hubie Brooks before him, Cordero was a bat-first player who ended up at short out of necessity. Big and strong at 6-foot-2 and over 200 pounds (he'd top out at 230 later in his career), he had limited range, however, and would need to hit a ton to justify his place in the lineup. Prospect hounds believed he could do it, as *Baseball America* ranked him the top prospect in the Expos' system in 1991 and 1992. Unfortunately, things didn't go so well that first year, as Cordero hit just .248/.308/.387: sub-par numbers at a time when scoring levels were starting to surge all over the league. Then again, Cordero was just 21, playing every day in the majors for the first time. The Expos were optimistic that he would improve with experience.

Cordero's rookie infield running mate was 25-year-old Wyoming product Mike Lansing. Here was a needle in a haystack, an infielder for the Miami Miracle of the Florida State League. Though Miami played against high Single-A teams affiliated with major league franchises, the Miracle were an unaffiliated team that operated independently. That unique status afforded Miami some unusual privileges, including being able to select some players during the lower rounds of the 1990 amateur draft. In the sixth round that year, the Miracle picked Lansing. Without the backing of a parent club, Miami occasionally needed to sell its best players to stay solvent. So when Lansing hit .286 with a .355 on-base percentage in 1991, he became intriguing bait—assuming anyone had bothered to notice. Since Alou had managed another team just up I-95 in West Palm, he'd gotten plenty of looks at Lansing. Alou recommended him to the Expos, and the deal was done. Though Lansing didn't win a steady everyday job right away like Cordero did, he proved to be a valuable superutility player in his debut season, hitting .287 with a .352 on-base percentage, 29 doubles, 23 steals, and solid defence at three different positions (third, short, and second) over 141 games.

The pitching staff had some new faces too. Kirk Rueter was an 18th-round pick out of Murray State in 1991. That modest pedigree made sense, since his fastball couldn't dent a loaf of bread. But Rueter knew how to pitch. He *lived* on the outside corner, inducing weak contact and getting calls at the edges of the strike zone. He also walked fewer than two batters per nine innings in the minor leagues, en route to a career 2.48 minor league ERA. And while no one expected big things from Rueter as a 22-year-old rookie, he put up terrific numbers in '93 after a July call-up, allowing just five homers in 14 starts, with a 2.73 ERA (and an 8–0 record, if you're into that kind of thing).

Jeff Fassero didn't start the year in the Expos' rotation either, instead coming out of the bullpen for the first half of the season. Once he did crack the starting five, he thrived. From his first start on July 10 until the end of the season, Fassero struck out 93 batters, walked 30, and allowed just four homers in 97⅔ innings—good for a 2.30 ERA. Fassero's origins were even less glamorous than Rueter's. A 22nd-round pick by St. Louis in 1984, he languished in the Cardinals' farm system. After the 1990 season he became a six-year minor league free agent, one of baseball's most overt examples of an unwanted player. But the Expos scooped him up on January 3, 1991, and four months later he was in the majors as a 28-year-old rookie. Two-and-a-half years later? He was the best starting pitcher on one of the best teams in the National League.

This was the Expos returning to their scouting and player-development roots, bringing in waves of new talent to bolster the major league roster. If anything, this was the next evolution of the organizational success of the mid-'70s to early '80s—with the Expos not only nurturing future stars, but also turning lightly regarded prospects into high-quality big-league players.

"You knew what you were doing [in player development] was going to count at the major league level," Duquette said in a 2012 interview, "because *there were no other options*. That was how we were going to win with a small payroll."

With Alou at the helm, a battalion of holdover 20-something players coming into their own, plus that infusion of new blood, the Expos won more games in 1993 than in any season since 1979. Duquette spoke of a rebuilding plan that had 1994 as the target date for NL East contention. Montreal got there a year ahead of schedule.

Just like in Alou's debut season, though, they didn't start off as contenders. Hosting the Giants on July 5 and 6, the Expos lost by scores of 10–4 and 13–5. That knocked Montreal down to 43–40 for the year, 11½ games out of first place, with more runs allowed than runs scored. After a five-game winning streak to end the first half, Montreal returned from the break and promptly started another losing skid, dropping six of seven games on the West Coast (including three more losses to a loaded Giants team). The Expos were back to 11½ games out, with 66 to play. A mediocre season, it seemed.

Then, crazy things began to happen. The Expos worked out a trade with the Braves, sending Dennis Martinez to Atlanta for power-hitting first-base prospect Brian Hunter. The Braves were in an electric pennant race with the Giants—one that would end with Atlanta winning 104 games and San Francisco finishing a game back with 103. Atlanta wanted pitching reinforcements, and Hunter became expendable after the Braves acquired star slugger Fred McGriff in a deadline deal. But Martinez vetoed the trade, exercising his right to do so as a player with 10 years of major league experience and five with the same team. El Presidente turned down the deal because the Braves' starting rotation was brimming with talent, and there was no guarantee that Martinez and his 4.23 ERA would have a place.

Though Martinez missed out on that incredible NL West race, he ended up getting a taste of pennant fever in Montreal instead. From July 22 to September 16, the Expos won 36 out of 51 games. That included a stretch in late August and early September in which they won 16 times and lost just once. Many of those victories were cliff-hangers, with a now formidable bullpen holding the fort night after night until the offence could rally. They posted one of the league's best records in one-run games at 32–24, and went on a run in which they won seven of eight in extra innings, reversing some ugly extra-inning results from earlier in the season.

Within that stretch came one of the most electrifying moments of all time at the Big O. On July 10, 1993, the Expos had traded for a left-handed pitcher named Denis Boucher. From a distance, this didn't seem like a big deal, considering Boucher's mediocre stuff and 6-plus ERA through his first 19 major league starts. What made the trade newsworthy was that Boucher was a native of Lachine, Quebec, making him the rarest of Expos species: a local boy with a shot at making the team.

On September 6, Boucher got that chance with a start at home against the Rockies. To many, the timing seemed curious. Boucher would later recall how several teammates expressed frustration with the move, since the Expos were now in the middle of a pennant race and Boucher hadn't exactly shown championship-calibre performance to that point in his career. The fans, however, felt otherwise. Boucher's first start as an Expo drew 40,066 fired-up souls to the stadium—a crowd twice the size of the one that showed up for the team's previous home game a week earlier.

The crowd gave Boucher a massive ovation when the lineup was introduced, again when the Expos took the field, again when his name was introduced as the game's starting pitcher, and one last time after he carved through the top of the Rockies order on just five pitches, inducing three straight weak groundouts. Boucher and Joe Siddall (a native of Windsor, Ontario) made history that day as the first all-Canadian battery in the major leagues.

"I always tell people it's good it was a day game, because if it happened at night, it would have been too much waiting and anticipating," Boucher said. "It was a good thing I was well pre-pared for that game. I'd been up with the team for a full week before that, and I was prepared to pitch. I didn't let emotions, fans, everybody yelling get the best of me. I just never let myself look up and be in awe of this giant, packed stadium. I've watched it on tape a few times since then. Still get chills."

Milestones aside, Boucher was outstanding, tossing six innings and allowing just one run on that crazy day, en route to a 4–3 Expos win. In fact, Boucher's five September starts added up to some excellent numbers: just three walks allowed in 28⅓ innings, and a tiny 1.91 ERA. Not bad for a guy who'd been labelled by some as a publicity stunt.

By the time the first-place Phillies came to town for a three-game series starting on September 17, the Expos had sliced the NL East gap to five games, with just 15 to go. Montreal was surface-of-the-sun hot by then; sweep the Phillies and the final two weeks of the season would be the most exciting home stretch at Olympic Stadium in a decade. The series opener was a zoo, as 45,757 fans packed the house. The Expos took a 3–0 lead into the sixth, only to see Martinez, then Rojas, combine to give up a seven-spot. The game went to the bottom of the seventh with Philly leading 7–4. A pair of singles sandwiched around a ground-out put runners at first and second with one out. With the pitcher's spot due up, Alou signalled down the bench. He wanted Curtis Pride to hit.

One of the hallmarks of Felipe Alou's managerial style was to value skill over grey hairs; if a rookie was more talented than the 13-year veteran, the rookie would get the call—even in a big spot. You couldn't find a much bigger spot than this one, nor a greener player than Pride. The Expos were eight outs away from falling to six games behind the Phillies, which would effectively end their season. Meanwhile, Pride was barely even a rookie. He'd been called up just a few days earlier, appeared in just two games, and would now make just his second career at-bat, his first at home in front of the giant, rabid Big O crowd. The first pitch from Phillies right-hander Bobby Thigpen was a fastball out over the plate. The lefty-swinging Pride smoked it, lashing a screaming line drive to the gap in left-centre. By the time the Phillies flung the ball back to the infield, two runs had scored.

The crowd went completely berserk—I know, because I was there. As the Phillies made a pitching change, we all stood and cheered.

And cheered.

And cheered.

Pride stood at second watching us. He walked over to Jerry Manuel, who was coaching third base. Michael Farber recounted the scene from there.

"Do I have the green light?" Pride asked.

"Tip your cap," Manuel said.

"What?"

"They're cheering you. Tip your cap."

Pride, who is deaf but reads lips, would later say that he couldn't hear the crowd's thunderous cheering—*he felt it through the turf.*

"The way they kept cheering," Manuel told Farber after the game, "it's as if the crowd wanted to break a barrier. They wanted him to know how they felt, to get beyond the wall. That's the greatest thing I've ever seen."

Same here. The first game I ever saw in person came in 1982, just after what would prove to be the only playoff experience in Expos history. When you spend the next 22 years cheering for a team that never wins anything, finding a favourite moment gets tricky. I didn't have Reggie Jackson going deep three times in a World Series game, Kirk Gibson limping off the bench for a game-winning homer in '88, or even Joe Carter's World Series walk-off in '93.

What I had—what all Expos fans of that generation had—was that Phillies series. Grissom followed Pride's double with a game-tying single two batters later, then the Expos won it on DeShields' sacrifice fly in the 12th, the capper on a four-and-a-half-hour thriller. The Expos lost the next day, then won the series finale on a walk-off two-run single down the left-field line by Wil Cordero. More than 50,000 fans showed up that Saturday, another 40,000-plus on the Sunday. People still talk about Cordero's hit, RDS colour commentator/excitable fellow Rodger Brulotte's call of "Cordero, Cordero, COR-DE-RO!!!!!" still ringing in people's ears.

No, the Expos couldn't quite catch the Phillies that year (again), finishing just three games out in second place. Regardless, my pinnacle of joy as an Expos fan was that Curtis Pride double. The deafening noise all around, as 45,757 of us yelled so loud we lost our voices, and our minds. A stuffed Olympic Stadium sending out a big F-U to those who'd mocked the Expos and their supposed lack of fan support. And Pride standing there on second, this rookie, this bit player who couldn't even hear, tapping his chest, telling us that he couldn't process what was happening with his ears . . . but he could with his heart. In all my years as a baseball fan, this was the moment I wished I could stick in a bottle, and keep forever.

CHAPTER NINE

"We knew no one could beat us." (1994)

One of the greatest trades the Expos ever made took impeccable timing, luck, and an extremely misguided self-appraisal by a free agent. It also required a little bit of sneakiness.

The Los Angeles Dodgers finished 81–81 in 1993, an underwhelming result even if it was an 18-game improvement over 1992. They needed to get better, and couldn't afford major holes in the lineup. The Dodgers' starting second baseman in '93 had been Jody Reed, a free agent at season's end. The Dodgers wanted Reed back, and dangled a three-year, $7.8 million contract. He'd made $2.5 million in '93, the fifth-highest salary among all second basemen that year, so the offer was a minor raise on a per-year basis. But the deal would also last three years and run through his 34th birthday, a dicey proposition given his most recent season. In 1993, Reed hit .278 with two home runs and just 28 unintentional walks in 132 games. He didn't run all that well, either. And while he was a solid defensive second baseman, he wasn't elite: more like the kind of player who could start for a last-place team, or be a utilityman on a contender. If he was already overpaid in '93, he'd be royally overpaid under the terms of this proposed deal.

Reed and his agent, J. D. Dowell, rejected the offer. In the annals of baseball history, this would go down as one of the worst decisions ever made by a free agent. Dowell never got the $10 million-plus he sought for his client, and Reed instead had to sign a one-year deal with the Brewers for just $350,000 in base salary. In one way, the Dodgers dodged a bullet by not having to pay their mediocre second baseman that much money. But Dowell's miscalculation would have a much deeper impact than anyone could have foreseen at the time. It would cost the Dodgers—and hand the Expos—a future Hall of Famer named Pedro Martinez.

When the plan to re-sign Reed failed, Dodgers general manager Fred Claire went after free agent Robby Thompson instead. Unlike Reed, Thompson was coming off a huge year, having hit .312 with 19 homers in '93 for the Giants, and winning the Gold Glove and Silver Slugger awards at second base. Also unlike Reed, Thompson got the big contract he was seeking, spurning the Dodgers' advances and re-upping with San Francisco for three years at $11.6 million (with an option for a fourth year). With Plan A and Plan B off the board, Claire instead turned to the trade market. His target: Delino DeShields.

"We thought Delino had an extremely bright future," Claire said in 2013. "He wasn't just a talented player, he was also a leader of that Expos team. He looked like he could be someone who would be with us for 10 years."

Dan Duquette was also a big DeShields fan. The Expos GM called him "our most recognizable player," a blazingly fast risk-taker who played with emotion and swagger. DeShields was a great fit playing on Olympic Stadium's AstroTurf, stretching singles into doubles, doubles into triples. Duquette and others saw potential for improvement too: just 24 years old, DeShields was fine-tuning his ability to turn double plays at second base, and honing his batting eye, having walked more times than he struck out for the first time in '93. A middle infielder that young, coming off a season in which he posted a .389 on-base percentage with 43 steals in just 123 games? Any team would salivate over someone like that.

Even with that skill set, DeShields wasn't untouchable in Montreal. With every passing day, Claude Brochu kept tightening the purse strings. Larry Walker even famously griped that the Expos players were now being asked to buy their own vitamins. With penny-pinching that extreme, any player with some service time under his belt and making more than the league minimum could be trade bait. DeShields was one of them, making $1.5 million in 1993 and now up for arbitration. Meanwhile, Mike Lansing was about to enter his second major league season, would make just $200,000 in 1994, and the Expos felt he was ready for a full-time job at second base. At the same time, Montreal also had a pitching vacancy to fill, with Dennis Martinez filing for free agency. If the Expos could find a team hungry for a new second baseman that also had a good, young pitcher to offer, a deal seemed possible.

The Dodgers were that team. Twenty-one-year-old Pedro Martinez had a great rookie campaign for L.A. in '93, firing 107 innings (99⅔ of those in relief), striking out 119 batters, and allowing just 76 hits and five home runs. He could be wild, walking 57 batters and losing control of his fastball at times. But that heater topped out in the high-90s and was accompanied by both a tantalizing curveball and a murderous changeup. Martinez's success wasn't anything new either—not after he'd stormed through the minor leagues, striking out more than a batter an inning despite ranking among the youngest players at each stop (and pitching in some extremely hitter-friendly ballparks).

In spring training of 1992, Claire made his policy on Martinez crystal clear to anyone who asked. "I won't trade Pedro Martinez," he said. "I don't care who they offer."

Tommy Lasorda wasn't quite sold, however. Pedro had pitched well in his first full season—that was true. But he also weighed just 164 pounds, and at 5-foot-11 (his listed height, but scouts claimed he was 5-foot-10 or shorter) lacked the kind of frame that would suggest he'd fill out in the future. The Dodgers manager didn't think Martinez had the size and strength to go deep into games the way a reliable starting pitcher should. Lasorda watched Martinez pitch well in relief in '93, then sent him out for a pair of starts in September. In his first start, Pedro surrendered five runs on 2⅓ innings; in his second, he gave up three more in five innings. Never mind that he'd thrown three innings or more in a game just twice all year, giving him no opportunity to stretch out his arm and re-acclimate to starting. Never mind that the first of those starts came in the mile-high air of Denver's Coors Field, a death trap for visiting pitchers. Those two starts confirmed the bias Lasorda already had in his head: Martinez was a fine reliever, but he didn't have what it took to be an effective starter in the majors.

Others in the Dodgers organization disagreed with Lasorda's assessment. One of those dissenters was Kevin Kennedy, Pedro's manager at Triple-A Albuquerque.

Kennedy hadn't managed Martinez for all that long. In 1991, a 19-year-old Pedro zoomed through three levels of minor league ball, starting in the Class-A California League and ending under Kennedy's watch in Albuquerque. The skinny right-hander made just six starts in that last stop, but that was enough to convince Kennedy that the Dodgers had a future star on their hands. As all minor league managers do, Kennedy wrote up reports on all the players he managed that season. He raved about Martinez's knockout stuff, and the way each of those pitches befuddled hitters with sharp, darting action. Kennedy also liked Pedro's ability to pound the inside and outside corners, to make batters swing and miss, and even his attitude on the mound: a combination of poise and aggression.

As the '91 Triple-A season ended, Kennedy was restless. He wanted to land a job in the majors—as a manager, preferably, but if he had to pay his dues for a few years as a coach first, so be it. He sent resumés to eight different teams, and after a few days, he started to get some responses. One was from Duquette. Come to Montreal, the Expos GM told Kennedy, I have a couple of things I want to run by you.

"That was the year the Expos had a lot of turnover, when Dave Dombrowski went to Florida and took John Boles and other people with him," Kennedy recalled. "Duquette flew me in, put me up at the [upscale] Queen Elizabeth [Hotel], took me to a Habs game, all of that. I really felt like I was being recruited, which was pretty cool. Dan said, 'I know you want to coach in the big leagues, but I have the minor league director job available right now. I promise I'll get you in the big leagues within two years.'"

Kennedy accepted the offer, and as Duquette entered his first off-season in his new GM job, he sought out Kennedy's counsel on players worth watching for future deals. Kennedy started telling Duquette about some of the players he'd managed. Then, a lightning bolt struck.

"I realized I'd never sent the Dodgers my reports," Kennedy told me. "I never had to, because I left the organization."

Instead, he handed the whole stack to Duquette. For the Expos, these surreptitious reports became a gold mine.

One of Duquette's biggest goals upon taking the Expos general manager job was to rebuild the bullpen, landing as many young, power arms as possible. One of the best pitchers on the '91 Albuquerque Dukes fit that mould. John Wetteland was a hard-throwing right-hander who struck out nearly a batter an inning that season. Of course, you can find hundreds of hard-throwing relievers in any given season—dozens of those with the numbers to match. As luck would have it, Kennedy didn't just manage Wetteland that season: he'd managed him for two years in rookie ball at Great Falls, and had named him the starter for the Texas League All-Star Game. He'd also managed him at winter ball in Puerto Rico, then again in the Dominican Republic. From 1985 through 1991, Kennedy either managed Wetteland or managed against him, getting to know his strengths and weaknesses intimately. His protegé was a starter for most of those years, but Kennedy could see that he didn't have the command or the temperament to start—that he couldn't survive the third time through opponents' lineups.

"He was so intense," Kennedy said. "There were times when you had to go out there and just tell him to breathe."

In 1991, the Dodgers sought to harness that intensity by making the right-hander a co-closer in Albuquerque. Suddenly Wetteland was finding the plate with more regularity. Freed from needing to pace himself over seven or eight innings, he started firing high-90s fastballs as a ninth-inning guy. On November 27, 1991, the Dodgers traded him to the Reds, part of a four-player deal that brought back Eric Davis, a star in the mid-to-late '80s who had bounce-back potential if he could overcome a string of injuries. In the end, Cincinnati didn't have much use for Wetteland—not when they already had the Nasty Boys trio of Rob Dibble, Randy Myers, and Norm Charlton. That gave the Expos a chance to buy low on a player they now coveted thanks to Kennedy. Only two weeks after acquiring him from the Dodgers, the Reds shipped Wetteland to Montreal (along with fringe right-hander Bill Risley), for Dave Martinez, Willie Greene, and Scott Ruskin.

Greene and Ruskin were the players acquired, along with Moises Alou, for Zane Smith 16 months earlier. This after the Expos nabbed Smith from the Braves for three players, including Kevin Dean (the first-round pick who never panned out, and instead went to prison). In a way, the Expos traded a guy who spent several years behind bars for Moises Alou . . . and John Wetteland.

The Expos had also gained intel on other players they would later acquire. One was Henry Rodriguez, an outfielder on the '91 Dukes who didn't put up exceptional numbers, but had done enough the year before in Double-A (28 homers) and shown a projectable enough power swing to make Kennedy—and Duquette's eventual successor Kevin Malone—believe he could one day produce in the big leagues. The Expos eventually acquired Rodriguez in a May 1995 trade, and promptly got rewarded in 1996 with one of the best power displays in team history.

Another of Kennedy's favourites was Darrin Fletcher. The lefty-swinging catcher played for Albuquerque in 1989 and 1990, but was dealt to Philly before the '91 season. There he ended up being blocked by Philadelphia's other left-handed-hitting catcher, Darren Daulton, which made him expendable. Two days before the Wetteland deal, the Expos flipped pedestrian relief pitcher Barry Jones for Fletcher, in the process acquiring a badly needed starting catcher.

Then there was Pedro.

No one needed smuggled scouting reports to see that Pedro had big-time potential when teams were banging down Fred Claire's door in the spring of '92. But in October of that year, Dodgers team doctor Dr. Frank Jobe performed surgery on Martinez's shoulder. Granted, it was his non-throwing shoulder, but just as Lasorda wondered if Pedro could handle a starter's workload, Jobe expressed even deeper concerns, wondering if the little righty's slight build would lead to a breakdown.

The glowing reports filed by Kennedy (who by 1993 had fulfilled his goal of becoming a major league manager, landing the job with the Rangers) convinced Duquette to take the plunge anyway. Especially since the Expos GM already had a bias of his own.

"I had the benefit of seeing Pedro when he pitched in rookie ball, in the Gulf Coast League," Duquette said. "He hit a couple of our batters. Surprise! Surprise! I said, 'Who *is* this kid?!' With that kind of abandon in his delivery, and competitiveness, and breaking ball . . . I loved him."

On November 19, 1993, the trade was made. Going to the Dodgers was DeShields, the talented second baseman Claire had been craving. Coming to the Expos was Pedro, the pitcher Duquette hoped could fill the void left by Dennis Martinez's departure.

"Pedro did an outstanding job for us in the role that he played," Lasorda said after the deal was made. "But in order to get a player the calibre and the quality of a DeShields, you have to give up something. . . .We had to have this guy because we felt we needed speed in the lineup. As an everyday player, we feel he will be more valuable to us than the relief pitcher."

The Montreal media didn't just agree with Lasorda's view that DeShields was the more valuable commodity: columnists launched grenades at Duquette and Brochu, accusing the Expos GM, and the team's principal owner, of being motivated by factors other than Martinez's ability.

"There's no puzzle why the Expos made the deal," wrote Pat Hickey of the *Montreal Gazette*. "Too many decisions are made to balance the books." Hickey's colleague Michael Farber was even harsher in his criticism. "[The] deal is rotten to the core. [The] Expos' one big deal will sicken fans." Pierre Ladouceur of *La Presse* claimed that "trading Delino DeShields to the Los Angeles Dodgers shows, once again, that the Expos executives are only thinking about reducing their payroll." Ladouceur's colleague

Philippe Cantin didn't mince words, either: "So begins the fire sale; where will it end?"

It was certainly true that trading DeShields for Pedro would save the Expos some money. But Duquette was optimistic: his predecessors had drafted and developed stars like Larry Walker and Marquis Grissom. They'd acquired important contributors like Jeff Fassero and Mike Lansing on the cheap, and snagged talented international amateurs like Wil Cordero and Mel Rojas. Promising up-and-comers included Cliff Floyd, Rondell White, and Kirk Rueter. Duquette himself pulled off successful trade after successful trade, landing Ken Hill and Butch Henry for the starting rotation, Sean Berry to play third, and Fletcher to catch. Nearly the entire Expos bullpen in 1994 came from Duquette deals, with Wetteland joining Jeff Shaw, Tim Scott, and Gil Heredia as nifty steals.

Pedro, however, was the capper. His doubters thought he was too small, and too fragile. But Duquette saw him as the final ingredient for a great team. As soon as he'd completed the deal, he called Brochu. The GM's prognostication for the 1994 season was short and sweet.

"We're going to win."

Duquette wouldn't stick around to see his prediction fulfilled. In January 1994, the Massachusetts native got an offer from the Red Sox to become their new general manager. As promising as the Expos were, Duquette couldn't turn down a chance to come home, and—if everything went right—break one of the most notorious championship droughts in sports.

In his stead, the Expos promoted scouting director Kevin Malone. There's no such thing as a perfect ball club, but Malone inherited a team that was pretty close. The 1994 Expos had a lineup full of on-base hounds, finishing third in the league in OBP that year. They had speed, with five players swiping enough bases to pro-rate out to 20 or more over a full season. They had one of the deepest and most balanced starting rotations in the league, with three lefties and two righties, finesse pitchers and power pitchers. Potential doubles and triples frequently died before ever hitting the turf, thanks to an outfield stuffed with human vacuum cleaners.

Then there was the bullpen. Though managers had always appreciated having both righties and lefties available in relief, Tony La Russa ramped up that interest in the '80s and '90s, aggressively playing matchups in the late innings, finding success with those tactics, and thus fostering a new wave of relief specialists. By 1994, every manager pined for a lefty reliever who could match up against sluggers like Barry Bonds and Fred McGriff in high-leverage situations.

Every manager, that is, but Felipe Alou. Just as he valued talent over experience when constructing a lineup, the Expos skipper sided with talent over handedness in building a bullpen. The Expos' top five relievers that year were all right-handers. He didn't need any lefties, if his righties were going to get everyone out.

"Wetteland was really as good against lefties as he was against righties with that big, hard curveball and that fastball he could blow by anybody," Alou said. "Shaw had that great slider and great sinkerball and pinpoint control. Mel Rojas was a starter who was mediocre, but the machine that was the Expos' player-development system made him into a great reliever, then a closer, with one of the best splitters in baseball. It's all a credit to the Expos' way of developing players. Not only our own players, but anybody who came to us."

With one of their youngest rosters ever (averaging just 26.2 years old), talent, depth, no obvious weaknesses, and a manager who could push the right buttons—the Duquette prophecy looked like it might get fulfilled.

The Expos' first big highlight came in the ninth game of the season. Pedro Martinez pitched brilliantly in his first start as an Expo, tossing six innings of one-run ball, giving up just three hits, and striking out eight. But he still got the loss, because his teammates couldn't score even a single run against Steve Trachsel and the Cubs. However, in his next start—his first in front of the home fans at the Big O—he became a legend.

As talented as he was in these early days, Martinez was still raw. He could throw his curve and changeup when ahead in the count 0–2 or 1–2, and get hitters to chase for strike three. But he hadn't yet figured out how to throw the ball over the plate consistently for strikes. What would make him so terrifying later in his career was his ability to snap off any one of his devastating pitches in any count—knowing the hitter had no chance one way or another— but that wasn't yet the case at age 22. His fastball was the pitch that really gave him problems; it also caused nightmares for his opponents. If there was one pitcher in the league that year liable to buzz your head with a 97-mile-per-hour fastball, it was Pedro.

Opinions vary on how and why that happened. The sympathetic view was that he really didn't have any idea where the ball was going, that early in his career.

"Felipe used to say, 'We're trying to teach him how to pitch inside, and he doesn't know how yet,'" said long-time Giants broadcaster and former ESPN play-by-play man Jon Miller. "He had that movement on his pitches that would get in on a right-handed hitter. He'd aim inside, and the pitch would go *way* inside."

"I remember they brought out a dummy," Martinez told me in a 2013 interview. "[Pitching coach] Joe Kerrigan wanted me to throw inside with the dummy standing there. I threw a few well, then I missed one and dented the dummy's head. Everybody laughed, but Kerrigan did not find it funny. He wouldn't support me, and didn't want to continue to work with me on pitching inside. Felipe was really supportive of me. After the dummy thing, he conducted all my bullpen [sessions]. Felipe and Bobby Cuellar [Kerrigan's replacement as pitching coach in 1997] helped a lot as far as correcting all those things."

The less charitable opinion about Pedro's wild streak was that he was throwing at people on purpose, using his wildness as a cover for plunking batters—or just scaring the hell out of them.

"By the time we got to 1997, his stuff was absolutely electric, the best stuff I've ever caught," said Darrin Fletcher, Martinez's catcher for four seasons in Montreal. "Leading up to then, absolutely—Pedro was a headhunter trying to hit everybody. He stopped when he realized, 'You know what? I don't even need to pitch inside. I'm just going to blow everybody up.' What an unbelievable arm he had."

The line between Pedro's intimidation and his losing control was so fine, he could even elicit mixed reactions from the same person in the same conversation. When I sat down with Dave Van Horne for a 2013 interview in Florida, the long-time Expos broadcaster first defended Martinez.

"I remember how Pedro made such good progress almost on a daily basis, even though he only pitched once every five days, being in the starting rotation," said Dave Van Horne. "I mean, he was working at it every day. They were working a lot on command of all of his pitches, but primarily the fastball, which had a tendency to get away from him. It would fly, it would sail, it would dip, it would dart, it would do a lot of things. He just couldn't control it very well."

Then, a few minutes later . . .

"I don't think Pedro ever wanted to put himself or his teammates in a situation where his feelings toward a hitter could put the outcome of the game in jeopardy no matter how he felt," said Van Horne. "But if he felt that a hitter had abused him, the hitter somewhere along the line was going to pay a price. I think if you looked at each start in which Pedro hit a batter, you could almost figure out whether it was purposeful or not."

Either way, it made hitters paranoid, to the point that some of them thought they might get hit every time up. That fear made a few hitters do some crazy things. But nothing crazier than what the Reds' Reggie Sanders did in that first Martinez start at Olympic Stadium.

Sanders was a dangerous hitter at that time, coming off a 20-homer season and a year away from a 1995 campaign that would cement him as one of the best sluggers in the game. He'd banged out three hits and knocked in five runs through the first two games of the series; and though Martinez didn't have a beef with him, he sure as hell wasn't going to let Sanders get comfortable in the batter's box and wail on pitches for a third game in a row. On Sanders' first time up, Martinez backed him off the plate with a fastball, causing Sanders to start jawing at him. A few moments later, Pedro struck him out swinging on a fastball. None of Sanders' teammates could get anything going either: from the first pitch, Martinez was mixing pitches beautifully, inducing lots of weak groundballs with soft stuff on the outside edge, then painting the inside corner with hard stuff. From the second inning through to Sanders' second at-bat in the fifth, no Cincinnati player could even work a three-ball count against Pedro, let alone get on base.

Sanders' second at-bat looked like a lot like his first. Refusing to let Sanders dig in, Martinez threw a fastball inside. The pitch wasn't dangerous, but did leave Sanders with another peeved expression his face—no posturing and whining this time, at least. Then Martinez fanned Sanders again on the fastball, eventually striking out the side in the fifth. The slaughter continued in the sixth and seventh, with the Reds rarely even making decent contact, and Pedro in complete command. Kevin Mitchell finally managed a deep flyball to start the eighth, but Moises Alou squeezed it for the first out of the inning.

That brought Sanders to the plate for the third time. Overmatched, he quickly fell behind 0–2. In just his fifth major league start, Martinez could now smell a perfect game. He had five outs to go—four if he could put Sanders away with one more strike. Martinez got the sign for a fastball, the same pitch he'd used to punch out Sanders twice already. He reared back and fired . . . and watched in horror as the ball sailed on him, nailing Sanders in the ribs. Pedro turned away from the plate toward the Expos dugout and threw up his hands in disgust: he couldn't believe he'd lost his perfect game. A split-second later, he found something else beyond comprehension: that Sanders would be so completely clueless that he'd charge the damn mound—as if Martinez meant to throw at him on an 0–2 count, five outs away from a perfecto. Sanders got to Pedro, tackled him, and both benches emptied.

"I just remember the frustration back then," Martinez said. "Being accused so much, being warned after two or three pitches, getting fined. I remember people looking at me to see what they could find, if they can find some weakness. The fact that I was small made me really attractive to guys wanting to beat me up. They thought they might get the weak side of me by charging me. Unfortunately for them, it did not work."

Even Reds catcher Brian Dorsett defended Pedro. "That's the way you've got to pitch," he said after the game. "You've got to bust them in and keep them honest."

Pedro got through the rest of the eighth without giving up a hit, only for Dorsett to break up the no-hitter leading off the ninth, chasing the Expos' starter from the game. As soon as Felipe Alou popped out of the dugout, the crowd began cheering like mad. In Martinez's first start ever at the Big O, the little guy had proven he could dominate any lineup (the Reds were the highest-scoring team in the National League that year), and that he'd do whatever was necessary to own the inside corner. As he jogged off the field, the cheers intensified. He tipped his cap, revealing his glorious Jheri-mullet. From that moment on, Pedro's starts became appointment viewing.

Martinez didn't get the win that day, since the bullpen couldn't hold the lead he'd left behind. But a pinch-hit single by valuable reserve outfielder Lou Frazier saved the day in the bottom of the ninth, and the Expos walked away with a 3–2 victory.

The next four games didn't go as well, as the Expos dropped four straight in Colorado and San Francisco. All told, Montreal had lost nine of its first 13 games of the season. Making matters worse was the hot start turned in by the Expos' brand-new division rivals, the Atlanta Braves. Realignment shifted the Braves to the NL East after the 1993 season, which was bad news for the Expos and the other clubs in the division. Atlanta was coming off three straight NL West titles, with World Series appearances in '91 and '92. Though the Braves weren't lacking for impressive hitters, their biggest strength lay in their pitching staff. Tom Glavine, Steve Avery, John Smoltz, and Kent Mercker gave Atlanta better-than-average options all the way through the number-five spot.

But Atlanta's staff ace was the Brave every team feared. Greg Maddux was coming off two straight Cy Young–winning seasons. In 1993, he led the National League in starts, complete games, innings pitched, and ERA. Though no one knew it yet, he hadn't even reached his peak, and was just entering a two-year stretch that to this day ranks as one of the best in baseball history, en route to one of the greatest pitching careers of all time. Through the first three starts of his '94 campaign, Maddux tossed two complete games, totalled 26 innings, struck out 20 batters, walked just one, and produced a 0.35 ERA. With a big assist from Maddux, the Braves jumped out to a scorching 13–1 record to start the year, building an 8½-game lead on the Expos.

A Braves-Expos rivalry formed quickly in their first year as intra-division combatants. The two teams shared the same spring training complex, and the Braves had developed into a powerhouse thanks mostly to killer scouting and player development—the very blueprint the Expos were trying to follow. For Georgia-born Expos outfielder Rondell White (a first-round pick who was mostly a reserve in '94 but would develop into one of the team's brightest young stars the following year), beating the Braves meant everything.

"I remember me and my brother and my cousin, cheering on the couch for those Braves teams in the '80s. 'Chambliss! Chambliss!!!' or whatever player was doing something big at the time," recalled White. "Then I got to meet some of these guys growing up, my idols; the first player I ever met was [Braves second baseman] Glenn Hubbard, it was so exciting. So now I'm in the big leagues, getting ready to play Maddux, Glavine, and Smoltz, America's team, TBS, all that. Playing against them, trying to beat them, there was a lot of extra incentive."

There'd be plenty of incentive for everyone when the Expos and Braves met up for the first time in '94. After that slow start, Montreal blazed through the league, winning 12 of 14; and at the same time, the Braves went ice cold. By the time the Expos got to Atlanta, they had surged to within a half-game of first place: win two out of three and they'd take over the NL East lead.

The series opener featured a classic matchup, with the young stallion Martinez taking on the dean of National League pitchers, Maddux. The Braves won the battle handily, with Pedro lasting just five innings while Maddux went the distance, shutting out the Expos with a four-hitter. In game two, wildly underrated Expos lefty Jeff Fassero pitched a gem, going 8⅔ innings, allowing just two runs, and striking out 11. But it wasn't good enough, as Tom Glavine bested him with a four-hitter, en route to a 2–1 Braves win.

Hoping to avoid a sweep, the Expos sent Ken Hill to the mound in the third game. I can vividly remember the day the Expos acquired Hill. After the 1991 season, we'd heard rumours that Dan Duquette was shopping Andres Galarraga, that the Cardinals were the Big Cat's most aggressive suitor, and that the Expos were after a starting pitcher. We were convinced Duquette was chasing Rheal Cormier. A left-hander who lacked overwhelming stuff, Cormier started working as a lumberjack before getting drafted in 1988 to play pro ball. Still, two factors made us think he'd end up an Expo. First, Galarraga's stock had plummeted following a miserable '91 season. Second, Cormier was a Francophone, a New Brunswick native of Acadian descent—about as close as you could get to a Québécois player without actual Quebec ties.

The Expos hadn't actually mined their home province all that much for talent before, with Claude Raymond and Denis Boucher standing out as rare exceptions 22 years apart. This was a sore spot for some, including Jacques Doucet, who believed the team could benefit greatly from drafting and developing local boys to one day play at the Big O. Given the boom in fan interest when Boucher eventually made his home debut, and the stellar careers later enjoyed by Quebec natives like Eric Gagne and Russell Martin, Doucet probably had a point. But as things turned out, the Expos wouldn't go for the French-speaking Cormier this time either; they went for Hill instead. When the news broke and I ran into fellow Maple Ridge Boys member Elan at school, we could only manage one reaction: "Ken Hill? Ken Hill?!?!?"

A lousy marketing move, maybe, and not a deal people expected . . . but definitely the right personnel decision. Never a big strikeout artist, Hill nonetheless matured into one of the

Expos' best pitchers, chewing up innings, keeping the ball in the ballpark, and keeping his team in games on a regular basis.

"He was huge in Montreal," said Van Horne. "He helped settle down all the younger, more inexperienced pitchers, including Pedro. He was just a take-charge guy, a terrific teammate, and a quality major league pitcher."

A slump-buster too. Facing the possibility of a sweep in Atlanta, Hill blew away the Braves in the series finale, tossing seven shutout innings on just three hits. He then gave way to Wetteland, who notched one of many unhittable performances that year: six batters up, six down, five of them on strikeouts.

When the calendar flipped over to June, the Expos turned into world beaters. They pulled off three series sweeps that month, dominating the Cubs, Mets, and Pirates. Usually comfortable at Olympic Stadium (even during so-so seasons), the Expos started creaming opponents regardless of venue: they would eventually end the season with the best road record in franchise history, and one of the best road marks by any team in years.

A different hero seemed to emerge every night. Larry Walker was unstoppable, hitting .322/.394/.587, ranking among the league leaders in multiple offensive categories, and like Andre Dawson and Ellis Valentine before him, making life hell for opponents with his rocket arm. Marquis Grissom ranked third in the league in stolen bases, and ran down every flyball and line drive hit within a 30-minute Metro ride from his glove. Sean Berry, the starting third baseman who took most of his at-bats in the seven- or eight-hole in '94, hit .278/.347/.453 and stole 14 bases without getting caught. At age 22, Wil Cordero led all NL shortstops in batting average, slugging average, and home runs. Moises Alou was a force of nature, batting .339/.397/.592 and finishing third in MVP voting.

Even the reserves got into the act. On June 3, sparsely used veteran first baseman Randy Milligan cracked a two-run, pinch-hit homer in the top of the eighth at Wrigley Field, erasing a 1–0 deficit and carrying Montreal to a 3–1 win. Two days later, utility infielder Freddie Benavides knocked in the go-ahead run in the 13th inning against the Cubs, completing the series sweep. Lenny Webster, the right-handed-hitting catcher acquired to platoon with Fletcher, played brilliantly all year long, hitting a robust .273/.370/.448 with a stack of big hits.

"They had everything," said Bud Black, who competed against the Expos as a member of the Giants' pitching staff from 1991 to 1994, then later became a big-league manager. "They had young players who were performing. Speed and power. They were well managed and played hard. The athleticism, the energy that those guys played with was something that I really remember."

The Expos' second matchup against the Braves came in late June. Montreal had gone 16–7 for the month leading into the three-game set at home, staying within striking distance of Atlanta at just 2½ games out. Attendance had started modestly in '94, but began to pick up as the wins multiplied. By the time the Braves arrived, everyone in town had to have a ticket. Nearly 132,000 fans hit the stadium for the those three games, a huge number for any Big O series, but a borderline fire safety violation for a Monday-to-Wednesday set. School was out—always a major factor for an attendance base that skewed young—and everyone understood the magnitude of this series. Even the normally affable Youppi! got into the act, pulling out a giant foam tomahawk and spending most of the series mocking the Braves and their ridiculous tomahawk-chop war cry.

"I remember the headline in *Le Journal de Montréal* before that series: 'Aux Barricades, les Gens!'—'To the barricades, everybody!'" said Jeff Blair, who along with his *Montreal Gazette* colleagues provided plenty of breathless coverage that week themselves. "The attitude was, 'We're going to storm Olympic Stadium and support the boys.' I think that is a Montreal thing, to be something of a latch-on sports crowd . . . unless it's hockey. Montreal's an events city, it's a sexy city, it's a fast-paced city. It likes the big show. And, in the atmosphere of Olympic Stadium, I always found—maybe it was the slamming of the seats even when it was empty, or the horns, or the chickens on the scoreboard—but I always found the noise per capita so high. The place was loud when no one showed up. When it was full, it was unbelievably loud."

Getting the Game 1 assignment for the Braves was their 170-pound destroyer of worlds, Greg Maddux. To be the best, the Expos would have to beat the best. But shockingly, they got to Maddux right away, cashing the game's first run on a Grissom double and a Frazier single. Then, sorcery. Again and again, the Expos threatened to add to their lead, only to have Maddux conjure up a spell to escape the jam. After that first run, loading the bases with two outs yielded nothing. Neither did the two-out double in the second, the leadoff double in the third, or the leadoff single in the fourth.

The crowd of 45,291 was noisy, but also getting increasingly anxious. As the Braves scored in the top of the sixth on the old double-steal-of-home-and-second play to tie the game at 1–1, a nervous murmur sliced through the boisterous atmosphere. Then, when the Expos got Cordero to third to start the bottom of the sixth, only for Maddux to Houdini his way out of that one too, many in attendance were ready to smash their fists into a brick wall.

Going to games in that era, however, I always felt that the Expos' most memorable rallies happened in the seventh. This isn't surprising: though front-line starting pitchers had long been expected to go nine innings, or come really close, by 1994 the combination of deeper, more potent lineups, friendlier hitters' parks, and tighter strike zones forced starters to exert maximum effort on just about every pitch. (Those who extol the virtues of old-time pitchers and believe that pitch-count monitoring is for wimps are often guilty of selection bias, choosing to remember Nolan Ryan and forget the thousands of promising young pitchers who've broken down from overuse.) That tougher sledding for starters in the '90s, combined with a greater awareness of the value of relief pitchers, made the seventh inning a dangerous time for managers, who had to decide whether to pull tiring starters or let them work out of their own jams. Though the Expos didn't necessarily score a disproportionate number of their runs in the seventh inning (after adjusting for league norms), the Gary Carter double and the Curtis Pride double—two of the decade's biggest highlights—both happened after the stretch. And on this night against the Braves, the Expos would get another unforgettable seventh-inning moment.

Grissom, who would have a monstrous four-hit game, led off with a single—then stole second, *and* third. Frazier walked, then quickly stole second himself. Two batters later, the bases were loaded with one out. Cordero then lined out to left, scoring Grissom and giving the Expos a 2–1 lead. The resulting ovation was probably one of the five biggest ever for a Big O sacrifice fly. But that wasn't the inning's roof-raiser—not by a long shot.

The next man up was Cliff Floyd. The Expos' first-round pick in the 1991 draft, Floyd was a 6-foot-5, 220-pound specimen, the number-one prospect in the game according to *Baseball America*. He had Ellis Valentine's tools, without the drama. Because the Expos already had the game's best young outfield in Moises Alou, Grissom, and Walker, Floyd became the primary first baseman in '94, despite being a 21-year-old rookie who was far more comfortable playing the outfield. He'd flashed some terrific minor league numbers while playing as one of the youngest players at every stop, but was now struggling as a near-full-time player in the big leagues—understandable for someone that inexperienced. Coming into that night's game, Floyd was hitting .277 with just 16 walks and two home runs in 238 plate appearances, making him one of the weakest threats in the Expos' loaded lineup. Facing Maddux with two outs and two on, with so much riding on the outcome of the game, seemed a terrible mismatch.

Floyd worked the count to 2–2. Then Atlanta catcher Javy Lopez put down the sign for a changeup. This was Maddux's heartbreaker, indistinguishable from a fastball out of his hand, then dying a quick death right before the batter tries to swing. This particular changeup was especially nasty, dropping all the way to Floyd's ankles: almost certainly, a big swing and a miss was about to happen.

Instead, Cliff Floyd smashed it to smithereens. Braves right fielder David Justice just turned and watched, the ball taking off like a rocket, landing in the right-field bleachers, and turning 45,291 brains to mush.

"I remember exactly where I was when that happened," recalled Alex Anthopoulos, a native Montrealer and diehard Expos fan who later went to work in the Expos' front office, and eventually became GM of the Blue Jays. "In Cape Cod at a friend's place, trying and trying until we finally found a radio. All of '94 was just so great. I never had as much passion for any team as I did for that team."

The players remember that game, and that series—in which the Expos took two out of three—as a turning point for the season.

"Later that night, we heard that Maddux tore up the locker room, just broke everything," Floyd told me over brunch in 2012, grinning at the memory. "I just thought, 'Now we have them right where we want them.'"

The big wins kept piling up. With a stroke of *Zelig*-like luck, I kept ending up at the ballpark for them. The Carter, Pride, and

Reggie Sanders games were all in Montreal, so it made sense that I'd be there for all of them. Yet somehow I got to see another pivotal Expos moment, 3,000 miles from home.

Immediately after the Braves series, the Expos flew to the West Coast for an 11-game road trip to close out the first half of the season. By the time they reached the final stop of the trip, a four-game series in San Diego, they still stood a game and a half behind Atlanta. Then the annihilation began. In Game 1, the reliable Ken Hill came through again, twirling a five-hit shutout that was over by the top of the first—a three-run homer by Fletcher giving the Expos all they'd need en route to a 7–0 win. Game 2 was an even bigger clobbering: Montreal took a 9–0 lead after just three innings, then rolled to a 14–0 wipeout led by Kirk Rueter, Jeff Shaw, and a balanced attack that saw every starter bang out at least one hit. The Padres briefly made Game 3 interesting, keeping the score tied 1–1 until the sixth. Then Walker cranked a two-run homer, more than enough for Montreal's underrated number-five starter, Butch Henry, to secure a 5–1 win. The Expos were now tied for first place, with a chance to pass the mighty Braves for the first time.

The series finale came on a beautiful, sunny Sunday afternoon. Jeff Fassero took the hill against Joey Hamilton, the Padres rookie in the midst of a terrific first season. Through his first nine starts in the big leagues, Hamilton had allowed only 14 earned runs, working out to a 1.94 ERA. Nobody could hit the guy. But the Expos didn't just hit him. They pulverized him.

When Moises Alou cranked a long home run to left in the first to open the scoring, I cheered silently in my seat, trying not to antagonize the perfectly nice Padres fans all around us. When San Diego countered with two runs in the bottom of the inning, I stewed. When Grissom blooped a double to right to cash Berry and tie the game in the top of the second, I gave a little fist pump. But later that inning, I wouldn't be able to hold it in any longer. A Frazier single and a Walker walk loaded the bases for Cordero, who from May 30 to July 9 (the third game of the Padres series) had hit .368/.416/.664, with 10 homers and 15 doubles in 152 at-bats. He'd already homered, doubled, and reached base six times in the series. You'd say this was the last guy Hamilton wanted to face in that spot, but half the lineup was on a multi-week stretch in which they'd put up video game numbers. Hoping to get ahead in the count, Hamilton slung a fastball. Cordero crushed it, a high shot down the left-field line that carried well over the wall. Grand slam.

I lost it—popping out of my seat, belting out a 20-second, un-Canadian "WOOOOOOOOOO!!!!!!!", jumping up and down, and nearly knocking over the old lady next to me. But who could restrain themselves at a time like this, after so many years of frustration? Montreal preserved that lead the rest of the way, with Alou tacking on a second homer in the ninth, clinching an 8–2 win. Meanwhile, on the other side of the country, the Braves fell at home to the Cardinals 6–1. The Expos went into the All-Star break right where we'd dreamed they'd be at the start of the season: all alone atop the National League East.

The time for trepidation was over. Players, fans, media—everyone was convinced this was going to be the Expos' year, that nobody was going to catch them, not even the Braves.

Darrin Fletcher: "At the start of games, we just seemed to get a two- or three-run lead in the first three innings all the time. We had Walker-Grissom-Alou, a freight train of hitters coming up in that lineup. Then we had Wetteland and Rojas, who made it almost impossible for teams to come back on us. Five guys made the All-Star Team, and we should have had more. We just flipped it to the on switch all year long."

Larry Walker: "Most of my career, you'd go to the park that night, and hope you were going to win it. In '94, we pretty much knew we were going to win it. Losing wasn't part of the equation. After the break, we played the Braves and beat 'em again. I remember leaving Atlanta, and we were just laughing. Like, 'This is our competition?!'"

Rondell White: "After one of those games in Atlanta, we were in the showers, and someone yelled out: 'The Braves are hamburger, when are we going to eat some steak too?!'"

Cliff Floyd: "We were a one-heartbeat type team. We stood up for one another. Our energy level was high. There was no thinking that we were going to lose. We knew we were going to win every night. We knew no one could beat us."

Nobody did. Not in the All-Star Game, when Alou belted a game-winning double in the bottom of the 10th to win it for the National League. Not on August 1, when Grissom launched a walk-off, inside-the-park home run to beat the Cardinals. (Google "Marquis Grissom walk-off inside-the-park home run." I'll wait.) And not from July 18 through August 11, a 23-game stretch in which the Expos lost a grand total of three times.

Only one thing could derail the second playoff berth in Expos history, and a shot at their first World Series ever.

Money.

By 1994, Major League Baseball's owners couldn't agree on how to share it, or even *if* they should share it. Teams with the weakest revenue streams were finding it harder and harder to survive financially. The richest teams had no interest in sharing with the poorest ones—not unless they got a major concession: a salary cap that would restrict players' earning ability, and put more of that money into owners' pockets instead. If players would bear the cost of keeping poorer teams afloat, the richer teams would sign off. If not, the owners would simply unilaterally impose their changes.

On June 14, Richard Ravitch, chief negotiator for the owners, unveiled their proposal. The payroll cap, as expected, was the deal's biggest feature. But the plan included multiple other features designed to tamp down salaries and transfer more money to owners. Salary arbitration, the system that allowed players to negotiate for higher pay after three seasons of service time (or two-plus seasons, in limited instances), would be eliminated. Players would be allowed to file for free agency after four years, instead of the existing rule requiring six years of service time. But free agency itself would become restricted, with teams claiming the right to match other clubs' top offers on players who became free agents after five or six years—thus erasing the existing system in which players had free rein to shop their services as they saw fit. As a sop in exchange for these concessions, owners said they'd guarantee that players receive 50 percent of league revenue. One problem: that would be a steep drop from the 58 percent that players were projected to get from the estimated $1.8 billion in MLB revenue for the '94 season.

The owners' proposal wasn't entirely without merit. The 58–42 revenue split in '94 was atypically large, and teams were still years away from the explosion in local TV revenue that would dramatically swing the balance of financial power in the owners' favour. Also, it was certainly true that several small-revenue teams were under the gun financially—none more so than the Expos. The combination of spotty attendance, sub-par local media deals, and numerous other factors had forced the Expos to slash expenses. Montreal, especially, needed a more generous revenue-sharing system in the worst way.

But there was just no way it was going to come out of players' pockets—not after they'd fought for so long to finally get unfettered free agency. And certainly not after the owners had colluded to hold down free-agent salaries in the '80s—with one of the most hawkish being Milwaukee Brewers boss Bud Selig, who was now pushing to restrict salaries again as baseball's acting commissioner. Feeling there was no other way to avoid having owners impose their will, the players went on strike on August 12.

For the Expos, who'd surged to a 74–40 record that was the best in all of baseball, this was certainly a tough break. But the consensus in the clubhouse was that the strike wouldn't last. A couple of weeks, maybe. Worst case, they'd be back playing around Labour Day.

"Felipe told us to stay in town," said Floyd. "Stay in town, and they would call us and keep us updated."

Nearly three weeks went by before the two sides finally sat down to try to hammer out a deal. Despite the presence of federal mediators, however, the talks went nowhere. On September 8, four weeks into the strike, the Players Association offered a plan that would levy a 1½ percent tax on the highest-payroll teams, which would then get funnelled to the poorest clubs. Also included in the plan was a measure that would have teams share 25 percent of gate receipts. The owners turned the deal down.

Throughout baseball, anger and frustration were building—nowhere more so than in Montreal. The Expos had struggled in one way or another for their entire existence. The expansion team that Bronfman and his partners had fought for nearly got handed to another city. Plans for a new ballpark got delayed and delayed, until the Expos finally ended up with a gigantic, money-losing lemon in Olympic Stadium. Star players started bolting. Bronfman sold the team. Brochu and his consortium ran the organization on a shoestring budget, with the Expos carrying the second-lowest payroll in baseball.

Yet somehow, against all odds, this underfunded team had run roughshod over the rest of the league, potentially setting up the first World Series trip in the club's existence. Losing that chance would be unfathomably painful. The lost revenue of a cancelled season (and playoffs) would have dire consequences for the Expos' bottom line, which would likely lead to money-driven panic moves. It would deny an incredibly talented and supremely entertaining group of players the chance to play out their dream season. Above all else, it would break the fans' spirits, turning thousands of Montreal baseball supporters against the game forever.

On September 14, the death blow was delivered. The season was cancelled. For the first time in 90 years, there would be no World Series.

"There was no other way to put it," said Floyd, "other than just . . . devastation."

Claude Brochu didn't it see it that way, however. He expressed disappointment over the season ending and the Expos being denied a shot at a playoff run. But he was also adamant about getting a revenue-sharing system that he hoped would help the Expos remain viable over the long haul.

"I think for baseball, it was the greater good," Brochu said. "You can't just be thinking in your own self-interest. You shouldn't be a part of ownership if that's the way you're thinking. We needed [revenue sharing] or we couldn't survive. It was a life-or-death struggle. So, I don't buy that, that I didn't look out for the best interests of the team. That's exactly what I did, and I was ready to sacrifice the season to do it, despite how good the team was."

I asked Brochu if he regretted the cancellation of what might've been a World Series in Montreal.

"I think it would have bumped up [revenue] to some extent, and maybe it would have been a little easier [in 1995 and beyond]. But I would have had to look at the financials. We were getting killed. We had no central revenue, no television money, no big crowds. I've done a calculation. I thought, if we had gone through to the World Series, we might have broken even."

For Brochu, the bottom line was that revenue sharing would improve financial conditions across the league, ushering in what he called "the golden years." Baseball would indeed experience a resurgence after the strike, thanks in part to revenue sharing, but also to Cal Ripken Jr. breaking Lou Gehrig's consecutive games streak, as well as the Sosa-McGwire home-run race that captivated fans throughout North America. But the Expos never got to share in baseball's bounty. Even if Brochu's long view had merit, Montrealers were livid over what had happened to their team. No one wanted to hear excuses or rationales.

I sure as hell didn't. I cried like a damn baby the day they cancelled the season. I even did something I never thought possible: I gave up on baseball. If this was how the game I loved was going to treat fans—especially Expos fans—then screw it, this wasn't worth the heartache.

But baseball was Expos' play-by-play man Dave Van Horne's livelihood, and he had to press on. He got back to work when play resumed, though he did stage a kind of silent protest. Van Horne carefully wrote the names of the entire 25-man roster on a little index card, then placed that card in his wallet, where it would sit through the harsh winter that followed that '94 disaster, into 1995 and onward.

Ask him about it today and Van Horne will pull out that card, read through the names, and flash a sad smile. Twenty years after baseball sabotaged the best team in Expos history, he remembers what might have been. That card—that incredible roll call—will sit in his pocket for as long as he lives, a reminder of a dream destroyed.

CHAPTER TEN

Expos University (1995–1999)

Y ou could spend half an afternoon recounting the many dark days in Expos history.

October 19, 1981: Blue Monday, the closest the Expos ever got to a World Series. December 10, 1984: the day they traded Gary Carter away, Charles Bronfman's frustrations with the game and rising salaries leading to the ouster of a legend. June 14, 1991: the official completion of the franchise sale, a transfer of ownership from Bronfman to the Claude Brochu–headed consortium that led to dire times. And of course, August 12, 1994: the day the players went on strike, denying the best Expos team ever its shot at glory.

But for sheer on-field impact, it's tough to beat April 5–8, 1995, one of the most destructive three-day periods for the Expos—or any other franchise. Just a few days earlier, on March 31, district court judge (and future Supreme Court Justice) Sonia Sotomayor issued an injunction against the owners, preventing them from using replacement players in regular-season games.

That ruling ended the strike, which had lasted 232 days. It also prompted Brochu to make a call, to Kevin Malone. The controlling partner's message to the general manager was a simple one: get rid of three of the team's best players, and do it immediately. Marquis Grissom, Ken Hill, and John Wetteland were about to become ex-Expos.

Brochu's reasoning made sense, on the surface anyway. The cancellation of the last 48 games of the 1994 season, along with the playoffs and World Series, had blown a big hole in the Expos' finances. Brochu claimed the team lost $15 million in '94 as a result, though there's no way to verify that, since baseball teams aren't required to open their books (and never do). Grissom, Hill, and Wetteland would cost a shade over $8 million combined in '94 and then would all get raises in '95 (they'd end up making $13 million between the three of them that year). Add Larry Walker, the best player of the four and a free agent who wasn't going to be re-signed under any circumstances, and Brochu and his partners would be dodging about $18 million in salary commitments for the 1995 season.

Meanwhile, fans had grown incredibly bitter and frustrated after everything that happened in '94, and though the Expos had tried to respond to that frustration by slashing season-ticket prices, total attendance was sure to drop precipitously. Aside from the fans' disenchantment, there was the likelihood that the team wouldn't be as good (or as exciting), and that the abbreviated, 144-game season would wipe out nine home dates. Rising operating costs and plummeting income, Brochu says, forced his hand.

"If the whole ownership group had said, 'All right, we'll put the money in, keep them,' then I would have considered it," Brochu explained. "But when we first worked out the [new partnership deal], I'd asked everyone: 'All right, are you prepared to put any money in?' 'No.' Everybody looked down. It was, 'No.' Clear. 'No,' and that was it. When they said that, I had to commit to having no cash calls. So I said to Kevin, 'We cannot go into this season with these four guys—we can't do it. I can't take the risk, we're going to lose too much money.'"

Of course, the Expos' cash crunch was partly Brochu's doing. He'd voted along with his fellow owners for the plan that ultimately (and predictably) alienated the players and caused the strike in the first place. A dissenting vote might not have mattered anyway, given other owners' commitment to their cause. But even if you could understand Brochu's point of view, you could understand the fans' side too: that the man in charge of their favourite team had sold them out.

And now he was selling the team's star players. Teams trade established veterans for prospects all the time, and it often works (the Expos themselves had done it, trading Rusty Staub to the Mets 23 years earlier, an unthinkable move at the time that worked out well anyway). But ditching four front-line players at once was a lot more extreme. Still, Malone could make it a manageable proposition; all he needed was some time, and a little bit of leverage.

He got neither of those things. The Expos would play their first game on April 26 that year—meaning Malone had less than four weeks to make his moves. Practically speaking, he had even less. The deadline to offer players arbitration was April 7 (normally the arbitration date would be months earlier, but the strike had pushed everything back), and Brochu didn't want to offer arbitration only to have the big four accept, leaving the Expos on the hook for their 1995 salaries. That gave Malone just *one week* to dispose of four of the best players in the league.

Malone tried to lobby his boss for more time, but Brochu refused. Okay, then how about keeping one or two of the four players. Same reply—no.

"We'd traded quality guys before, just never in those circumstances," said Malone. "Everybody in baseball knew we had to move these guys. Getting full value was going to be very difficult."

Not difficult. Impossible.

On April 5, Malone traded Ken Hill back to his former team, the Cardinals. In return, the Expos got three players: pitchers Kirk Bullinger and Bryan Eversgerd, and outfielder DaRond Stovall. These were relatively young players, with Eversgerd's 67⅔ innings pitched in 1994 the only major league experience among them. But they were not really prospects: Stovall had the highest pedigree as a fifth-round pick, and none of the three ever made *Baseball America*'s top 100 or any other prospect list. They would later bear this out, with Bullinger and Eversgerd combining to throw just 28 innings for the Expos, and Stovall garnering just 78 at-bats . . . for his entire major league career.

Malone's second trade that day sent John Wetteland to the Yankees. In return, the Expos got only one player: Fernando Seguignol, a 6-foot-5, 257-pound giant of a first baseman with great raw power—and no earthly idea how to tell a ball from a strike. The English translation for the French word *guignol* is clown, an appropriate description in this case, given how badly the Yankees clowned the Expos in the trade. But hey, the move came with *some* good news. New York sent back $2 million in the deal, which Brochu and his partners used to balance their self-imposed microscopic budget, because putting another cent of their own money into the team to build a winner would surely have triggered the immediate bankruptcy of Bell, Desjardins, and all the other gigantic conglomerates that owned a piece of the Expos.

The next day, the third domino fell, as Malone shipped Marquis Grissom to Atlanta. In return, the Braves delivered three players: outfielders Roberto Kelly and Tony Tarasco, and pitcher Esteban Yan. Tarasco lasted just one season in Montreal, and quickly proved he had no business starting in the big leagues. Yan never suited up for the Expos at all; Montreal sold him to Baltimore the next spring, and he later went on to play for six additional teams, lasting 11 mediocre seasons in the majors. His biggest contribution to Expos folklore came in an episode of *The Simpsons* years later, when Bart and Milhouse, pretending they were big-league ballplayers, conjured up the two most obscure names possible: "I'm Tomokazu Ohka of the Montreal Expos! And I'm Esteban Yan of the Tampa Bay Devil Rays!" As for Kelly, he played just 24 games in Montreal before getting flipped to the Dodgers; at least Malone was able to turn that lemon into lemonade, acquiring Henry Rodriguez.

The nail in the coffin, however, was Larry Walker. Here was an elite player—a *Canadian*—who loved playing in Montreal. At 28 years old, Walker was just coming into his own, posting his best season in '94 and finishing 11th in MVP voting that year. If anything, he was underrated in some circles, playing away from the media spotlight in Montreal and putting up his best numbers during a season that got washed away. Baseball's cognoscenti, though? They knew *exactly* how good Walker was, and how great he would become.

"Tony La Russa still uses Walker as a comparison when he's talking about players—'This guy reminds me of Walker,'" said Jeff Blair. "Charlie Manuel would always use him as a comparison. Jim Fanning said he's the best instinctive ballplayer he'd ever seen."

Unlike Hill, Wetteland, and Grissom, Walker was a free agent, meaning the Expos couldn't trade him. What they could do was offer him arbitration. Normally, a player of Walker's calibre would turn down the offer, preferring to sign a lucrative, long-term deal rather than reach a one-year agreement; the point of the arbitration offer would be to get compensatory draft picks when Walker left, thus acquiring potential building blocks for the future. The problem—incredibly—was that Walker wanted to stay. He wanted nothing more than to get another crack at competing in '95, with the same killer '94 teammates around him. Under normal circumstances, this would be a boon to the team offering arbitration, the chance to retain a great player without committing the massive sums of money that a star testing the free-agent market for the first time would normally command. But rather than embrace the idea of Walker coming back relatively cheaply, Brochu feared it: "relatively cheaply" was still too expensive for the consortium. The Expos didn't offer Walker arbitration, meaning they'd forfeited the valuable draft picks that would come if another team signed him. The day after the arbitration deadline, the Rockies inked the Maple Ridge Boy to a four-year, $22.5 million contract.

While Expos fans wailed in protest of the team's fire sale, Brochu shrugged it all off. He naively believed that he could build another team that would be as good as the '94 Expos.

"I said look, 'People are going to hate us, but they'll forget. They won't be mad at us forever. They'll come back.' I had confidence that we had that ability, that we'd rebuild, but this time with more money [from revenue sharing]."

Though Brochu believed he was taking the long view, his was really a short-sighted glimpse of the situation. Had the Expos opted to retain Hill, Wetteland, Grissom, and Walker, they would've gone into the '95 season as favourites to win it all. Some fed-up fans would've stayed away regardless, but others who might have been on the fence after the strike would've returned to the ballpark—eager to see a great group of players make the postseason run they'd been denied a year earlier. That would have meant a softer landing with regard to both ticket sales and ticket prices. A playoff berth would have helped rebuild the Expos' tattered brand far more quickly than Brochu's plan. And with more young talent knocking on the door—Rondell White already up in the majors, and a new batch of prospects rising quickly—they could've kept on winning.

Even if things didn't go as well, if the Expos didn't win as expected or fan support didn't return as hoped, Brochu could've ordered Malone to trade away the team's best players later in the year. That way, the GM would have had plenty of time to size up the trade market, solicit offers from multiple suitors, and acquire the kind of young talent that could form the foundation for the next winning ball club in Montreal (exactly as Brochu hoped). There might have been some near-term financial losses, sure. But if the ultimate goal was to ensure the team's long-term success, landing something better than Tony Tarasco and a handful of magic beans would've been the way to go.

"I ran into Claude Brochu at a '94 reunion," said Cliff Floyd. "He brought up everything that happened. You just look at him, and you go, 'You could've had a dynasty. You could have hung your hat on this team for all time.'"

That's just not how Brochu operated. To him, the cautious move was always the correct one.

"The difficulty I had with Claude Brochu is that the entertainment of sports means doing everything you can to try to win," said Mark Routtenberg, former president of Guess Canada and a minority partner with a small stake in the team. "What's going to happen on the field, you don't know. You never know. It's still worth the gamble—if you lose, it's okay with the fans, because at least you tried. But if the fans feel you're never trying to get there, that there's no entertainment value, then they're going to stop supporting you."

To nobody's surprise, the Expos stunk in '95. With payroll slashed 35 percent, Montreal limped to a 66–78 record, finishing dead last in the NL East. Attendance tumbled 26 percent compared to '94 levels, shrivelling up as the year went on and

319

bottoming out on September 11, when just 9,715 fans saw Pedro Martinez toss a four-hit shutout at the Mets. After all the promise of 1992, all the excitement of 1993, and all the domination in 1994, 1995 was a total disaster.

Watching what the four departed stars did for other teams only made everything more depressing. After starting the season in St. Louis, Hill got dealt to Cleveland later in July. He pitched reasonably well down the stretch, then churned out one of the biggest starts in Indians history: seven innings of shutout ball that tied the American League Championship Series at 2–2, and set Cleveland up for a trip to the World Series two games later. The winning pitcher in the clinching Game 6? Old friend Dennis Martinez, who at age 41 fired seven shutout innings of his own to beat the Mariners and his former Expos teammate Randy Johnson. Meanwhile, Wetteland went from being one of the best closers in the National League to taking his place among the American League's elite with the Yankees. With Wetteland's help, the Yanks returned to the playoffs themselves for the first time in 14 years—and won the World Series a year after that, with Wetteland saving all four victories and being named World Series MVP. Finally, all Walker did in '95 was hit .306/.381/.607, launch 36 homers, and lead the Rockies to their first-ever playoff berth, in just their third season of existence.

None of those arcs hurt quite as much as Grissom's, though. When Malone announced that Grissom was up for bid, the two teams that showed the most interest were the Marlins and the Braves. Malone ultimately chose Atlanta, walking just a couple hundred yards across the West Palm Beach complex that the Expos and Braves shared to hammer out a deal.

"It definitely makes them a much better club," Malone said after the trade was made. "I think this basically will bring a world championship to the Braves at some point."

Not some point—that very year. Grissom didn't hit all that well during the '95 regular season. But he was an absolute terror in the playoffs. First, he hit .524 with three home runs in a four-game League Division Series win over Walker's Rockies. When the Braves made it to the World Series against Hill's Indians, Grissom starred again, hitting .360 in the six-game series. With two outs in the ninth inning of Game 6 and the Braves leading 1–0, Atlanta closer Mark Wohlers threw a fastball on the outside corner. Indians second baseman Carlos Baerga cracked a flyball to left-centre. The ball drifted, drifted, then finally landed . . . in Grissom's glove.

The Braves would go on to torment the Expos (and the rest of the National League East) for another decade, winning 11 straight NL East crowns, 14 division titles in 15 years all told. Expos fans couldn't help but wonder if that could have been *them* celebrating every year—if 1994's best team in baseball could have become a dynasty—had Brochu convinced the team's cheapskate owners to spend a few damn dollars, or taken a leap of faith that short-term financial pain would lead to long-term success. If instead of seeing their favourite players sprinkled around the league, making World Series–clinching catches, those stars could've stayed in Montreal and brought a championship to *la belle province*.

My self-imposed divorce from baseball didn't last long. My girl-friend, Angèle, bought me a 1959 Felipe Alou rookie card as a birthday present, just a few days after the '94 season was can-celled. The gift reminded me that I loved baseball and its history, that one season didn't mean everything in the grand scheme of things, and that the game would move on. As of this book's spring 2014 publication, she and I have been married for 16 years. In the end, I was with the Expos for the long haul as well: it's just that the same couldn't be said about the players.

Some earlier-era players hung around longer. Gary Carter and Andre Dawson spent parts of 11 seasons in Montreal, Tim Raines 12, Tim Wallach and Steve Rogers 13—with Rogers playing his entire career as an Expo. By the '90s, though, the life cycles had begun to shrink. Walker and Grissom were Expos for six seasons, Wetteland and Hill just three. Even front-office people started to leave more quickly. Dave Dombrowski had become baseball's youngest general manager when he came to Montreal in 1987, only to leave for Miami four years later. Dan Duquette spent four seasons as farm director, two-plus as GM, then left for that dream job in his home state of Massachusetts with the Red Sox. Kevin Malone took over as scouting director in '91, but would leave his GM job in '95 after becoming disillusioned by that season's fire sale.

All these players and decision makers had studied at baseball's signature academy for young talent, then gone out into the world to pursue bigger opportunities. As Michael Farber put it, they'd all graduated from Expos University.

"We'd lose players to other teams, and it got to the point where we were *always* underdogs," said Darrin Fletcher, who stuck around for six seasons, longer than most Expos players in the '90s (he wanted to get his master's degree before leaving). "We were the beneficiary of low expectations, that we had low-risk, high-reward type teams. We didn't have any pressure. Felipe fostered that. As players, we felt we were fighting against not just the rest of the league, but even against our own organization, since they were constantly purging our roster. That motivated us. We used it to our advantage."

Motivation is great. Talent is better. Only three of the starting eight from 1994's lineup were still everyday players for Montreal in '96. To fill the many holes created by players leaving via trades and free agency (not to mention the departing coaches and front-office staff), the Expos turned to their perennially productive minor league system.

☞ THE BIG, BAD, BRAWLIN' SENATORS ☜

The 1993 Harrisburg Senators were one of the biggest, baddest minor league teams that ever played. That year, the Expos' Pennsylvanian Double-A affiliate featured 22 players who went on to play in the major leagues. The Senators had four first-round picks on the roster: Cliff Floyd, Rondell White, Shane Andrews, and Gabe White. They went 94-44, winning the Eastern League's regular-season crown by 19 games. This wasn't merely a great team, though. The '93 Senators had the same cockiness that defined the '94 Expos. They strutted onto the field every night knowing they were going to win.

"We took pride in beating the shit out of people," said Floyd, smiling at the memory. "It was no-holds-barred. If you look back at our team down in Harrisburg, it was unreal. Literally, it was stupid. We had guys like Tyrone Woods who had 16 bombs and would just sit there on the bench. Same thing with Oreste Marrero. These were really good players and we'd have to spot-start them at third or wherever because there was no room in the lineup. If you threw anything around the plate, we were going to knock that shit as far as we could. The owner got so mad, because he kept having to buy more baseballs. We would just launch them."

Sooner or later, a team that good—and that arrogant—was going to piss somebody off. The London Tigers were that some-body. The first seven times Harrisburg played London in 1993, the Senators won each and every matchup, several of them by lopsided scores. The Tigers were a lousy team that year, and would go on to finish 12 games below .500. But coming into their eighth game against the Senators that season, they'd grown sick and tired of getting pushed around. The two managers had known each other for years (they were even consecutive managers for the Reds' Chattanooga affiliate), further stoking the rivalry. Harrisburg's manager was Jim Tracy, who'd been recruited by Dan Duquette specifically to manage that team, given how heavily invested the Expos were in those players' success. London's manager had not only played against Tracy in the minors, he also had some familiarity with Tracy's new organization. Fellow by the name of Tom Runnells.

By 2009, Tracy would be managing the Rockies and Runnells—17 years after the Schwarzkopf impression heard 'round the world—would be his bench coach. In 2012, I sat the two of them down in spring training and had them (along with Floyd and Rondell White, in separate conversations) reminisce about one of the wildest brawls in baseball history.

"We were sick of 'em all right," said Runnells. "Of course, why wouldn't you be? When you're sitting there getting beat, just thrashed every day by this team."

"So we had two guys on, and Floyd was the hitter," recalled Tracy. "Floyd just crushes one, hits it quite a long way, and puts us ahead. Then Oreste Marrero comes up. Wonderful, wonderful human being, we nicknamed him "Full Metal Jacket" because he had forearms bigger than Steve Garvey's and was probably the strongest guy on the team. So Marrero is the next hitter after Floyd and . . . I mean, Floyd's homer was titanic, it really was. Then Marrero gets a 3–2 pitch . . . out of the strike zone up, and he hits one to centre field even further than Floyd did. Long gone."

"They're thumpin' us, again," said Runnells. "We've got these little guys playing third, short, second, couple good players out in the outfield, whatever. Not the greatest club. And they're crushing us."

"So now Mike Hardge comes up," continued Tracy. "He was a second baseman that had a little bit of flair."

Hardge was just 5-foot-11, 183 pounds. He hit just six home runs all year and was never a big power hitter, especially not compared to many of his slugging behemoth teammates.

"Mike Hardge was my first roommate ever—he was the jokester of the team," said White. "I used to make the comparison to Rickey Henderson. He was *super* cocky. After those two home runs, he pointed his bat at the bleachers."

The other Harrisburg players knew he was just clowning around. London's manager didn't think it was funny. At all.

"My buddy over here (Runnells), he walks out to home plate and he's yelling," said Tracy.

"You have to show some respect, come on!" said Runnells. "So okay, I go back to the dugout. I turned to [pitching coach] Sid Monge and I said, 'Sid, we're gonna go to blows right now, so just get ready.' The next pitch, boom! Hardge gets drilled, and here we go."

"I'm trying to think of who was on that London team that stood out to me . . . Danny Bautista!" said Floyd. "Danny Bautista straight knee-mugged everybody. He was just a mean dude. He hated our pitcher. Tracy was yelling, 'Stay back!' I guess Tracy was worried about us getting hurt. A brawl was the last thing he wanted. It was sort of like, hey man, don't hurt nobody and let's get away from this."

"The next thing I know, [6-foot-2, 225-pound Harrisburg outfielder] Glenn Murray's got me in a headlock," said Runnells. "And I know some of these guys from the Expos days when they were younger kids. And they knew me! Glenn's got me around the head and I've got him around the waist, you know, like, what am I gonna do here? And I said, 'Glenn, we are not fighting, we are not going down.' And the next thing I know, I'm on the ground."

"I would venture to say of all the brawls that I've seen or been involved in as a player, coach, or manager in baseball, this one is at the top," said Tracy. "It was unbelievable. It lasted for a good 15 to 20 minutes. Every time we thought we got it settled down, there'd be another fight breaking. How many players were kicked out? Nine or ten? It was unbelievable."

Amid all that pandemonium, players and managers on both sides clearly remember one enduring image. While big stars like Floyd and White stayed out of the scrum, Harrisburg left-hander Joey Eischen lost it. He grabbed two London players and put them both in headlocks, marched around the field, and wouldn't let go.

"He was mad because nobody was going to fight him—they were saying, 'Stay away from this guy!'" chuckled Floyd. "Then he got those two guys and wouldn't let go. After the game, we were like, 'Damn, we've got some newfound respect for Joey Eischen!'"

Five players from that Harrisburg team—White, Andrews (the starting third baseman who'd replaced Sean Berry), Floyd, Kirk Rueter, and hard-throwing Venezuelan right-hander Ugueth Urbina—played key roles on the '96 Expos, with White now installed as the everyday centre fielder, Rueter back in the rotation, and Floyd relegated to part-time duty after injury cost him much of the '95 season. The holdovers from the '94 team included Moises Alou, Fletcher, and Lansing in the lineup, Martinez and Fassero in the rotation, and Rojas in the bullpen, now in the closer role vacated by Wetteland. Several new additions made the team much better, much faster than you'd have expected after the disastrous '95 campaign.

Mark Grudzielanek took over at shortstop in '96, after the Expos traded Wil Cordero to Boston. An 11th-round pick who never projected as a big prospect, Grudzielanek played well,

hitting .306, scoring 99 runs, and making the All-Star Team. On the pitching side, the 22-year-old Urbina split time between the rotation and bullpen, and did a decent job in the process, striking out nearly a batter an inning. The hunch my friends and I once had about Rheal Cormier proved to be right as well—we were just four years too early. The Expos got Cormier from the

Red Sox in the Cordero trade, and the Acadian lefty gave them 27 respectable starts.

Three other newcomers quickly became fan favourites as well. The Expos acquired David Segui on June 8, 1995, in a one-for-one trade that sent pitching prospect Reid Cornelius to the Mets. Cornelius never panned out in New York, but Segui did in Montreal, immediately. Already having a strong season for the Mets at the time of the swap, Segui mashed the ball for the Expos, hitting .331 in 58 games.

As lousy as Montreal was in '95, Segui was a rare bright spot. His 59th game as an Expo came at Shea Stadium. The Maple Ridge Boys were there, on the first edition of what would become an annual Expos road trip tradition. With the first baseman returning to New York to play his old team, we couldn't resist the chance to act like jerks.

In the top of the first, the Expos put runners on first and second with one out, bringing Segui to the plate to face Jason Isringhausen. Despite his high batting average, Segui was clearly playing over his head, and wasn't a particularly great hitter for that era, possessing only moderate power at a time when first basemen were launching 35–40 homers a year seemingly at will. We didn't care. We wanted to let the Mets fans have it.

As they announced Segui's name on the loudspeaker, the four of us got up, and at the top of our lungs, in the middle of the crowded first-base-side box seats, belted out: "M-V-P! M-V-P!"

The first pitch from Isringhausen was a fastball right down Broadway. Thwack! Segui smoked it, a bomb to right field that cleared the wall with room to spare. Three-run homer. "M-V-P! M-V-P! M-V-P!!!!!" If you could have only seen the looks on the Mets fans' faces as we chanted Segui all the way around the bases. After the game, a 3–1 Expos win, the four of us spilled out of the stadium. As the trademark post-game Shea Stadium song played

over the loudspeakers, we sang, horribly out of tune: ". . . I want
to be a part of it! New York, New Yooooork!" Unlike powerhouse
teams like the Yankees and Red Sox, the Expos never got much
support on the road. So we were only too happy to make asses of
ourselves at Shea. Anything for the cause.

Another newcomer, Henry Rodriguez, made a much bigger
impression in '96. After coming over in the Roberto Kelly deal in
May 1995, Rodriguez played just a handful of games for the rest
of that season.

Then, in '96, he went nuts. In 145 games, Rodriguez slammed
36 home runs and 42 doubles, and made his first (and only)
All-Star Game. Glomming onto Rodriguez's easy smile and prodigious power, fans began paying tribute to the team's new left
fielder. Every time he cracked a long ball, *les partisans* hurled Oh
Henry! bars on the field—another goofy tradition you could only
find at the Big O.

Then there was F. P. Santangelo. The Michigan native became
a hero in Ottawa, which was great news for fans of the Lynx (the
Expos-affiliated Triple-A franchise that launched in 1993), but not
so much for Santangelo: if you hang around a Triple-A team long
enough to get your number retired, as Santangelo did, that's not
a good sign for your chances in the big leagues. After three years
at Triple-A, six in the minors all told, he wondered if he'd ever
achieve his dream of playing in the Show.

Santangelo was finally offered a shot in the spring of '95. With
the strike lasting through the winter and into the spring, the
owners planned to use replacement players to start the season.

"We went to home plate at the minor league complex in
Lantana, Florida," Santangelo told me in 2012. "Kevin Malone
was speaking. All the A-ball teams, Double-A, Triple-A, all the
coaches, everyone was there. He said, 'I'll make this easy on you
guys. I made you do it, blame it on me. If you've got a problem

with that, you can leave right now.' I was the only guy who put a bag over my shoulder and left. When I got to the majors I wanted it to be the happiest time of my life. Getting a hit off a scab truck driver wouldn't do anything."

Santangelo got lots of support for his stance from his former minor league manager, Felipe Alou. People noticed, including the *Montreal Gazette*'s writer Jeff Blair.

"People ask me, 'What is the thing you remember about Felipe, one act or one thing that Felipe Alou did that you remember,'" said Blair. "What I'll always remember is when they put the screws to Santangelo, when they wanted him to be a scab. This is a guy who had been in the minors for all of those years, he's finally offered a chance, and he doesn't know what to do. They're basically telling him, 'If you don't come, if you don't do this, you're not coming back.' So Felipe tells him: 'If they get rid of you, they'll have to get rid of me too.'"

They didn't get rid of Santangelo—or Felipe. And on August 2, 1995, the 5-foot-10 spark plug of a superutilityman finally got his break, playing in his first major league game. This was partly Alou giving Santangelo a chance after what was now nearly seven seasons in the minors. But Santangelo would prove to be a better player than most expected. In 1996, despite never being handed a starting job, he appeared in 152 games in left field, centre field, and right field . . . and at second base, third base, and shortstop. He was one of the Expos' most valuable players, hitting .277/.369/.407 and playing excellent defence. Doing everything he could to reach base, he became a hit-by-pitch machine, getting plunked 48 times between the 1997 and 1998 seasons—HBP numbers not seen since the early '70s, when Ron Hunt broke the all-time single-season record by getting drilled 50 times. We loved Santangelo, and even gave him a dopey nickname: if garden-variety hustle players got praised for their intangibles, we lauded F. P. for his "Santangibles."

This collection of players couldn't match up with their '94 predecessors, but against all odds, they became contenders. They got off to one of their fastest starts ever, winning 17 of their first 25 games, the last win a 21–9 whitewash of the Rockies at Coors Field that saw Grudzielanek, Segui, Fletcher, and Santangelo combine for 13 hits and 16 RBI. From April 5 through May 18, the Expos stood alone in first place in the NL East. The Braves wouldn't let that situation last for long, riding a 19–6 month of May to reclaim first place. But Montreal wouldn't fold, surging to a 47–33 record at the end of June, just three games behind Atlanta.

As July got under way, it was clear that the Expos had enough talent to hang in the race for a while. But they also had major weaknesses. Though Pedro and Fassero were in the midst of excellent seasons, the rest of the rotation was merely decent, with the number-five spot a revolving door of iffy options. The bullpen also lacked depth, with few reliable pitchers after Rojas thanks to post-1994 attrition. Given the excitement this underdog Expos team was starting to generate, and the brutal ending to Montreal's last playoff push, making some upgrades before the July 31 trade deadline seemed like a no-brainer. With a chance to capture fans' imagination and take a major step toward erasing the ill will of '94, new general manager Jim Beattie scoured the league for potential upgrades, then acquired . . . Mark Leiter, a 33-year-old right-hander with a 5.19 ERA.

You couldn't blame Beattie. Like every Expos GM in the post-Bronfman era, Beattie had his hands tied by ownership's steadfast refusal to ever spend real money, or even to take a little risk when all the stars aligned in the team's favour.

"We knew, if we were close, that we weren't going to get any real help," said Fletcher. "No chance."

Though the Braves pulled away as the season wore on, the Expos still had a shot at the playoffs, thanks to the Wild Card system that took effect in 1995 (after the intended first Wild Card year, 1994, ended prematurely). Montreal went down to the last weekend of the regular season with a chance to play into the postseason for the first time since 1981.

The attendance for the series opener (against the Braves; it *had* to be the damn Braves) was 33,133, nowhere near a full house, but at least a decent turnout given how badly burned many Expos fans felt after the strike. Atlanta pulled John Smoltz from the game after just five innings, and the Expos immediately jumped on the Braves bullpen, thanks to a two-run homer by Segui in the sixth. Unfortunately, neither Fassero nor Montreal's bullpen had it that night, either, and the Expos fell 6–4. There was still an outside chance, however: if the Padres could lose their next two games, and Montreal won their next two, it would force a one-game playoff. With the Padres playing an afternoon game on the West Coast, players gathered around in the clubhouse to watch. But it was not to be. By the time the first pitch was thrown at 7:38 that night at the Big O, the outcome had been decided: the Expos were out, again. They wouldn't have another winning season for the rest of the decade.

What followed the '96 season was yet another player exodus. Montreal traded Jeff Fassero away for three players who weren't nearly as good as Jeff Fassero. Cliff Floyd went to Miami in a deal that at least brought back a quality pitcher in Dustin Hermanson, but also proved to be a sell-low, as Floyd blossomed into a star with the Marlins. Meanwhile, Moises Alou and Mel Rojas left via free agency—the Expos couldn't even keep their manager's son and nephew.

The vicious cycle had to stop. No matter how productive the farm system might be, the Expos were going to keep coming up short if they had to ditch two or three of their best players every year. Though the league's revamped revenue-sharing program had helped kick a few million dollars Montreal's way, that new money was just enough to keep the ship from sinking. Salaries were rising across baseball, and local revenue streams were a mess, with the team's attendance continuing to lag near the bottom of the league, and TV and radio not offering much help. If the Expos were going to be saved, there was only way to do it: build a new ballpark.

Felipe Alou told me a story that crystallized the state of Expos baseball, and of Olympic Stadium, in the late '90s.

"I have a friend from the Dominican Republic who's a team owner there," said Alou. "My friend is a very successful man in business and baseball, a very rich man. One year he came to Montreal to talk with me and to see the Expos' operations. He came with some friends from the Dominican Republic and stayed at the hotel downtown, the Queen Elizabeth. He told me that he went around the city to see if he could buy an Expos hat. He couldn't find a store downtown that would sell him one. Then, he and his two friends took a taxi to go to Olympic Stadium. When they arrived, the driver knew where Olympic Stadium was, but didn't know where the entrance was.

"He told me that for the one week he was in town, he never saw one person with an Expos hat. The day he went to see a game the first time, we had 12,000 fans. He told me those 12,000 fans had to be the best fans in the world. When he arrived at the stadium—let's say we were playing the Cincinnati Reds—he and his friends got out of the taxi and walked around the stadium, and there were no signs anywhere that said, 'Tonight, the Expos play Cincinnati.' How could they get even 12,000 fans, he wanted to know, if he couldn't find a hat, he doesn't see a store downtown that sells hats, and when he comes to the ballpark you can't find the door, and there are no signs advertising the game? My friend said, 'No wonder they don't have fans here!' I believe he was right."

The erosion of the Expos' fan base in the '90s is a complicated issue that can't be boiled down to just one factor. The fiasco of 1994 hurt. Losing star players to other teams, over and over, hurt a lot. The Expos were one of the winningest teams in baseball from 1992 to 1996, even counting the miserable '95 season, but when they stopped winning largely because of players leaving, that gave fans more reason to stay away. By the later 1990s, the local press became a problem too. Some of the French press took anonymous tips handed to them by disgruntled local consortium members and blew them up into exposés of dysfunction between Claude Brochu and his partners. The English media criticized everything else, including the team turning into a cellar-dweller. A lot of the criticism was justified: the team *was* terrible and the discord inside the ownership group would play a significant role in future events, but the bottom line was that reading about the Expos became a daily exercise in negativity.

Much of the blame for the waning attendance, and the team's faltering image, lay with Olympic Stadium itself. The collapsed beam, the roof that never worked, and the cold, cavernous, uninviting atmosphere within the seating bowl were all turnoffs. The location in the East End, away from major population centres, was a major drawback. Fans who lived in the western suburbs lost interest in schlepping all the way to the stadium. People from other parts of the city didn't want to cross bridges or tunnels. The large business community downtown was geographically closer, but—with no fun restaurants, bars, or ancillary activities of any kind nearby—the Big O wasn't appealing to them either.

Brochu knew all this, and knew that getting out of Olympic Stadium and into a new, baseball-only park was the best way to help the team survive (maybe even thrive) long-term. To build support for that new stadium, Brochu needed to convince everyone—Major League Baseball, potential financiers in the

Quebec premier's office, and the media—that the Big O wasn't fit for baseball.

But there was a fine line between strategic anti-marketing and being so negative (and convincing) that fans took Brochu at his word and decided they, too, should stop going to the ballpark. The commissioner's office joined the anti–Olympic Stadium campaign, with Bud Selig insisting that the old park was untenable. In '97, attendance slid another 7 percent to an average of 18,489 fans a game. In 1998, the bottom dropped out: the Expos drew fewer than a million fans, the per-game average of 11,295 representing a 39 percent free-fall. Though many factors combined to squash attendance, for many fans it felt as though a restaurant owner was inviting you to eat at his restaurant, then telling you there are cockroaches in the soup. There *were* cockroaches at the Big O— literally and figuratively—but when Selig backed Brochu's play, it came off to many locals as an American outsider sticking his nose where it didn't belong.

Brochu started thinking about a new ballpark back in 1992— soon after the 55-ton chunk of the building crashed to the ground. By 1996, he'd started commissioning focus groups to provide feedback on what they'd like to see in a stadium.

I know, because I was *in* one of those groups. A friend of mine had received an invite to be part of it; not a baseball fan, he arranged to have the invite transferred to me. When I walked into the room, there were 11 others there, all brought in to render their ballpark opinions. Five minutes in, I was giving a long answer to one of the first questions posed to the group. Fifteen minutes in I was more or less the only voice being heard, the foreman of a jury that had 11 level-headed folks and one lunatic who did nothing but think about baseball. A lot of minutiae got discussed that day: ticket prices, giveaways, concessions. The two biggest takeaways were: 1) if you're going to build a new ballpark, make it either open-air or possibly open-air with a retractable roof that works; and 2) build the damn thing downtown, to capitalize on the massive, untapped market of office workers eager for an activity to add to their *cinq à sept* rituals. Make happy hour even happier, and people will pack the joint.

On June 20, 1997, Brochu publicly announced his new stadium plan. The park would be built in the heart of downtown, on a plot of land donated by the federal government, bound by Notre-Dame, de la Montagne, St. Jacques, and Peel streets. It would be a $250 million open-air park, with Brochu later stumping for an addition $100 million to be spent on an umbrella-like retract-able roof. Even the 22-year-old narcissistic me held no delusions of grandeur that Brochu had based the plan on my rants in the focus group, but it was still exciting to see that the Expos' big boss shared the same vision. Designed by Daniel Arbour & Associates and architecture firms NBBJ and HOK, the stadium would include 35,000 (heated!) seats, and an old-school brick facade with architecture that, to Brochu, evoked downtown's old Bonaventure train station. The new stadium, which later secured naming rights from Labatt Breweries, would open in 2001 as Labatt Park.

Local media, for the most part, supported the plan. Plenty of U.S.-based teams had threatened to relocate if they didn't get a new publicly financed stadium. But in the Expos' case, it wasn't so much a threat as a mortal lock. The owners had lost tens of millions of dollars, attempts to recruit new corporate partners had failed, and though revenue sharing had temporarily plugged the hole in the dike, the continuing dearth in local revenue streams meant status quo couldn't hold up much longer. "This isn't black-mail," read the resulting *Montreal Gazette* editorial in response to the stadium plan, "but rather simple logic."

Getting the media's support was nice. But what Brochu and the Expos needed far more were endorsements from those who would sign the cheques. To raise the $250 million needed to build the stadium, Brochu proposed a mix of private and public funding. On the private side, the Expos would attempt to sell $100 million worth of personal seat licences. PSLs became a trendy stadium financing option in the '90s, a plan by which the buyer pays a large sum of money to secure the right to buy season tickets. Brochu would eventually get $40 million in PSL commitments, an impressive number given that ground hadn't actually been broken on Labatt Park yet, and that PSLs are a shady scheme—one in which a licensee who no longer wants season tickets can either try to sell the seat licence . . . or forfeit the licence back to the team. (Either way, the team wins.) Brochu approached local businesses with the PSL plan first. He then proposed selling commemorative bricks, which individual buyers could inscribe with personalized messages for the low, low price of $299 a pop.

The bigger chunk of the money, $150 million, however, would come from the government. The plan discussed by Brochu and Quebec's finance minister (and later premier) Bernard Landry called for taxes on player salaries rather than direct, out-of-pocket contributions by the province. The plan made sense in theory: if the Expos were to leave, that tax revenue would be gone anyway. But it was also a presumptuous plan, one that assumed that tax money (and whatever "non-direct" revenue sources Brochu and Landry could dream up) would cover the full $150 million price tag, and that the project would have no cost overruns. Given Brochu's relatively tiny $250 million projection and the track record of many gigantic overruns on U.S.-based projects, the need for more money from the province seemed a lock. All of that before we even get to the $100 million Brochu said it would take to build a retractable roof (for that, the Expos' managing partner suggested ticket taxes, a wildly over-optimistic proposal).

Though Landry would remain supportive throughout the discussion process, his boss wasn't a fan of the plan. The day after the introductory stadium press conference, Premier Lucien Bouchard weighed in.

"When we're closing hospitals," said Bouchard, "I'm not sure we should be opening stadiums." Besides, he continued, "we already have a big stadium, which cost a few dollars and isn't finished being paid for."

While Brochu tried to figure out a way to convince the premier, the front office was failing in its attempt to convince the fans—especially when Pedro Martinez was traded away after the 1997 season.

Dealing one of the two most talented pitchers the Expos ever had (a Pedro vs. Randy Johnson debate would be a fun one) was part of one last rebuild before Labatt Park could open in four years. But the fans' reaction was much harsher than Brochu expected: after so many years of watching the Expos cheap out on players—Carter, Dawson, Walker, Grissom, Hill, Wetteland, Alou, and more—and then lose them, Pedro was the last straw. The wild but promising Martinez of 1994 had matured into the best pitcher in the league. He'd thrown nine perfect innings on the road against the Padres in '95 (losing the perfecto and no-hitter in the 10th, sadly), cranked his strikeout-to-walk rate to new heights in '96, then conquered the universe in '97. That season, Pedro tossed 241⅓ innings, struck out 305 batters, and posted a 1.90 ERA during a sky-high offensive year that we would later come to realize was the apex of baseball's steroids era. (The Expos were as complicit as any other club, with one player describing the clubhouse as "Grand Central" for steroids. Several Expos from that era later appeared in the Mitchell Report, a document released in 2007 that detailed performance-enhancing drug use by dozens of players, following an independent investigation led by former U.S.

senator George Mitchell.) On a lousy team that won only 78 games that season, Pedro *was* the show, pocketing his first of three Cy Young Awards at age 25. As bad as all the other trades and defections had been, never before had the Expos traded away someone with that electric a combination of youth, talent, flair, and lovability. Shipping him off to Boston was nothing short of a back-breaker.

"I was a season-ticket holder for a long time, with a group of people," said Mitch Melnick. "And when Pedro was traded I said, 'Fuck, I'm not givin' any more money. This is fuckin' ridiculous.' All they could get was Carl Pavano and Tony Armas? Fuck! We just traded a Hall of Fame pitcher!!!"

While fans fumed, Brochu's partners began to turn against him as well. Provigo's Pierre Michaud and pharmacy chain owner Jean Coutu in particular went from harsh critics behind closed doors to ripping Brochu in public—then to actively plotting against him to rebuild the consortium with someone else at the helm. Eventually even Jacques Ménard (one of Brochu's earliest allies when he started recruiting local businesses to buy the team from Charles Bronfman) and Mark Routtenberg (the one consortium member Brochu considered a true friend and saw socially) flipped sides. The reasons for revolt depend on who you ask: to the partners, Brochu's actions during his time as managing partner painted him as either incompetent, a glory hound, or both. To Brochu, the partners' rebellion amounted to sheer jealousy that he (as the Expos' public face in MLB's eyes), and not they, called the shots.

On September 2, 1998, Brochu and Ménard headed a group of four that met with Bouchard in Quebec City. This time, the premier delivered his message of skepticism face to face: he wasn't going to support a new ballpark for the Expos, not when the province was having problems ranging from the aforementioned hospital closings to the far more popular Montreal Canadiens facing financial woes of their own.

The Habs' struggles emphatically underscored the monumental challenge the Expos were facing. After the Expos briefly passed them in popularity in the early '80s, the Canadiens quickly reclaimed their status as the kings of Montreal, winning Stanley Cups in 1986 and 1993, and, with the exception of '94, dwarfing the Expos in fan fervour. But by the late '90s, the local economy was so shaky, and the supply of well-heeled potential local investors so low, that even the city's hockey gods couldn't find a suitor.

"You'd had all the cash leave the province," said Elliott Price, referring to the 1976 sovereignty referendum and the slow exodus of businesses afterwards. "Think about how crazy it is that nobody would buy the Canadiens. How could you not buy the Montreal Canadiens?!"

The Habs finally found a buyer in 2001, when American businessman George Gillett purchased the team and its arena, the Molson Centre, for the dirt-cheap price of $185 million. The Molson (now Bell) Centre had itself been financed privately: if the Habs had to build their own arena, a baseball stadium receiving public money was a tall order indeed.

But at the end of the '98 season, three thousand fans assembled downtown to rally to support the stadium proposal. On stage, Rusty Staub, Gary Carter, and the team's newest star, Vladimir Guerrero, got a massive ovation. Two of the highest-ranking Expos were notably absent, however. One was Felipe Alou, who was in a dispute with Montreal over a new contract and was being courted by the Dodgers. The other was Brochu, who was trying to resolve the Alou situation before returning to his primary goal of pulling a stadium deal out of a hat. Maybe it was for the best, given the fire sales he'd engineered and the beatings he'd taken in the press. Still, even without Alou there, those in attendance described the mood as optimistic. Even festive.

"The rally merely confirmed the general mood this week," wrote *Montreal Gazette* columnist Jack Todd, "which was that despite the mysterious status of Alou, the absence of Claude Brochu and reports that Brochu is on his way out as managing partner, the future of the Expos in Montreal looks brighter than it has at any time in the past three years."

A few days after the rally (and with Alou's three-year extension closer to being finalized), Brochu returned to Quebec City to meet with Bouchard once more. This time, Bud Selig himself came along to plead the Expos' case, but again, talks went nowhere. Brochu would allege that his partners had poisoned the well against him, telling Bouchard that he should back a stadium plan—but only if Brochu were no longer in charge. Whether legitimate financial concerns or backroom dealings caused Bouchard to balk (probably both, though much more of the former) made no difference for Expos fans. For them, what mattered most was that the dream of a beautiful new downtown stadium and the financial security it promised the team ($50 million a year in additional revenue to start, per Brochu's estimates) appeared dead.

By the end of the 1990s, Brochu's former partners had finally forced him out. That left the now ex-managing partner to collect a payout of $15 million (plus, according to sources, more down the road). With Brochu gone, Ménard led a search for a new managing partner, but as the search dragged on, everyone involved—including Major League Baseball—started to worry. If a new investor couldn't be found, that would mark the end of the Expos. After years of dodging bullets, *Nos Amours* were now perched on the edge of destruction.

Only two sources of hope remained. On the field, the Expos had Guerrero, a powder keg of talent who reminded old-time baseball fans of Roberto Clemente. Montreal was so confident in Guerrero's abilities, the team shocked the baseball world by actually spending some damn money, locking Vladi up for five years on a $28 million contract.

Off the field, Ménard and company realized that only one investor was willing to step forward. For years, he'd dreamed of owning a major league team. A decade after their first round of talks with him had gone nowhere, the Expos were finally willing to offer him that chance. The fate of the franchise rested in Jeffrey Loria's hands.

CHAPTER ELEVEN

The End (2000–2004)

History, Winston Churchill told us, is written by the victors. Clearly, Winston Churchill wasn't a Montrealer.

Claude Brochu's fall from grace was partly deserved: the way he handled some major decisions, especially the post-strike fire sale of 1995, irreparably harmed the Expos, both on the field and in the minds of jilted fans. But the structure of the team's partnership—in which Brochu was the public face of the team while his well-heeled partners lurked in the shadows—thrust a disproportionate amount of blame on Brochu. The partners represented some of the biggest, richest, most prestigious companies in Quebec. Any of them could have put in more money at any time to help the Expos navigate the many land mines the team faced during the '90s. They chose to offer nothing. Then, as time went on, they destroyed Brochu in the eyes of the public. These were powerful figures, each with many well-connected friends in the media, in boardrooms, in the premier's office—everywhere. By the time they were through with their smear campaign, Brochu had been cast as public enemy number one, while their own reputations remained unharmed in many people's eyes. History, as it would turn out, was written by the eventual losers.

Fans brought signs to the Big O calling for Brochu's ouster. Which was fine, of course: force your GM into trading John Wetteland for cash and Fernando freaking Seguignol, and you deserve every bit of the fans' scorn. But the backlash went far beyond signs at the ballpark. For the last couple of years of his time as the consortium's managing partner, Brochu had a bodyguard follow him everywhere. A *bodyguard*. Because he ordered some crappy baseball trades. Such was the power of his very loud silent partners, that they could manipulate public opinion perfectly to completely avoid blame for the Expos' downfall, with a few unhinged locals even making Brochu fear for his damn life. And such was the power of group psychology, that in the face of an extremely complicated situation in which many parties were to blame, the public could single out one person. When you're trying to build a mob mentality, a scapegoat is what you need more than anything. Claude Brochu was that scapegoat.

Like Brochu, Jeffrey Loria (and his stepson and team executive vice president David Samson) made plenty of mistakes in the two years that they owned the Expos. But the level of vitriol that Expos fans threw Loria's way back then (and even now) far exceeded the actual damage done by the team's new leaders. The demise of the Expos played out over 20 years. It started with Charles Bronfman's disillusionment, the Gary Carter trade, and the team losing its southern Ontario broadcast foothold to the Blue Jays, then got worse in the '90s when no one with money or real power would step forward to support the team. You could even argue that the root causes traced back another decade further, to architect Roger Taillibert breaking ground on Olympic Stadium, one of the worst facilities anyone could ever dream up for a baseball team. Those

are complex, nuanced explanations that weren't (and still aren't) easy for some people to digest. Much easier to pick a villain and pin it on him. First it was Brochu, and, after he left, Loria became that villain.

"No more business as usual." Those were Loria's first words in his first press conference. No more business as usual with the team's microscopic payroll. No more business as usual getting by with a season-ticket base so tiny you'd think it was for a series of elementary school plays. No more business as usual broadcasting games for next to nothing. In return for his investment, Loria wanted to own a baseball team that could compete with the rest of the league.

Once that short, blunt speech ended, Loria's first course of action was simple. He was going to spend real money, and buy real players.

Loria took control of the team on December 9, 1999, and just 11 days later, the Expos signed Graeme Lloyd to a three-year, $9 million contract. From a baseball standpoint, this was a spectacularly stupid move. Lloyd was a 32-year-old left-handed reliever who'd had only a couple of decent seasons. He was the kind of player who might get acquired by a stacked team looking for one more minor piece before making a run at the World Series. Every year, teams sign pitchers of Lloyd's calibre to one-year deals for fairly small sums of money. Yes, the Expos' bullpen had struggled mightily ever since the breakup of the 1994 powerhouse. Still, to spend this much on Lloyd smacked of an excessive desire on Loria's behalf to prove his commitment to winning—and of the New Yorker's quite obvious Yankees fetish (Lloyd was a former Yankee).

Two days later, the Expos made another bad baseball move. With eyes for another Yankee, they acquired 30-year-old Japanese pitcher Hideki Irabu from New York. In return, they gave up three young pitchers, two of whom (Jake Westbrook and Ted Lilly) went on to have long, successful careers: Lilly just retired after the 2013 season, and Westbrook, at press time, looked likely to sign somewhere and pitch in the majors in 2014.

About three months after the Irabu deal came yet another big move: in a three-way trade, the Expos shipped 25-year-old first baseman Brad Fullmer (a homegrown player with pop, making the league minimum and under team control for four more years) to Toronto, and got back Lee Stevens (a 32-year-old, arbitration-eligible first baseman about to make $3.5 million in 2000) from Texas. That season, Fullmer broke out, cranking 32 home runs for the Jays. Meanwhile, Stevens hit .265 with 22 home runs, and remained exactly what he was before and what he'd be thereafter:

a semi-functional, below-average major league first baseman who had no business making real money. Loria found Stevens' first underwhelming season so impressive that he gave the mediocre first baseman a two-year, $8 million contract extension too.

Thanks almost entirely to those three players, the Expos' payroll jumped to $33 million in 2000, nearly double the $17.9 million in 1999 and far above the team's previous all-time high of $19.3 million in '97.

No one held any illusions of superstardom when it came to Lloyd, Irabu, and Stevens. But it was certainly a change of course from the old plan, which included grand strategies such as: "Let's trade the best pitcher in the league, who's 25 years old and one of the most popular players we've ever had, so that maybe, if everything breaks perfectly, we can field a competitive club four years from now, when this hypothetical new stadium finally opens." For the Expos, the moves Loria had just bankrolled were most certainly *not* business as usual.

In December 1999, Loria told the *New York Times*' Murray Chass the Expos could turn their fortunes around "by establishing stability, commencing a new marketing program and bringing in a winning attitude and winning players." He continued, "We can build this franchise to where it was in the '80s and the early '90s." Loria talked a good game too.

But there was trouble from the start. After all those moves, the 2000 team was still terrible, losing 95 games. Michael Barrett, a catching prospect who got converted to third base, followed a decent rookie season in '99 with a terrible 2000, hitting .214 with just one home run. Orlando Cabrera, another young player with promise, cancelled out his solid defence at shortstop by hitting just .237 with a .279 on-base percentage. Twenty-two-year-old centre fielder Peter Bergeron, whom the Expos hoped might become an effective leadoff man . . . was not effective, hitting

.245 with limited power. The two biggest disappointments, however, were the ex-Yankees that Loria had coveted. Irabu was a human tire fire, posting a 7.24 (!!!) ERA, which made the fact that he couldn't stay healthy a big relief. At the same time, Graeme Lloyd might've had the unluckiest year ever foisted on an Expos player. He missed the entire season after having shoulder surgery; at the start of the season, his wife, just 26, died due to complications from Crohn's disease; then, in August, a tornado destroyed his home in Florida.

Spending all that money was a nice symbolic gesture—but symbolism wasn't going to win ballgames. Loria (and GM Jim Beattie) simply didn't spend their money wisely; if they were going to buy free agents or make trades, they needed to target better players. Or at least, rather than blow a ton of money on crappy veterans, they could've plowed some of that cash into the draft. The mid-to-late 1990s had been a wasteland of picks, a disaster for an Expos team that had made a living through scouting and player development, going all the way back to their aggressive offer to woo Gary Carter away from quarterbacking at UCLA. Even so, if the Expos had recommitted to spending big money on big prospects, that plan would've taken years to bear fruit (with the best high schoolers a good three or four years from making the Show, and maybe seven or eight years from approaching their peak). Neither Loria nor anyone else had the luxury of being *that* patient, not when the Expos needed to win back local support immediately or risk extinction. Unfortunately, with elite players increasingly adding the Expos to their lists of teams on their no-trade clauses and free agents avoiding the growing headache in Montreal, all that was left was to overpay for half-decent players and pray for a miracle. The 2000 season was the opposite of a miracle. It was a year so depressing that it immediately wiped out whatever little hope had been built up when the new owner arrived.

"[Loria] increased the payroll, improved the team, spoke to the Chamber of Commerce, and he thought that would lead to some movement with the new ballpark, that people would start committing to it," said Mitch Melnick. "Nothing happened. Nothing. People were . . . waiting. They wanted to wait to see if this team was really that much better with a new owner. It's not that they had doubts about Loria right away—those came later. But, it was like, 'I don't want to spend $10,000 if I don't know this team is going to be any good.'"

And the team still didn't have a baseball-friendly ballpark to draw people in.

In the summer of 1999—months before the ownership transfer officially took place—Loria, Samson, Jacques Ménard, and a local contractor had met with representatives from Major League Baseball and the sports arm of architecture firm HOK. The Brochu-era plan to build a traditional-looking stadium had been scrapped, and now, the new Expos contingent (led at this point by Ménard) wanted to build the stadium for much less than the cost of other parks: around $250 million. The new design was far more modern, with grand, curved contours and lots of glass, as well as a retractable roof. HOK had designed several throwback ballparks that opened in the '90s, its signature project being Oriole Park at Camden Yards in Baltimore. At the meeting, HOK representatives checked off the dozens of problems with the cheaper proposal, telling the contingent that the new plan was going to fail miserably.

You could see both sides of the issue. From MLB's perspective, messing with the successful formula that HOK had laid out in Baltimore and other markets seemed an unnecessary risk (not to mention the stadium *did* look somewhat flimsy, even if it had aesthetic appeal; the retractable roof might've ripped off the place after the first stiff breeze). But the Expos group saw things differently.

"I was at Morgan Stanley [before being asked by Loria to come work for the Expos]," Samson told me in a 2013 interview in Miami, "and these were my first experiences dealing with people in baseball. I learned that anything different is wrong. That's the view within baseball. That's the old, old-boys network. I didn't agree. Just because something is done in a different way doesn't mean it's wrong."

Of course, design still wasn't the biggest problem—funding was. Disagreements over design could be hammered out over time. Even the initial reticence from the local business community didn't seem like a deal-breaker. What was essential, though, was that the Expos secure financial support from Quebec City. This was Ménard's dossier: the interim head of the consortium was supposed to negotiate with Bouchard to secure the province's co-operation. Where Brochu had failed, Ménard vowed to succeed. When he approached Loria to take over the team, Ménard told the prospective new owner that the stadium deal's negotiations were all but done. When Loria and Samson actually took over the team, they quickly realized this wasn't true. The government hadn't agreed to any kind of financial plan. In the end, it never did, and Loria and Samson never got a single meeting with Bouchard or his underlings to convince them otherwise.

"In business you can do all the due diligence you want," said Samson. "But it's not until you're behind the wheel that you really know whether the tires work."

All four tires blew out at once. The team still stunk. The new ballpark never happened. And the next setback was an even bigger rude awakening.

Dissatisfied with local TV and radio deals that were much smaller than any other major league team's, Loria went to meet with the networks. He travelled to Toronto to meet with TSN, the national, all-sports cable TV network. TSN said it was willing to pay $5,000 a game, when—according to sources—the network was paying the Jays at least $200,000 a game.

"That meeting lasted about 30 seconds," said P. J. Loyello, Expos PR man from 1995 to 2002.

The next meeting was with CJAD, a prominent English-language radio station in predominantly French-speaking Montreal. CJAD's offer was: nothing.

"I think we're going to have an issue here," Ted Blackman, CJAD's program director, told Loria. "We don't offer money; we don't pay for these deals. We have a brokerage deal with the Alouettes, we have a brokerage deal with the Canadiens."

That was Montreal's sports landscape in the late '90s and into the next decade. The beloved Habs couldn't even get proper media deals, so what chance did the lowly Expos have? The prevailing sentiment at CJAD was "they need us more than we need them."

Meanwhile, Mitch Melnick was working for Team 990, an all-sports, English-language station. CJAD refusing to pay for Expos games presented an opportunity, so Melnick went to Team 990's general manager Lee Hamilton to take his temperature on a possible deal.

"He said, 'I'll be happy to make a deal . . . if they're willing to *pay* $1,000 per game,'" recalled Melnick. "It's Loria's first year, and Lee wanted him to pay $1,000 a game. Shell out $162,000, and he would carry the Expos."

No major league owner in their right mind, in any city, would accept that kind of deal—not when other clubs were pulling in tens of millions of dollars between radio and TV rights. Samson figured local broadcasters would come around, that after a hot start, *they* would approach the Expos to work something out. That call never came.

"Negotiation" was not the message that got conveyed to the public. After 31 seasons of Expos games on local English radio, there were none in 2000. Instead of radio, the Expos decided to broadcast their games in English on the Internet. This was a radical and cutting-edge move, but one that drew an audience that was just a fraction of the size of what they used to get on the radio. For everyone but a few tech-savvy early adopters, this was a devastating setback, not only to fans, but also to the voice of the Expos, Dave Van Horne.

"It wasn't very pleasant," Van Horne told Rich Griffin in a 2011 *Toronto Star* article. "My daily escape was the two and a half to three hours I was behind the mic to do the ballgame [broadcast over the Internet]. The rest of the time was spent wondering what I was going to do the rest of my life. A good part of that season was spent agonizing over what was next for me, for my family, for my livelihood. Openings at the major league level don't come up very often."

For many fans and local media members, the math was simple: before Loria, they could sit out on the porch on a summer night and listen to Van Horne's dulcet voice. Once Loria arrived, many people couldn't do that anymore. So obviously, Loria had to be at fault. A narrative quickly emerged: this aloof art dealer and his fast-talking, short-statured, Napoleon-complexed stepson—these *New Yorkers*—were sabotaging the team. This was a far easier stance to adopt than accepting the obvious: that the Montreal business community, and now Montreal's media outlets, wanted no part of the Expos.

"They [didn't stop having] radio because they were purposely torpedoing the franchise," said Melnick. "There was no radio because nobody wanted to pay for it. If there had been money from the media, and if the local guys had gone into their pockets and said, 'We're gonna build a ballpark,' things would have been different, absolutely."

The last tire to blow was Loria's relationship with his partners in the consortium. But in this case, it would be largely his own doing.

In May 2000, Loria issued the first cash call to his partners. For a typical partnership, this would be standard operating procedure: spending had gone up with Beattie's acquisition of players over the winter in the hopes of improving the ball club. More money would be needed for other expenditures in the future, as the cost of doing business in Major League Baseball continued to climb. To keep pace, both Loria—who'd bought a 24 percent stake in the team for $18 million Canadian (about $12 million U.S. at the time, with the lopsided exchange rate)—and his partners would need to chip in to pay the tab.

Loria put in his share. No one else did.

This was the Raymond Cyr philosophy, being played out in real time. Bell, Nesbitt Burns, Desjardins: the representatives from these and most of the other consortium members had viewed their earlier investments as charitable donations. They painted themselves as white knights who'd done right by the community by contributing the equivalent of a rounding error on their companies' profit and loss statements. But also like Cyr, they had made it clear that there would be no more money coming—ever. Not to keep the 1994 team intact; not to keep Pedro Martinez; not to make a stadium deal happen by financing a big chunk of it themselves—never. (Jean Coutu, grocery store chain Loblaw Companies, and Charles Bronfman's son, Stephen—who'd been approached about a majority position before Loria—made an exception to the "never" rule, investing $1 million each at the same time that Loria put his money in, with a commitment to invest another $9 million each later on.) Brochu had let this stand, running the ball club on the puniest of budgets in a quixotic attempt to both win games and avoid bankruptcy. Loria had different ideas, figuring that to make money, he and everyone else would have to spend some.

There was no other way to increase investment. With no English radio, minimal revenue from French radio, and not much more from all TV ventures combined, media money was nearly non-existent. Attendance had been dreadful, diving to 9,547 fans a game in '99, then ticking up to a still ugly 11,435 in 2000. Outsiders had begun to mock the fan base for its lack of support, but they were, frankly, way off base in their criticisms. After years of being told there were cockroaches in the soup, many Montrealers had done what anyone would do in that situation: go to a different restaurant. To get any kind of positive momentum going, all of the partners would have to bite the bullet, hoping that a little spending now would lead to better results down the road.

Loria's partners, however, pleaded for a different course of action. The easiest way to raise money, they argued, would be to trade the team's highest-paid player. Once again.

Yes, to keep the Expos going, the most popular opinion in the room was to trade a 25-year-old superstar, the franchise player signed to a team-friendly contract who'd become the one and only reason for fans to bother showing up at all. To solve our problems, they said, let's dump Vladimir Guerrero.

☞ THE UNFORGETTABLE ☜
VLADIMIR GUERRERO

Vladimir Guerrero's first major league home run was, like so many of his other feats over the years, a revelation. The date was September 21, 1996, and the Expos, for a change, were contending down to the wire: they'd end up with a chance to make the playoffs all the way 'til the second-to-last day of the season. With one out in the ninth, Montreal trailed Atlanta 5-3. On the mound for the Braves was Mark Wohlers, a nearly unhittable closer who dialled up his fastball into the high-90s. The Expos needed to mount a rally, and this was just the third game of Vlad's career. To Don Sutton, the Braves' colour commentator, leaving Guerrero in this spot was the wrong move. Though it wasn't his team making the decision, Sutton seemed almost *angry* about it.

"Here's a kid coming in against the best closer in the league, and you're only down by two," Sutton lectured. "This is a white flag."

Half a second later, the first pitch Guerrero saw was a fastball. It was low, a couple of inches below the knees, and was outside, off the plate by a couple more inches. This was the kind of pitch that a hitter *might* swing at to protect the plate with an 0-2 count: maybe a weak swing, choked up on the bat, to foul the ball away and keep the at-bat alive. Wearing no batting gloves (as was his habit for the rest of his career), Vlad hacked at the pitch. Down two in the ninth and needing at least a baserunner to bring the tying run to the plate, this was an impetuous swing—something you wouldn't see from almost any other hitter in the league in that spot. We'll let Braves play-by-play man Skip Caray, and Sutton, take it from here.

Caray: "Fly ball, pretty well hit to right field. Back goes Dye into the corner, looks up . . . that ball is gone."

Sutton: "Like I said, it's a brilliant move. No it's not, it's a *lucky* move. That's something . . . that just absolutely . . . happened . . . and it turned out well . . . for the Expos."

Caray: "Trying to think with Alou, I guess he figured the kid's a good fastball hitter, and there's a good fastball pitcher out there. It certainly worked."

Sutton: "This looked like a good pitch, out away from him. It may not have been a strike! But boy, he leaned out there and drilled it."

Trying to rationalize Guerrero and where he could be used was a futile, even counterproductive exercise. Your eyes would process what would happen, but your brain just couldn't accept it. It had to be *lucky*. Vlad defied everything you thought you knew about baseball. How could it be anything other than luck?

There was nothing typical about him. Vlad grew up unfathomably poor in the southeastern Dominican Republic town of Nizao. As Dan Le Batard wrote in his excellent 2002 Guerrero profile for *ESPN The Magazine,* little Vlad drank from puddles because the shack he lived in had no running water (or electricity). When a hurricane blew the tin roof off their hovel, Vlad's family of seven squeezed into one tiny room, sharing two beds, then waited and waited for the hurricane-caused flooding to subside, while subsisting on milk and sugar dropped from rescue helicopters. Rather than go to school, he toiled the fields, harvesting tomatoes, melons, and onions. School was a luxury, and he frequently missed classes as a young child; his education ended for good after the fifth grade.

"I feel guilty about that," Vlad's mother told Le Batard, "but we had to eat. The storm didn't kill anybody in our town, but the hunger after it did."

When he wasn't working, young Vlad was playing baseball. And when his older brother Wilton got invited to a Dodgers training camp, 16-year-old Vlad (he'd lied and said he was a year older) tagged along. The raw skills were obvious: 6-foot-3 with a rocket arm, brimming with athleticism. The governing expression for Dominican players was (and still is), "you don't walk off the island"—meaning to impress scouts, you need to swing away. Even by those standards, Vlad was a freak of nature, a player so long-armed, and so strong, that he could reach out and hit balls four, six, even eight inches off the plate. And hit them *hard.* Vlad roped the ball all over the field that day under the Dodgers' watchful eyes, and earned a 30-day contract. It might have been longer, but the Dodgers didn't know what to make of the kid: he'd shown up with no shoes, then injured his hamstring trying to leg out a double. According to legend, Vlad realized he wouldn't be able to run after the injury. His next time up, he hit a home run instead—so he could trot slowly around the bases.

At any rate, the Dodgers never followed up. So Vlad returned to doing manual labour, while playing any form of baseball he could on the side. It was Fred Ferreira—dubbed "The Shark of the Caribbean" because of his knack for finding and signing diamond-in-the-rough players—who discovered Vlad next. The Expos' international scouting director signed him in March 1993. Then came a breathtakingly fast ascent.

Vlad hit .314 in rookie ball in 1994. The next year, in the Single A South Atlantic League, he hit .333, cracking 21 doubles, 10 triples, and 16 home runs in 110 games. The prospect hounds started salivating, and *Baseball America* named Guerrero the ninth-best prospect in the game before the 1996 season. That '96 campaign was the stuff of legends: as excited as we were to follow the Expos through their surprise 88-win season, all we kept hearing about was Vlad. This being 1996, you couldn't get reams of information on faraway prospects online like you can now. Instead, the news would leak out in dribs and drabs, a tiny two-line mention in agate type, or a cryptic quote buried at the end of a Sunday notes column. Harrisburg, Pennsylvania, was just an eight-hour drive from Montreal. But it was more fun to let your imagination run wild, picturing Vlad destroying the Double-A Eastern League with his cannon for an arm, his gazelle-like strides, and that lethal weapon of a bat. His final numbers that year were obscene: .360/.438/.612, with 32 doubles, eight triples, and 19 homers in 417 at-bats . . . at age 21.

When word spread that the Expos were going to call him up for the end of that season, we went nuts, and started plotting to get to every one of his games. Meanwhile, Montreal's coaching staff held a meeting to discuss how to handle this guy, this once-in-a-generation talent—who was also the least disciplined player many of them would ever see.

"I'll never forget that meeting as long as I live," said Jim Tracy, who'd been promoted to become Felipe Alou's bench coach. "Felipe called the staff into his office. And with that deep-ass voice of his, I heard this message: 'Leave him alone.' That's what he said. 'There's going to be mistakes. The ball's not going to be thrown to the cut-off man early on. His plate discipline is going to be very raw at best. Leave. Him. Alone.'"

That's what everyone did, from the first day of his career 'til the last. What followed was a highly abnormal existence for a major league ballplayer. Vlad lived with his mom, bulking up on her cooking, then brought her to the ballpark with giant dishes full of food for the rest of the team. When the Expos later acquired Wilton from the Dodgers (he'd made it to the big leagues too, albeit in much less spectacular fashion), Mom and the two brothers lived together in Vlad's downtown apartment. Vlad was painfully shy, speaking only Spanish and turning away interview requests, feeling embarrassed at his lack of education (his nickname, since childhood, was "El Mudo"—"The Mute"). He never watched video of opposing pitchers, never studied their tendencies, and often didn't even know their names. His one study habit—if you could call it that—was to step into the batter's box on his PlayStation. One of the oldest axioms in sports is to practise the way you play. No problem for Vlad: he swung at everything on PlayStation, too.

But damn it, Felipe was right. The world left Vlad alone, and he rewarded all of us with an unforgettable career.

The numbers were magnificent, certainly, including a 2002 season in which he missed a 40–40 campaign by a single home run (it looked like he got his 40th too, but for a missed call by an umpire). But the best way to describe his incredible career is through other people's stories. Those who watched Vlad play walk around with indelible memories.

Bill Geivett (former Expos farm director): "In 1994, [Vlad] was in the Gulf Coast League, in rookie ball. We were gonna go over to watch the Mets, and then I was going to watch the West Palm Beach team play at night in Kissimmee. So, we drive over to watch the Mets, and I want to see all the guys, but I want to see this Guerrero kid that I've been hearing about. So I go out there, and the first pitch he sees, he hits it over the fence. Then I watch him make a play in the outfield, and he throws it in. I said, 'Let's go. I've seen enough.'"

Jeff Blair: "Rondell was down in Harrisburg on injury rehab, and he claims he saw a pitch where the ball bounced in front of home plate. Whoever threw it stumbled. The ball bounced in front of home plate . . . and Vlad knocked it over the centre-field fence. Over the wall, at least 400 feet. The greatest description of Vladimir Guerrero I ever heard was that he swings like he's hitting a tennis racket. All he has to do is get some part of the bat on the ball, and he's going to crush it."

Jim Tracy: "We were sitting there in the dugout and I saw Pete Harnisch throw a two-strike split-finger. It hit the dirt. [Vlad] swung, and hit it. It looked like a three-wood going out toward left-centre field, and it got stuck between two pads on the outfield wall. I remember Barry Larkin standing at shortstop, as he's in his position, and when the ball got hit I saw Larkin just start to move. By the time he turned around, the ball was literally stuck in the pads for a ground-rule double. Felipe looked over at me and said, 'Hey, Trace, did that ball bounce?' I said, 'Yes, Skip, once before he hit it, and once after he hit it.' When he was a kid and came to the big leagues, you could throw a ball somewhere in the vicinity of the first-base dugout, and there was no guarantee that he wouldn't take a swing at it."

Doug Glanville (former MLB outfielder): "I was with the Phillies, and Amaury Telemaco was pitching. He's going over the scouting report. What should you throw him? Outside? No. Inside? No. After a couple of minutes, they just told him, 'Throw the pitch, and pray.'

"Another time, Vlad hit a line drive off a knuckleball. At the Vet. Desi Relaford was playing shortstop. He put his glove up *after* it whooshed by his head. I didn't even react and it was by me, hit the wall. Hardest-hit ball I've ever seen."

Manny Acta (former Expos third-base coach): "He drank like a fish. Ate a ton. Fifty thousand cans of beer, and a bag of rice. Never bothered him. He'd show up to the park hung over, and hit bombs, like it was nothing."

Glanville: "2001, it's the ninth inning, tie game, and Rheal Cormier is trying to unintentionally intentionally walk him. First pitch, in the dirt. The second, at his eyeballs. Third pitch is at least eight inches outside. He reaches out . . . opposite-field walk-off."

Rheal Cormier: "There's no pitch he can't reach. I've seen him hit balls a foot outside off Greg Maddux for a home run the other way. The guy is not human. He should be in another league."

Acta: "Vlad comes to the park one day, rubbing his palms together. 'Kevin Brown is pitching today, I'm going to crush him.' Keep in mind Kevin Brown might've had the nastiest sinker of his generation. He has a decent Hall of Fame argument. First pitch: monster home run. [Vlad] comes back to the dugout, cackling. Cackling!"

What I remembered most vividly about Vlad was his arm. There's a YouTube video of him long-tossing a ball at Yankee Stadium, from the left-field foul line, over the wall in right-centre . . . at least 370 feet. The problem was, he was *so* confident, so cocksure he could throw out anyone, anytime—that it occasionally cost him.

May 30, 1998, Expos vs. Pirates at old Three Rivers Stadium. I'm on one of my classic baseball road trips with the Maple Ridge Boys, high on Primanti and a chance to see Vlad break some other team's heart. Unfortunately for the Expos, their closer Ugueth Urbina doesn't have it that day. Four batters in, he's loaded the bases with one out, putting the Expos' two-run lead in jeopardy. Jason Kendall raps an outside fastball to right, and the ball bounces in front of Vlad, scoring the runner from third easily. We rise to our feet anticipating what's going to happen next: Vlad's going to charge in, field the ball, and fire a chest-high strike home, cutting down the potential tying run and saving the game for the Expos. Sure enough, Vlad charges . . . fields the ball cleanly . . . winds up . . . and airmails the catcher by 10 feet. The bases clear, Pirates win.

He had hubris, and he had balls. That's what made him so much damn fun to watch, win or lose. He never got a championship in Montreal—or anywhere else. That doesn't change what he was: a player who was truly beyond belief. When I'm old and grey, and most of my other memories have escaped me, I'll still tell my great grandkids about Vladimir Guerrero. Some people you just never forget.

No self-respecting owner would unload a player *that* good, three and a half years before the end of the player's contract, just to save a few million bucks. That included Loria. The art dealer's Manhattan gallery featured exquisite works of art by some of the masters, such as Amedeo Modigliani and Henry Moore. But Loria was a baseball fan to the core, and he knew a superstar when he saw one. Whenever someone from the baseball world would visit his gallery on East 72nd Street, Loria would point to a big installation that looked completely out of place in the art world. It was a life-sized cardboard cutout, of Vladimir Guerrero. That, he'd tell anyone within earshot, is my most valuable piece of art. There was no way Vlad was getting traded.

The partners immediately realized the gravity of the situation. If Loria answered the cash call and everyone else ignored it, they might end up looking like unsupportive misers. As a compromise, they *loaned* Loria the money to pay down the team's debt and keep operations running. After that first cash call, Coutu told reporters that Loria was "trying to take the team away from us." Meanwhile, several consortium members ran to their PR firms, knowing that if Loria made additional cash calls and they didn't answer them, they'd need to do some heavy spinning to come out looking like the good guys—just as they had in the Brochu days. Then, a few months after that first cash call in May 2000, Loria issued another one.

Now, the partners were becoming seriously concerned. Raymond Bachand of the Fonds de solidarité des travailleurs du Quebec asked Loria to step down, with his initial $18 million investment handed back to him. Loria refused: by answering the second cash call himself with no one else putting forth any money, he'd just diluted the value of his partners' shares, gaining a larger share of the team himself. That process continued into 2001, while the atmosphere at the Big O somehow got even gloomier (the Expos lost 94 games and drew fewer than eight thousand fans a game, one of the lowest totals for any team in decades). Loria kept putting out cash calls, watching them go unanswered, and scooping up a bigger and bigger controlling interest in the team. By the time Loria finally left the Expos in 2002, he'd accumulated a staggering 93 percent equity share, after purchasing less than one quarter of the ball club to start.

At the very least, we can say that Loria was both a shrewd and ruthless businessman. From the start, he had Samson do most of the talking on day-to-day operations, swooping in only when he needed to grab greater control of the team. Realizing very quickly that his partners wouldn't match his investments, Loria saw an opportunity to assume nearly total financial control of a very rare and precious commodity—a Major League Baseball team—and he seized it. On the surface, there didn't seem to be anything illegal about what he had done; taking advantage of others for being stubborn and cheap isn't against the law.

But as you might expect, Loria's outfoxed partners saw something far more nefarious. They became convinced that Loria had planned this all along.

"We [lobbied] Bud Selig near the end," Stephen Bronfman told me in a 2011 interview. The partners insisted to the commissioner that Loria was a carpetbagger. "Bud would say, 'Well, we don't like him either,'" continued Bronfman. "It was a lot of cockamamie."

Bronfman's father Charles, who'd been friendly with Selig for decades, had tried to speak up on the consortium's behalf, but to no avail. All of it made the partners wonder if there was a conspiracy in place—if after dealing with the embarrassingly small crowds, annual losses, and bad publicity coming out of Montreal for so many years, Selig might've set a plan in motion to yank the Expos away. There'd been rumours for years that the team might move, with the most frequently rumoured destination being

Washington, D.C.: if Loria and Selig were in fact in cahoots, Loria nabbing 93 percent of the team would've certainly made it easier for the league to move the Expos.

"I believed in the conspiracy theory," Stephen Bronfman told me in 2011. "I think they were embarrassed with the Expos' situation, and they wanted to move the team. I think there was something in the works to do something with the situation here. They didn't like what was going on."

A set of events at the end of the 2001 season made clear that yes, Major League Baseball and most of its owners wanted the Expos gone. On November 6, 2001, the owners voted 28–2 in favour of contracting two teams, the Expos and the Minnesota Twins (who had a stadium problem of their own in the outdated Metrodome), with the Expos and Twins being the lone dissenting teams. The plan called for the two clubs to play lame-duck seasons in 2002, after which they'd end operations, with their players getting scattered to the other 28 teams via a dispersal draft.

Then, in early 2002, MLB completed a most suspicious three-way franchise swap. John Henry, the owner of the Marlins who wanted to upgrade to a better situation, got awarded ownership of the Boston Red Sox despite not being the high bidder when the team went up for sale. To make the deal work, Henry sold the Marlins to Loria for $158.5 million, and, completing the loop, Loria sold the Expos to Major League Baseball for $120 million plus a $38.5 million interest-free loan. For his two-year investment in Montreal, Loria reaped an enormous profit, *and* positioned himself to take over a less troubled team without laying out a penny of his own money on purchase day. He also put the Expos' fate directly in MLB's hands, just as the consortium members left behind had suspected.

In July 2002, the partners filed suit against four people: Loria, Samson, Selig, and MLB chief operator officer Bob DuPuy. The way they did it was a massive overreach, however. They filed a Racketeer Influenced and Corrupt Organizations (RICO) Act lawsuit: the kind of strategy that governments often use to prosecute organized crime. Though the sequence of events that took place between Loria's arrival in December 1999 and his official exit in February 2002 certainly looked suspicious—from Loria consolidating most of the team's shares, to the contraction announcement, all the way to the shady franchise merry-go-round that benefited everybody except the Expos—the plaintiffs couldn't prove a conspiracy by RICO standards. The case ultimately got kicked to an arbitration panel, which ruled in favour of the defendants.

With MLB taking over in 2002, it finally looked like the end of the Expos. The team was either going to move, or if the league kept its word, be eliminated completely. All that remained, it seemed, was one final season.

The last days of the Montreal Expos were sad, surreal, and even occasionally exciting. What began as a plan to put a failing franchise out of its misery as quickly as possible turned into a long, drama-filled slog, the likes of which baseball had never seen before—and never will again.

It started with the vote for contraction. Only the targets dissented, which meant that the Toronto Blue Jays were one of those 28 teams that voted to wipe out their Canadian neighbours. That lack of solidarity offended many Expos fans, especially those with long memories. John McHale had fought like hell to get Toronto a major league franchise. For years, the Expos and Jays played the annual Pearson Cup exhibition game, further stoking the friendly rivalry between the two cities. During the 1992 World Series in Toronto, Paul Beeston could have picked just about anyone to throw out the ceremonial first pitch before the Jays' first home game, but he picked Charles Bronfman, honouring the Expos' owner for bringing baseball to Canada in the first place. The arrival of interleague play made for some fun matchups, too: On Canada Day, 1997, Jeff Juden outduelled his childhood idol— and eventual Cy Young winner—Roger Clemens at SkyDome, to this day one of my favourite baseball memories (and possibly the most Canadian day ever for a fan, given that my buddy Jon and I sprinted three kilometres from the game to Molson Amphitheatre to catch the last 45 minutes of a Rush concert).

But as was the case with Brochu, Loria, Selig, and all the other villains of Expos lore, the circumstances weren't as simple as some people made them out to be. Baseball's owners always had a way of building consensus and aiming for unanimity, and just as a Brochu vote against the salary cap and other salary-squashing measures wouldn't have stopped the '94 strike by itself, a token vote in the Expos' favour wouldn't have stopped the landslide of sentiment that led to contraction getting ratified. Still, Toronto could have done *something*. Years earlier, the Pittsburgh Steelers voted against the NFL moving their rivals, the Cleveland Browns, to Baltimore. Browns owner Art Modell got his wish and wrested the team away anyway. But Cleveland fans never forgot that their rivals stood with them in their time of need. The Jays didn't do that. They kicked the Expos while they were down, and it hurt like hell.

With the spectre of contraction looming, MLB assumed control of the Expos in February 2002. That gave the team, now wards of the state, just a few weeks to prepare for the start of the season. To do so, the Expos would need to use every resource at their disposal. Unfortunately, they had virtually none. Jeffrey Loria had taken *everything*. He grabbed the computers, the scouting reports, the radar guns, and the personnel—including Jim Beattie's GM replacement Larry Beinfest, P. J. Loyello (to head up PR), and several other baseball ops and business-side execs. Plus he would have a reunion with Dave Van Horne, who'd taken his trademark "Up, Up, and Away!" home-run call to Miami in 2001 after Loria yanked the Expos off English radio, then continued on with the Marlins when Loria arrived in '02. Another life-sized Vladimir Guerrero cutout once sat innocuously in the Expos' business offices at Olympic Stadium: Loria took that too, as if it might appreciate like a Monet painting.

It was all a lucky break for at least one individual, though. That's when Omar Minaya got the call. How'd you like to be the new general manager of the Montreal Expos, Bud Selig asked. Minaya jumped at the chance. Dominican-born and New York-raised, Minaya was 43 years old, and had spent nearly a quarter century in professional baseball. He'd gone from 14th-round draft pick to minor league ball, played in the Dominican and in Italy, scouted for the Texas Rangers, then eventually landed with the New York Mets, where he'd climbed to the position of assistant general manager. He'd long hoped to become a GM, and now the *commissioner* was calling, offering him the chance to become the first Latin-born general manager in Major League Baseball. He had to say yes. Just one problem.

"I had 72 hours to put the whole staff together," Minaya said. "In 72 hours, training camp was going to open."

Minaya wasn't exaggerating. Thanks to Loria, and to remaining staffers jumping at new opportunities with the Expos seemingly about to fold, the team had only six employees left on the baseball operations side: farm director Adam Wogan, Randy St. Claire (who worked as a pitching coach in the minor leagues and would later get promoted to major league pitching coach), Triple-A manager Tim Leiper, long-time trainer Ron McClain, long-time office assistant Marcia Schnaar, and Monique Giroux (who worked for the Expos from day one, starting as an intern, then eventually transitioning to media relations and staying to the bitter end).

Thirty-three years after that first frantic spring, the Expos had come full circle, scrambling to cobble together enough people and infrastructure to resemble a viable major league team. Minaya hired anyone he could find. He brought in support staffers who'd been fired by the Marlins after Loria had poached many of Montreal's key people. He gave young people a chance, including Dana Brown, who rose from the role of scout with the Pittsburgh Pirates to scouting director with the Expos, just as he hit his 35th birthday. But Brown was ancient compared to Alex Anthopoulos. Hired in May 2000 as an intern, Anthopoulos started out making copies, sorting mail, and driving people to the airport for seven bucks an hour. By 2002, he'd shown enough initiative to get . . . another internship for seven bucks an hour, this time in the storage room, organizing game tapes. Not long afterwards, at age 25, he got promoted all the way to assistant scouting director.

This was Expos University to the highest degree: with the smallest staff of any major league team, first-semester freshmen like Anthopoulos suddenly found themselves taking graduate-level baseball seminars. "You had so much work thrown on you, and I was just a sponge, soaking it all up," said Anthopoulos. "It was, by far, the most fun I ever had in the game."

For all the pressure on the front office to put a respectable product on the field under brutal circumstances, fun was the operative word for many people who worked for that 2002 team.

"There was the risk of the team contracting, sure," said Tony Siegle, Minaya's assistant GM. "We all worked late, seven nights a week. We went home to change underwear, that was it. We didn't care! It was great."

The team on the field was fun to watch, too. The Expos had lost 90 or more games for four straight seasons, and the most buzz-worthy development of their truncated off-season had been inviting a washed-up Jose Canseco to spring training. No one expected much. To everyone's surprise, the Expos stormed out of the gate in 2002, winning 17 of their first 27 games and grabbing a tie for first place as of May 1. But they were doing it without Felipe Alou. The beloved manager, after a quarter century with the Expos organization, had been fired in May 2001; the truth was that it suited both sides well by that point, given how bitter everyone had become. The new manager, Hall of Famer Frank Robinson, got much of the credit for inspiring the troops. In reality, Robinson was a poor tactician who bunted far too often, and while many praised his wisdom and experience, others didn't appreciate his sometimes grumpy personality.

The bigger contributing factor was the same ingredient the Expos had used time and time again to build teams amid constant attrition: the farm system. Guerrero was the star, leading the league in hits and total bases, winning the Silver Slugger Award and finishing fourth in MVP voting. Now, though, he had an able supporting cast. Jose Vidro shed much of the baby fat and the defensive yips that made him a questionable prospect, settling in as the starting second baseman and hitting .315 with 19 homers and 43 doubles. His double-play partner, Orlando Cabrera, still wasn't a great hitter, but his bat had improved, and that, combined with his terrific defence at short and 25 stolen bases, made him a solid everyday player. Another homegrown player, Brad Wilkerson, smacked 20 homers with a .370 on-base percentage. Smartly returned to his natural position of catcher, Michael Barrett's all-around game improved, and he formed a reliable tandem behind the plate with Brian Schneider.

The pitching staff also featured several productive players from the Expos' system. The staff ace was Javier Vazquez: talented but incredibly raw as a rookie in '98, Vazquez had become a favourite of Felipe Alou's, despite a 6.06 ERA that year. He shaved a run off that mark in his second year, then another in his third. By 2002, he'd become one of the best young pitchers in the league, a workhorse who went on to make 32 or more starts for 10 years in a row, following his predecessor Pedro Martinez's lead by featuring a knockout changeup. The young players who didn't come from the farm system were usually acquired from other teams in exchange for Expos veterans who'd started to get too expensive. That included Japanese right-hander Tomokazu Ohka (yes, Esteban Yan's counterpart in that Bart-and-Milhouse joke), who posted the lowest ERA of any Expos starter that year at 3.18. Mix those ingredients with a cheap and effective bullpen committee led by lefty Scott Stewart, and suddenly the Expos had the makings of a contender.

Minaya made a bunch of additional little moves. Desperate for a utilityman, he flipped future All-Star Jason Bay for middling infielder Lou Collier. He also brought back several old favourites, including Andres Galarraga, Henry Rodriguez, and Wil Cordero. But he wanted to do something bigger. By June 1, the Expos' hot start had faded, and Montreal found itself a game below .500—but an eight-game winning streak later that month hoisted the team into second place. Expos Nation sprang to life. Writing for BaseballProspectus.com at the time, I banged out a 1,700-word column stuffed with fake trades, knowing full well they weren't going to happen. The Expos were literally owned by 29 other teams, with Tony Tavares serving as team president and MLB's advocate in Montreal's front office. That arrangement meant that any move that added salary would have to be approved by the Expos' direct competitors. Given this terrible conflict of interest, and Montreal's history of making exactly one significant go-for-it deadline deal ever (the Mark Langston trade, which cost Randy Johnson), the realistic prediction was for nothing to happen, and for the team to quickly slide back into irrelevance.

But times had changed. By this point in the year, it was clear to nearly everyone that contraction was off the table: the Twins weren't going to go quietly, and no other suitable contraction partner could be found, thwarting MLB's stated goal of deleting two teams at once to avoid having an odd number of clubs. Only Minaya hadn't been expressly told to operate any differently, so his mindset had to be that this was the Expos' final year, one way or another. Minaya also wanted to establish his bona fides as a bold, winning general manager—someone who'd be a strong candidate for another GM job once his time in Montreal was done. Time for a blockbuster.

On June 27, the deal was announced. Going to the Cleveland Indians were three terrific prospects: shortstop Brandon Phillips, left-handed pitcher Cliff Lee, and outfielder Grady Sizemore. Coming back to the Expos: Bartolo Colon, one of the best starting pitchers in the game. The trade sent shockwaves through the league. Minaya had been able to defray Colon's salary by including Loria's favourite overpaid first baseman, Lee Stevens, in the swap, so money wasn't the issue. Still, the package of talent sent to Cleveland was one of the biggest ever shipped in a deadline deal. The three prospects all flourished too: as of the end of the 2013 season, they'd combined for 10 All-Star appearances and a Cy Young Award.

Minaya didn't give a damn. His mandate was to win, and win now. If the team got contracted at year's end, Phillips, Lee, and Sizemore wouldn't be ready to become stars in the big leagues anyway. If the Expos eventually moved to D.C., well, that probably wouldn't be on his watch, not unless the new owners wanted to hang onto the past. And in Minaya's mind, maybe, just maybe, a miracle playoff run could turn the tide in Montreal.

"We were trying to save the team by trying to contend," said Minaya. "I didn't know where things were with potential buyers or anything. But we felt if we got into the playoffs, the town would have supported us, and the private sector would offer more support. We saw it in Seattle [with the Mariners gaining momentum toward a new stadium after their playoff run in 1995]. And our goal was to win. Getting to the playoffs would have created that demand from politicians, entrepreneurs, to say, 'Hey, we gotta step up as a city to save this.'"

The Expos were 6½ games out when the trade went down. By the All-Star break, they'd fallen to 9½ games back. That didn't stop Minaya. With the additional playoff possibility of the Wild Card out there, and with most of his chips already shoved into the middle of the table, he made another huge move: an eight-player trade that reeled in both top power hitter (and '94 Expos wunderkind) Cliff Floyd and Wilton Guerrero (for his second tour of duty in Montreal and a reunion with Vlad). Montreal responded by . . . losing some more. The 'Spos won only six of their next 18 games, falling back below .500 and out of the race. Floyd got shipped to Boston 19 days after the splashy deal that brought him to Montreal, and Colon got flipped over the winter for a package of talent nowhere near as strong as the one sent to Cleveland. The Expos ended the season at 83–79, a nice accomplishment given the turmoil of February, but not a playoff season. No politicians, entrepreneurs, or anyone else in Montreal made a peep. Same as always.

Mercifully, contraction didn't happen, so Minaya and company stayed on for another year. Like the year before, 2003 brought more fun than anyone expected. But it also included two monumental punches to the face.

The Expos played well, even while Guerrero missed 50 games that year due to injuries. He got plenty of support: Cabrera put up the best numbers of his career, Vidro and Wilkerson were steady contributors, and Vazquez and Ohka were sharp once again.

The big addition this time, however, was Livan Hernandez, the veteran right-hander acquired in a steal of a deal with the Giants right before Opening Day. Montreal needed a bigger payroll to support this talented squad, and MLB, to its immense credit, obliged. In 2002, the team's payroll had risen to an all-time high of $38.7 million; in 2003, it jumped to nearly $52 million. Cynical fans might've wondered if they'd have been better off with the team being owned by the league all along, instead of the cheapskate local owners who helped drive the Expos into the ground. Montreal started the season with a bang, and through 50 games, the club stood at 32–18, just two games out of first.

Then came the first punch in the face. Since the Expos were going to move soon anyway, and since attendance remained lousy in Montreal (fans by this point knew it), Major League Baseball got the brilliant idea to move 22 home games to San Juan, Puerto Rico. The move did have some benefits, as despite playing in tiny Hiram Bithorn Stadium, the Expos drew more fans per game in San Juan than they did in Montreal, with Puerto Rican players Jose Vidro, Javier Vazquez, and Wil Cordero being particularly big hits. Still, for the Expos fans that had remained loyal throughout all the chaos, having more than a quarter of the team's home games yanked away—when this might've been the team's last season—was unnecessarily cruel.

It affected the players, too. After that hot start, the Expos ran into the most ludicrous travel stretch imaginable, with a schedule that went like this: four games in Miami (including a doubleheader); three games in Philly (including a doubleheader); six games in San Juan, Puerto Rico; three in Seattle; three in Oakland; three in Pittsburgh (including a doubleheader). Montreal (could you even still call them the "Montreal" Expos?) went 8–14 over that period, losing six of the final seven games at the tail end of the 25 days away from home.

"At first I was thinking, 'Wow, we get to go to Puerto Rico,'" said Jamey Carroll, who was a wide-eyed rookie infielder on the 2003 team. "It was the sense of anticipation for going somewhere new. It was kind of fun. But at the same time, after awhile we started getting tired of it. We started getting numb."

Ever resilient, the Expos shook off their travel blues, and late in the season, they began to rally. Sitting at 60–60 on August 12, they won seven of their next 11 games: suddenly, the Expos were in striking distance of the Wild Card, heading into a pivotal four-game series at home against the Phillies. It was a last gasp of excitement, one that, against all odds, actually drew people back to the ballpark. In the series opener, more than 30,000 fans saw the Expos hammer the Phillies 12–1. Game 2 was one of the most electrifying contests in franchise history. Down 8–0 heading into the bottom of the fifth, Montreal stormed all the way back, finally taking the lead in a seven-run seventh (once again, the seventh inning was Magic Time). Cordero, one of the heroes of the big late-season Phillies series 10 years before, came through again this time, stroking a pair of two-run doubles. Final score: Expos 14, Phillies 10.

"It's unreal," said Frank Robinson after the game, citing both the comeback win and the Expos' big comeback in the Wild-Card race, in which the team now trailed the Phillies and Marlins by just two games. "You see it happening but you don't believe it."

Montreal built on those first two wins, taking the final two games of the series to complete the sweep. Simultaneous losses by the Marlins left the Expos where no one thought they could possibly be that late in the season. On August 28, 2003, they were tied for the Wild Card, with a chance to make the playoffs for just the second time ever—very possibly in their final year of existence.

"It was Believer Fever," said superfan Katie Hynes, referring to that season's slogan, as the Expos made believers out of fans who'd (justifiably) given up on the team years earlier. "I'll always remember on the Tuesday night, falling behind 8–0. Then that comeback. My nephew, who was six, on my brother's shoulders. We were jumping around, yelling. It was incredible."

I'd love to write you a happy ending here. I'd love to tell you that Hollywood got hold of that improbable Expos season, then punched up the script with a huge September, a run to the play-offs, and somehow, some way, a World Series for the ages.

None of that happened. The Expos flew to Miami, then lost three straight nail-biters to the Marlins and their old pal Jeffrey Loria. Three games back and heading into September, they'd at least get a little help from minor league call-ups, since every team gained the right to promote up to 15 players on October 1, right? Most teams called up at least four or five players, some clubs seven, eight, or more. The Expos promoted . . . *zero*.

Eric Knott was a relief pitcher on that '03 team. He didn't have a great season by any means. But he could've at least provided some depth for a bullpen that had worn down over the course of the year (in part due to neck strains caused by watching countless Rocky Biddle fastballs get drilled into the bleachers). He didn't get that chance.

"We had just swept Philly, so this was a few days before rosters expanded," said Knott. "We were packing up to play the Marlins, tied for the Wild Card. Then all of a sudden, they pulled me and a couple others from the bus. They were sending me down, right when the roster was supposed to expand. A few weeks later, at the end of September, I got a letter from the commissioner's office. Due to budget restraints, it said, we regret to inform you we had to send you down."

And there it was. The Expos were still in the race heading into the season's final month. But with one last chance for salvation, Montreal—the team and the city—learned that Major League

Baseball had forsaken them. That after funding a competitive team for nearly two seasons, the league wouldn't approve a few hundred thousand dollars (a few bucks more than a rookie's salary) to give them one more fighting chance. If Expos fans were ever going to hold an ounce of forgiveness in their hearts—for 1994, for the fire sales, for Claude Brochu and Jeffrey Loria and belittling by ignoramus talking heads and every other kick in the ass baseball had handed out—that forgiveness flittered away on September 1, 2003.

The Expos did get a reprieve for one more year. But the 2004 season offered nothing but pain. At the end of the 2003 campaign, Vladi left to go win an MVP for the Angels. Vazquez got dealt to the Yankees, and went on to play eight more seasons in the big leagues. All that remained in '04 was to count down the final days, say goodbye, then shed some tears.

"I was at the last game at the Big O," said P. J. Loyello. "The game ends, and I go in the clubhouse and I see Bob Elliott. Bob had covered the Expos back in their heyday. So Bob says, 'Tell me about your memories of Olympic Stadium and the Expos.' And I just broke down. He did, too."

"After that last game in Montreal, the season ended in New York," said Mitch Melnick. "I was there with Elliott [Price] and his brother. Those last two years I was doing colour commentary for select road games, and this was one of them, the last one. As we got toward the end of the game, it just kept building. Then we just lost it. It was pretty heavy. This was the end."

"Things changed after they left," said Johnny Elias. "There are amateur leagues going on everywhere, and they're still very popular. But the sense of looking up to somebody, that feeling is gone. For baseball fans, when the Expos left, there was a big hole left behind."

In the end, the Expos had needed a champion, someone with money and power who could run the team through the harsh 1990s, then reap the benefits in the next decade when an explosion in national and local TV deals and a vastly expanded revenue-sharing program made even the poorest teams prosperous and relatively secure. No one ever showed up. That, more than anything, is why baseball didn't work in Montreal. In the league's eyes, Montreal had failed baseball. The cold, hard truth was that for the most part, this was absolutely right.

But to the fans who stuck with the team for all those years, it was the opposite. They'd given their hopes and dreams, their childhoods and adulthoods and their golden years, supporting a team that could be tough to love. In a panel discussion five years after the Expos left Montreal, Dave Van Horne rattled off the nicknames of some of the players who'd made up that tough-to-love team: Rusty and Beetsy, Singy and Jorgy, Stoney and Frenchy, Bocc and Cy and LP, Hawk, Cro, and Rock, Woodie, Ross the Boss, and the Kid, Eli, Gully, Scotty, Charlie, and Scoop, the Cat and Marquis, Walk and Mo, El Presidente and Pedro, Cliffy and Rondell and Orlando and Michael and Brian and Jose and Vladi. These were the guys those fans had cheered for day in and day out, only to see it all slip away.

To the Expos diehards, Montreal hadn't failed baseball. Baseball had failed Montreal.

Epilogue

Ten years after the Expos left Montreal and became the Washington Nationals, the memories live on.

A few weeks after that last game in Montreal, the Boston Red Sox won the 2004 World Series. One of Boston's most popular players was Pedro Martinez. When a TV reporter tracked Pedro down in the clubhouse and thrust a mic in his face, a million thoughts had to be rushing through the pitcher's head. He had to acknowledge his new adopted city, and the joy everyone in Boston felt after ending an 86-year World Series drought, one of the most notorious streaks in sports history. Most of all, he had to express his own feelings after winning his first championship. This was the culmination of more than a decade of dominance in the majors. It was also the celebration that he—and all of Montreal—might've had 10 years earlier if the stars had aligned a little differently. Amid all that chaos, his teammates jubilantly celebrating behind him, the camera's blinking eye pointing at him, and all those thoughts to process, he offered this:

"I would like to share this with the people of Montreal that are not going to have a team anymore. But my heart . . . and my ring is with them too."

Sometimes, those memories come flooding back in a chance meeting. Like when Jeff Blair flew to San Francisco in 2007 to cover Barry Bonds' pursuit of the all-time home run record. There, he ran into some old friends.

"Kirk Rueter was doing some work for the Giants," recalled Blair. "He showed up at the clubhouse one day and F. P. Santangelo was there. So we just started talking, just shooting the shit. Then Felipe sees us, so he comes over too. I remember Lee Jenkins was there covering Bonds, too. Lee's standing there watching this conversation for five, ten minutes. 'Does that happen all the time?' he says. 'Yup. Pretty much.'"

The dozens of ex-Expos players that I talked to for this book told hundreds of stories about their time living in Montreal. They all loved it. Many of them had come up through the minor league system, making Montreal their first stop in the big leagues. They remember living in the Manhattan building downtown, a high-rise that housed countless players over the years, and was a short Metro ride from the ballpark—a shorter walk to the city's famous nightlife. Yeah, the stadium stunk, and going through customs before and after every road trip was a pain in the ass, and, in rare cases, Doritos were hard to find. But player after player spoke in glowing terms about the city and its fans; how they wished they could've remained Expos for longer, but for the economic realities of the game. At the end of many of these conversations, they would offer a fleeting, wistful thought: Wouldn't it be great, they'd say, if baseball came back to Montreal someday?

It always seemed like idle chatter. Now? Well, maybe not.

Three days after this book gets published, there will be a Major League Baseball game at Olympic Stadium, the first of a two-game series. One of the participants will be the Mets, whom the Expos played in both their first and last games. The other will be the Blue Jays. The Jays were the ones who pushed to make the games happen, in fact—hoping to extend their appeal into Quebec, a large untapped market of potential fans, most of whom didn't latch onto Toronto (or any other team) after the Expos left.

But there will be other forces at work that weekend as well. One of them will be Warren Cromartie.

On February 16, 2012, Gary Carter died from a hyperaggressive form of cancer at the age of 57. Seven and a half years after the Expos' last game, Carter's untimely death dug up feelings many fans didn't even realize still existed. There was grief over Carter's passing, as people remembered not only a great player, but also a beacon for the community. Carter was a symbol of Montreal baseball in its glory days, and remembering those days suddenly made people want to relive the past. Cromartie was deeply affected by Carter's passing. And he saw an opportunity to help fans channel those feelings of nostalgia.

"I came to Montreal and wanted to spend some time in the city," Cromartie told me. "It had been years since the Expos left. I got off the plane and this family recognized me. 'Where can we go to look at something [related to] the Expos?' they asked me. It really knocked me back. I had to think about it. Then I realized there's nothing in Montreal with 'Expos' on it. That hit me real hard. It's like the Expos were never there. So I said to myself, 'You know what, let me try to get people talking about baseball again here.'"

Not long afterwards, Cromartie launched the Montreal Baseball Project (MBP). In the summer of 2012, MBP hosted a gala in Montreal, honouring Carter and the 1981 team that he helped lead to within a game of the World Series. More than half of that '81 team showed up: Andre Dawson and Tim Raines, Bill Gullickson, Ellis Valentine, and many others.

That event begat other events, and other people becoming interested in rekindling the Expos flame. Matthew Ross has helped galvanize local interest via his ExposNation fan page, which to date has more than 167,000 likes on Facebook. He's organized two trips to Rogers Centre for Jays games, bringing two hundred Expos fans with him for the first one, nearly a thousand for the second. There was a pitch-and-catch event with Steve Rogers in 2013. Fun ventures that for an hour, or maybe an afternoon, got a small subset of Montrealers jazzed up about baseball again.

Now, everyone's thinking bigger. MBP commissioned a $400,000 feasibility study on whether a major league ball club could work in Montreal under current economic conditions. The study found that, yes, a team could be viable. The proliferation of sports channels in Canada presents a media revenue opportunity that didn't exist during the Expos' dying days. Rogers snatching hockey broadcasting rights away from Bell Media and its TSN subsidiary—thus creating a giant hole in TSN's programming— could increase demand for another sport (and another team) to cover. The improvement in Montreal's economy, MLB's far more generous revenue-sharing program . . . these and other factors could make baseball a success in Montreal.

Still, as of January 2014, it's a spectacular long shot. Montreal doesn't have a stadium that's suitable for baseball. No billionaire— or multi-billion-dollar company—has expressed any interest in bankrolling a hypothetical baseball team. At the moment, no team is for sale, nor are there any plans for expansion on the horizon. Moreover, Major League Baseball has a long institutional memory, and the league might not be keen on revisiting the only city ever to lose a team in the past 40-plus years. So for now, it will remain a twinkle of a thought. MLB will go about its business; Montrealers will tend to their own.

Until then, the spirit of the Expos will live on. The organizers of those Jays-Mets exhibition games are expecting huge crowds. For those two days, we could see 60-, 70-, maybe 80,000 or more fans pack the Big O. There'll be some Jays fans, sure, maybe a few Mets fans, too. But the majority will be Expos fans, summoned to the ballpark after 10 years away, clutching Youppi! dolls, donning the old baby-blue jerseys, and wearing the old pinwheel caps—the ones everyone used to mock, now a fashion statement for a new generation, many of whom barely remember *Nos Amours*, if at all. Whatever the future holds, those two days will be a party, the kind Montrealers used to throw when their team was hot, when everyone wanted a piece of the action.

Here's hoping there'll be more parties to come.

ACKNOWLEDGEMENTS

In the fall of 2007, I got an email from Random House, sent by someone I didn't know. That person liked my work, and wanted to know if I'd be interested in writing a book. This email would eventually transform my entire career. My life, really.

I'd wanted to be a professional sportswriter for years, dating back to high school in Montreal. That pursuit proved to be a monumental challenge: graduating from Concordia University in 1997, I found a landscape that offered few to no opportunities for aspiring sportswriters. I'd landed a job as an intern, then as a cub reporter covering community news for the *Montreal Gazette*. But cracking the sports desk was likely to take years, and finding assignments more invigorating than high-school field hockey several more. This wasn't the *Gazette*'s fault—not with a strong staff of beat writers and columnists in house. Rather, it was the harsh reality associated with a limited publishing world that hadn't yet made many inroads on the Internet. In those days, there were only two writers regularly producing the kind of content on the web that I devoured: Rob Neyer for what was then called ESPN SportsZone; and Bill Simmons, writing for something called Digital City Boston (one of several moderate-traffic online regional hubs owned by AOL).

In the 10 years that followed, my fledgling career as a community news reporter evolved to include daily stock market coverage for *Investor's Business Daily*. Hoping to at least nudge my way closer to sports, I concocted a plan to join the group of brilliant writers and analysts at Baseball Prospectus. In late 2001, Rany Jazayerli, one of the group's original members, wrote a post asking for people to join the Strat-O-Matic league that he and fellow BP writer/original Joe Sheehan helped start. I figured if I could join that league, maybe I could make friends with Rany and Joe—and somehow talk my way into writing for BP.

This was not going to be easy, though. Expecting a handful of emails for the four slots he needed to fill, Rany instead got more than a hundred replies, so he made everyone fill out long, detailed applications. Respondents had to describe everything from their ideal 25-man Strat-O-Matic roster to details about their baseball backgrounds. Three of the replies were slam dunks from immensely qualified applicants who'd been playing Strat for years, with tons of experience playing the online game that members of Rany's North American Strat-O-Matic Association (yes, NASA) used. A close race ensued for the fourth league vacancy, and the application Rany ultimately chose came from an avid baseball fan who had never played the online version of the game. In fact, he hadn't played any Strat-O-Matic at all since he was 14 years old, giving it up right around the time he discovered girls. Still, Rany liked one line in particular on that person's application: it asked that he take pity on me, since I was a Montreal Expos fan.

The Expos got me in that league, and a few months later, I wrote my first piece for Baseball Prospectus, where I spent four great years. Working for the group afforded some tremendous opportunities, including contributions to the Baseball Prospectus annual, working with a ludicrously talented group of writers on a book called *Baseball Between the Numbers*, and doing occasional freelance work for ESPN.com. But as great as those gigs were, I still hadn't achieved my goal of writing about sports for a living.

So when that email from Random House arrived, 10 years after graduation, I couldn't believe my luck. Or really, anything about the email. It took several more emails before I figured out the connection, and grew to trust the guy on the other end. Turned out Paul Taunton used to read an old Montreal Expos message board at BaseballBoards.com (later FanHome.com, now ExposForever. com, part of the Scout network of team sites), where I used to post. This was years before I started writing anything about baseball: I was at that point a dude in his early-to-mid 20s who'd read some Bill James and Rob Neyer, and had a big (virtual) mouth. As it happened, my fellow boardie had become a big Expos fan while attending McGill in the late '90s, and found my stats-infused, obsessive posts about Expos first baseman Lee Stevens interesting. (To say that I hated the relatively big money the Expos were paying Stevens would be an understatement.)

Paul kept tabs on me during my years writing for Baseball Prospectus and ESPN.com (and later FanGraphs and Bloomberg Sports). When Random House formed a partnership with ESPN Books and he went looking for a relative unknown who could write a compelling book about baseball, his attention turned to a fellow Expos fan. We batted around ideas for months, and finally the perfect one came thanks to Steve Wulf at ESPN (a terrific writer, as well as a savvy editor): a hybrid sports/business book on the unlikely darlings of 2008, the Tampa Bay Rays. That book became *The Extra 2%*, and a few months after publication, I got an email from Grantland deputy editor Dan Fierman asking if I'd like to contribute to the site. A few months after that, I got my wish: 14 years after university, I'd finally landed a gig as a full-time sportswriter.

Though you could argue that other factors played into the fulfillment of my professional dreams, it all boiled down to the Montreal Expos, to my insane, unwavering devotion to the team, and to some 3 a.m. message board diatribes about Lee Stevens. I'd probably be filing TPS reports if not for the Expos. They formed the foundation of my sports fandom, and it's thanks to *Nos Amours* that a math-obsessed kid who carried a Little Professor calculator around when he was three years old cultivated that love for numbers into a career writing about the analytical side of baseball.

I owe thanks to Paul Taunton for seeing potential in a wise-ass message board poster, for helping shape *The Extra 2%* into what it became, and, soon after that book came out, for suggesting we work together on a book about the Expos, this time on behalf of Random House Canada. I'd also like to thank his colleagues Ruta Liormonas, Deirdre Molina, Brittany Larkin, Linda Pruessen, Five Seventeen, Erin Parker, Sean Tai, Sheila Kay, Anne Collins, Marion Garner, Matthew Sibiga, Brad Martin, Kristin Cochrane, Duncan Shields, James Young, and the rest of the team at Random House Canada.

Rob Neyer has gone from being a role model after whom I patterned my career to the person responsible for first reads on both *The Extra 2%* and *Up, Up, & Away*. This is a stroke of incredible luck for which I can never thank Flying Spaghetti Monster enough. Rob has beaten a huge number of bad writing habits out of me over the past five years, doing so with patience and encouragement. I was a better writer after *The Extra 2%* than I was when I started it, and I'm a better writer today than I was when I started *Up, Up, & Away*. Thanks to Rob, I've even learned the correct usage of "may" versus "might," for the longest time my mortal grammatical enemy.

Bill Simmons went from being an early, shining example of what was possible for an Internet-based sportswriter to someone much closer: a great supporter of my work, and also my excellent boss. Dan Fierman, Mike Philbrick, Mal Rubin, Sarah Larimer, and Chris Ryan have all been terrific editors and confidants. When Dan was about to hire me, he first spelled out the cardinal rule of Grantland: "No assholes." Hopefully I've lived up to my end of the bargain; everyone I've met at Grantland certainly has. As the two people with whom I've worked most closely over the past three years, Mike and Mal in particular have been amazing. Every writer should be lucky enough to work with such great people.

Much love to every other Grantlander, including Bill Barnwell, Zach Lowe, Kirk Goldsberry, Katie Baker, Sean Fennessey, Rafe Bartholomew, Rembert Browne, Mark Lisanti, Patricia Lee, Andy Greenwald, Jonathan Abrams, Brian Phillips, Sean McIndoe, David Cho, Andrew Sharp, Bryan Curtis, Emily Yoshida, Mark Titus, Jay Kang, Robert Mays, Charlie Pierce, Holly Anderson, Sal Iacono, Dan Silver, Justin Halpern, Michael Baumann, Shane Ryan, and Rany Jazayerli (I follow him everywhere); as well as my terrific podcast producers Dave Jacoby and Joe Fuentes. Thanks also to my producers and colleagues at *Baseball Tonight*, including Mike McQuade, Pete McConville, Fernando Lopez, Mark Schuman, Gregg Colli, Justin Havens, Adnan Virk, Boog Sciambi, Karl Ravech, Keith Law, Buster Olney, Jayson Stark, Tim Kurkjian, Manny Acta, Alex Cora, Doug Glanville, Barry Larkin, Chris Singleton, Mark Mulder, Curt Schilling, and John Kruk.

My literary agent Sydelle Kramer has been by my side for years. She's a fount of ideas, she knows the publishing industry better than just about anyone, and she cares deeply about her clients.

Thanks to all the players, managers, scouts, general managers, front-office executives, owners, writers, broadcasters, team employees, and fans who shared their stories. There were interviews in malls and coffee shops, stadiums and living rooms, offices and bars. There were also numerous phone chats with people I'd never met who agreed to share their thoughts because they believed in the project and were willing to play along with an overzealous Canadian with lots of questions. It's tough to single anyone out without offending dozens and dozens of others, but I will say

ACKNOWLEDGEMENTS

this: the one-hour chat I had with Felipe Alou at the back fields of the San Francisco Giants' minor league complex is something I'll remember and cherish for the rest of my life.

An all-star team of transcribers helped convert many interviews into ready-to-use material for the book. First and foremost, massive thanks to Blake Murphy and Ryan Szporer, who carried the biggest share of the workload. I'm also indebted to Jared Book, Kyle Casey, Cedric de Jager, Minda Haas, Corey Sylvester, and Matt Swain. Additional assists were offered by Gabriel Brison-Trezise, Forrest Carpenter, Jordan Cunningham, Jacob Grill-Abramowitz, Fred Katz, Maxime Paiement, Jamie Vann Struth, and Adam Wray. My brilliant and resourceful wife, Dr. Angèle Fauchier, helped manage hundreds of interview files and reams of source material, while also setting up workflow on my Scrivener writing platform. Lifesavers, all of you.

Speaking of incredible generosity, Russ Hansen met me one sunny afternoon at the Redondo Beach Cafe, then unveiled a treasure trove: years of phenomenal photos and materials, all of which I was free to use at my discretion. Russ' photos appear in this book, making it that much better. Likewise, Terry Mosher overwhelmed me with a gracious offer of his own: the opportunity to go through his entire collection of Expos-related editorial cartoons, choose whichever ones I liked, then sprinkle them throughout the book. That's how the great Aislin and his award-winning images came to populate *Up, Up, & Away*. Thanks also to Loretta Stephens for her assistance with photography.

I mention this book's many sources in the references, but want to point out two in particular that proved invaluable. First, SABR's BioProject produced a staggering number of terrific biographies on former Expos players, managers, and execs that served as vital source material. Though the BioProject deploys many different writers, Rory Costello and Norm King wrote some particularly

390

fruitful ones with Expos themes. While we're here, let's toss out a blanket endorsement for SABR and everything that organization does; if you're not yet a member, you should fix that *tout de suite*. A second go-to source was the *Montreal Gazette*, my first-ever full-time employer. I kept going back to the *Gazette's* archives, again and again, to pull out quotes and facts about the Expos: from mid-'6os articles describing the city's quest to land a Major League Baseball team to 2004 editions of the paper that chronicled the end of the franchise in *la belle province*. Getting the opportunity to interview esteemed *Gazette* writers such as Michael Farber, Jeff Blair, and Stephanie Myles only enhanced the experience.

One more group of people I'd like to single out: the many members of the Montreal media who so richly recounted their experiences covering the ballclub. Dave Van Horne told so many terrific stories about his 32 years broadcasting games that I wished I had three books' worth of space to recount them all. Between his years covering the team from *La Presse*, followed by his own three-plus decades of broadcasting games, Jacques Doucet was there for the Expos' entire history. He invited me into his home and regaled me with stories for the next three hours; several times during those three hours, we both found ourselves in tears.

As you're reading this book, I'll probably be blabbing on a show somewhere about baseball. There's no way to cover everyone, so consider this a blanket thanks to all who've afforded me the opportunity to talk about the game. The great people at TSN 690 in Montreal in particular have been putting me on the air for so many years. Elliott Price, Shaun Starr, Mitch Melnick, Dave Kaufman, and Matthew Ross, *merci mes amis*.

Over the years I've gotten to know so many great people and brilliant minds in sports journalism and related industries that I'm already lamenting those I might forget to mention. To name just a few: Benjamin Hochman, Dave Cameron, R. J. Anderson,

Tommy Rancel, Jason Collette, Matthew Berry, Nate Ravitz, Kevin Goldstein, Dave Appelman, Matt Meyers, Mark Simon, Susan Slusser, Derrick Goold, Amanda Rykoff, Craig Calcaterra, Dave Dameshek, Bob Elliott, Jay Jaffe, Emma Span, Nick Piecoro, Chris Liss, Jeff Erickson, King Kaufman, Will Leitch, Ben Kabak, Tommy Bennett, Henry Abbott, Kevin Arnovitz, Dave Schoenfield, Greg Foster, Jesse Spector, Dirk Hayhurst, Jeff Passan, Kevin Kaduk, Tony Khan, Adam Thompson, Wendy Thurm, Tim Marchman, Randy Sklar, Jason Sklar, Gar Ryness, Jay Farrar, Annakin Slayd, Ben Lindbergh, and Brian Kenny.

Dialling up the way-back machine, thank you to all my Montreal pals who ate poutine with me and helped make up ridiculous songs for Expos players, both in the bleachers at the Big O and on road trips. First and foremost, those include the original Maple Ridge Boys, Elan Satov, Brian Benjamin, Andrew Kensley, and Eric Kligman. Other eggers-on included Derek Marinos, Jamie Itzkovits, Jon Selig, Lenny Godel, Ron Wexler, Ronen Pomeranc, David Itzkovits, Stephan Ouaknine, Avi Satov, and Double Mic himself, Michael Siegman. Also, I might've lost my mind during this book process without the friendship and Don's Club Tavern accompaniment offered by the Denver WINS crew.

Family! Thanks Dad, Roz, Mom, Drew, Dan, R. J. Katie, Theo, Quinn, Logan, Samantha, Jesse, Lauren, Nicole, Bess, and all the loved ones no longer with us. You are all wonderful.

Finally, Angèle, Ellis, and Thalia—thanks for brightening my days with your love and warmth. Once again, you've made gigantic sacrifices that enabled me to write this book, for which I'm eternally grateful. I'm the luckiest husband and dad in the world.

REFERENCES

This book took nearly three years to come together, and would not have been possible without the co-operation of many interviewees. From a two-hour breakfast with Cliff Floyd in a Miami-area coffee shop to spending an hour and a half in Tim Raines' manager's office before a Newark Bears game, the generosity and candour shown by all of these people are the lifeblood of this book—even in cases where they're not quoted directly. Those interviewees are:

Abramovitch, Scott 07/07/11
Acta, Manny 01/27/13
Alou, Felipe 03/13/13
Anthopoulos, Alex 02/09/12
Antonetti, Chris 03/08/12
Aplin, Jamie 09/02/12
Assaf, Jeb 09/02/12
Basu, Arjun 10/31/12
Beacon, Bill 02/22/13
Beattie, Jim 10/24/11
Benjamin, Brian 01/23/13
Blair, Jeff 12/06/11
Boucher, Denis 12/07/12
Bragan Jr., Pedro 12/20/11
Brochu, Claude 06/15/12
Bronfman, Charles 07/18/11

Bronfman, Stephen 07/19/11
Burke, Tom and Tim 07/21/11
Capozzi, Nick 09/02/12
Carlson, Michael 2/20/12
    and 5/12/12
Carroll, Jamey 07/08/11
Casavant, Denis 10/15/12
Claire, Fred 12/13/13
Cook, Murray 01/03/13
Cosentino, Sam 09/11/12
Costello, Rory 06/08/12
Cromartie, Warren 11/28/2011
    and 5/16/13
Dawson, Andre 01/05/13
DeShields, Delino 12/12/12
Dever, John 09/25/12

Dombrowski, Dave 02/10/12
Doucet, Jacques 7/20/2011
    and 1/21/2013
Duquette, Dan 02/15/12
Elias, Johnny 10/13/12
Fanning, Frank 09/02/12
Fanning, Jim 07/06/12
Farber, Michael 12/19/11
Farrar, Jay 05/08/12
Fletcher, Darrin 12/21/11
Floyd, Cliff 01/16/12
Francona, Terry 01/31/13
Geivett, Bill 09/25/12
Gerstein, Brian 09/02/12
Glanville, Doug, 09/24/13
Godel, Lenny 09/02/12
Griffin, Rich 12/07/11
Hansen, Russ 09/21/12
Hughes, Gary 01/17/13
Huntington, Neal 02/23/12
Hynes, Katie 10/12/12
Iorg, Dane 08/24/12
Itzkovits, David 6/24/12
Izturis, Maicer 07/07/11
Juden, Jeff 07/10/12
Kaplan, Ari 07/25/13
Kaufman, Dave 05/08/12
Kearce, Christy 02/22/13
Kennedy, Kevin 11/27/13
Kensley, Andrew 06/24/12
Kligman, Eric 06/24/12
Knott, Eric 07/26/12

Kruk, John 12/19/11
LaCava, Tony 02/10/12
Le Lay, Richard 07/03/13
Lee, Bill 10/14/12
Linker, Andy 12/29/11
Loyello, P. J. 05/16/13
MacPhail IV, Lee 01/22/13
Makos, Elias 02/03/12
Malone, Kevin 12/18/12
Masteralexis, Jim 09/07/12
Martinez, Dave 06/21/12
Martinez, Dennis 06/28/12
Martinez, Pedro 09/05/13
McClain, Ron 01/16/13
McDonald, Rob 12/20/11
McGinn, Dan 02/08/13
Melnick, Mitch 06/18/12
Miller, Jon 5/31/12 and 6/5/12
Mills, Brad 05/31/12
Minaya, Omar 01/22/13
Monday, Rick 09/21/11
Mosher, Terry (Aislin) 08/22/13
Myles, Stephanie 07/19/11
Nicholson, Bob 10/10/12
O'Brien-Locke, Adam 08/24/12
Price, Elliott 05/08/12
Raines, Tim 07/15/11
Raymond, Claude 05/10/12
Richman, Alan 06/24/11
Rogers, Steve 07/13/11
Rose, Pete 03/16/13
Ross, Matthew 09/18/13

Routtenberg, Mark 07/22/11

Runnells, Tom 03/12/12

Samson, David 05/16/13

Sanderson, Scott 8/30/13

Santangelo, F. P. 11/19/12

Satov, Elan 09/02/12

Schnaar, Marcia 02/09/12

Scioscia, Mike 07/07/11

Siddiqui, Adil 09/02/12

Siegle, Tony 12/21/11

Singleton, Ken 09/19/11

Slayd, Annakin 05/08/12

Spector, Jesse 08/23/13

Staub, Rusty 07/15/12

Stoneman, Bill 07/07/11

Strom, Brent 07/17/12

Tavares, Tony 12/07/12

Touchette, Serge 01/21/13

Toulch, Fred 09/10/12

Tracy, Jim 03/12/12

Trupiano, Jerry 10/14/13

Usereau, Alain 04/05/12

Valentine, Ellis 11/19/12

Van Horne, Dave 1/18/2012
   and 5/16/13

Walker, Larry 01/10/13

Wallach, Tim 07/08/11

Wexler, Ron 06/24/12

White, Rondell 06/04/12

Youmans, Floyd 05/21/13

I read a stack of books, in both English and French (thanks UTT and Herzliah for 11 years of trilingual education!), to gain a better understanding of the Expos' history—much of it occurring either before I was born or when I was too young to understand it. Those books include:

Brochu, Claude, Daniel Poulin and Mario Bolduc. *My Turn at Bat: The Sad Saga of the Expos*. Translated by Stephanie Myles. Toronto: ECW, 2002.

Doucet, Jacques and Marc Robitaille. *Il était une fois les Expos*, Vol. 1 and 2. Montreal: Hurtubise, 2011.

Gallagher, Danny and Bill Young. *Remembering the Montreal Expos*. Toronto: Scoop Press, 2006.

Luchuk, David. *Blue Jays 1, Expos 0: The Urban Rivalry That Killed Major League Baseball in Montreal*. Jefferson, NC: McFarland and Co., 2007.

Dawson, Andre with Alan Maimon. *If You Love this Game . . . An MVP's Life in Baseball.* Chicago: Triumph Books, 2012.

Snyder, Brodie. *The Year the Expos Almost Won the Pennant.* Toronto: Virgo Press, 1979.

Snyder, Brodie. *The Year the Expos Finally Won Something!* Bel Air, CA: Checkmark, 1981.

Turner, Dan. *The Expos Inside Out.* Toronto: McClelland & Stewart, 1983.

Usereau, Alain. *The Expos in Their Prime: The Short-Lived Glory of Montreal's Team, 1977—1984.* Jefferson, NC: McFarland and Co., 2012.

Williams, Dick and Bill Plaschke. *No More Mr. Nice Guy: A Life of Hardball.* New York: Harcourt, 1990.

I drew from interviews and reporting done by various publications, including but not limited to: the SABR BioProject, the *Montreal Gazette*, *La Presse*, *le Journal de Montreal*, the *Montreal Star*, *Canadian Press*, *Associated Press*, *Sports Illustrated*, *The Sporting News*, *The New York Times*, the *Los Angeles Times*, the *Toronto Star*, the *Toronto Sun*, the *Globe and Mail*, the *Boston Globe*, and ESPN.com. I also borrowed some Expos-related passages from posts that I wrote for various publications, including Grantland.com, BaseballProspectus.com, and JonahKeri.com.

Other valuable resources included: Baseball-Reference.com, The Book Blog, HardballTalk, Deadspin.com, SBNation.com, FieldofSchemes.com, TheClassical.com, *Inc. Magazine*, *The Wall Street Journal*, TheBigLead.com, CBSSports.com, Fangraphs.com, FanHome.com (formerly BaseballBoards.com), BaseballLibrary.com, MLB.com, *Paths to Glory* by Mark Armour and Daniel Levitt, *The Bill James Baseball Abstract* (several editions) by Bill James, plus a long list of friends, colleagues, industry peers, and cool followers on Twitter.

INDEX